Revolution to Revolution

Revolution to Revolution
Jamā'at-e-Islāmī in the Politics of Pakistan

Abdul Rashid Moten
Department of Political Science,
International Islamic University
Kuala Lumpur, Malaysia

Islamic Book Trust, Kuala Lumpur
in association with
International Islamic University Malaysia
2002

© Abdul Rashid Moten 2002
ISBN 983-9154-42-7

Published by
Islamic Book Trust
607 Mutiara Majestic
Jalan Othman
46000 Petaling Jaya
Selangor, Malaysia
Email: ibtkl@pd.jaring.my
Website: www.ibtbooks.com

Cover Design by
Bounce Graphics
bounce@tm.net.my

Printed by
Academe Art & Printing Services
Kuala Lumpur

CONTENTS

LIST OF TABLES

FOREWORD

Islam is at once a religion and a civilization which mandates a social order based upon the eternal principles laid down in the Qur'ān and the Sunnah. The Muslim community is mandated by Allah (*subhānahu wa taʿālā*) to construct a humane, universal society which stands for justice and the unity of soul and matter, this world and the hereafter, power and ethics, material progress and spirituality, religion and science, thought and action. Following the example of Allah's last Messenger, Muhammad (*sallāhu ʿalaihi wa sallam*) as the exemplar par excellence of moral-spiritual virtues, the Believers (*al-Mu'minūn*) strive incessantly for the actualization of the ethical state and society for the sake of achieving a just, peaceful and prosperous existence on God's earth. Consequently, throughout Muslim history there have been movements aimed at purging society of alien or non-Islamic accretions and to establish a viable civilization, a righteous order guided by the sharīʿah. This is exemplified by the Salafiyah movement of Muhammad ibn Abd al-Wahhab of Arabia, the Sokoto Jihad led by Shaykh Uthman ibn Muhammad Fudi in what is now known as Nigeria, the Mahdiyah movement led by Muhammad Ahmad ibn 'Abd Allah in the Sudan, and various Islamic puritanical and reformist movements in the Malay-Indonesian Archipelago. These movements resulted in a definite trend towards shunning local religious accretions and returning to the pristine and simple form of Islam which consists of obeying the injunctions of Allah (s.w.t) as embodied in the Qur'ān and of following the Sunnah of Muhammad (s.a.w) as described in detail in the books of ḥadīth.

The Muslim world has witnessed considerable turmoil since the beginning of the twentieth century. A large part of the world of Islam was under British, French and Italian domination. The

Osmanli Caliphate had come to an end and the fortunes of the Muslim world were at the lowest ebb. The Muslim reaction to this was seen in an increasing upsurge of religious motivation and spread of religious education among the people and in a series of religio-political movements in various parts of the Muslim world. The Tablīghī Jamāᶜat, known also as the "Faith Movement"; the Jamāᶜat-e-Islāmī in Pakistan, and the Islamic Revolution in Iran are some of the noteworthy examples of contemporary Islamic movements.

The Tablīghī movement initiated by Mawlana Muhammad Ilyas is perhaps the largest non-political group devoted to the cause of Islam through what may be called a "moral rearmament." Divorcing politics from its scheme of activities, it aims at regenerating the benevolent spirit of Islam through purification of intention, strengthening the faith, meticulous observance of prayer, acquisition of religious knowledge and following the Sunnah in personal and collective life - all with the aim of effecting change from collective piety.

The Jamāᶜat-e-Islāmī in Pakistan founded by Sayyid Abul A'la Mawdudi in Lahore in 1941 is an ideological movement. Its aim is to identify, select and organise those who respond to the call of Islam on one platform and to train them for moral, intellectual and social upliftment. Through these people, the Jamāᶜat embarks on an all-out campaign for the regeneration and reconstruction of the collective life of the community on Islamic principles and to change the social, economic and, most importantly, the political leadership of the country. The Jamāᶜat believes in conducting the movement for reform openly and peacefully within the boundaries of the law and existing constitution.

The Iranian revolution led by Ayatullah Ruhullah Musavi Khomeini believes in the *jihād* for the establishment of a just social, economic and political order. Imam Khomeini's *jihād* consisted of an uncompromising opposition to the tyrannical regimes and mobilisation of masses to rise against the regimes through various means. Khomeini rejected the piecemeal reformist approach and advocated the revolutionary method of uprooting the injustices from human society. The relative ease with which Reza Shah Pahlawi was toppled in Iran was the most dramatic manifestation of the revolutionary potential of Islam in modern times.

Islamic movements, including the three outlined above, can be grouped into two broad categories: one, which has primarily religious orientations and the other which is dominated by socio-political considerations. The Tablīghī movement can be categorized under the first category, while the Islamic Revolution in Iran and the Jamāᶜat-e-Islāmī movement in Pakistan are examples of the second. It must be pointed out at the outset that all these movements are inspired by the visions of a return to pristine Islam. Firstly, they are alike in perceiving Islam not as a religion composed of certain rituals but a comprehensive way of life. Secondly, they believe in the universality of Islam and, as such, emphasize the unity of all Muslims, transcending all barriers of race, colour and territory. Thirdly, they reject ideologies like capitalism, socialism, nationalism and secularism as man-made and hence incapable of ensuring happiness for mankind. Muslim societies suffer, according to them, because they succumb to ungodly ways of living and relegate religion to personal, private life. Fourthly, they abhor blind imitation (taqlīd) and advocate independent reasoning in matters of legal judgements (ijtihād). Finally, they stress the need for continuous, ceaseless struggle to fulfil the divine obligation of founding a social order based on divine imperatives.

It can be seen that the three movements have various manifestations. The strategies they pursued have serious implications as to their final outcome. The achievements of the Jamāᶜat and the Tablīghī movement pale into insignificance when compared to the movement in Iran and the victory it gained. One of the reasons is that unlike that of Sunni Muslims, a strong revolutionary component has been inherent in the shiᶜī school of thought. The shiᶜī consider only the Imams and those whom they appointed to be the legitimate holders of authority. All others are illegitimate, and therefore must be resisted. When opportunities are ripe for rebellion they would seize the occasion in the name of the Imam, and at other times they would be forced to conform to the dominant realities. Though the Sunni movements have so far not been able to achieve their goals, several indicators suggest that their popularity is on the rise. Does this mean that the movements are destined to attain the goal they set out to achieve? Considering the rate of growth, one is tempted to assume that the movements will be able to fulfill their aspirations at some point in the future. However, a more accurate assessment requires a critical evaluation of the objectives of the movement and the types of strategies employed to achieve these objectives, as well as the nature of the problems and difficulties they face.

The book *Revolution to Revolution: Jamāᶜat-e-Islāmī in the Politics of Pakistan* by Professor Abdul Rashid Moten of the Department of Political Science, International Islamic University Malaysia attempts a critical evaluation of the objectives, strategies and achievements of a contemporary Islamic movement. With particular reference to the Jamāᶜat-e-Islāmī in Pakistan, the author deals with four different and yet strictly interrelated issues. He alludes to the historical origins and ideological premises of Western supremacy, briefly discusses the democratic agenda of the Western powers, explains the Muslim response to the Western dictates and analyses the consequences of adopting the Western models for realizing Islamic aspirations. There are many scholars of Islamic movement who have embarked upon this type of analysis. What is interesting about Professor Abdul Rashid Moten's work is that he deviates from the mainstream. Instead of examining the impact of an Islamic movement on the society and the polity of a particular country, he reverses the sequence and asks what happens to an

Islamic movement when it enters into the political arena avowedly to capture political power. The study found, in the case of the Jamāᶜat-e-Islāmī, that one particular outcome of its decision to get involved in politics is the transformation of the revivalist movement into a political party. This transformation is associated with the leadership and elite structure of the Jamāᶜat. The irony is that despite the transformation, the Jamāᶜat has not been able to capture power. The only realistic course of action for the Jamāᶜat thus remains delinking, which means an opting out of structures of the capitalist world system pursued in Pakistan, and a total devotion to the alleviation of the problems of suffering millions. Only such an admittedly long and presumably uneasy method of *daᶜwah* might provide a real hope for the people of Pakistan and in the long run create a firm basis for ushering in a just and humane Islamic political order.

From the intellectual point of view, the author asks questions and points to problems that are quite often distorted or even completely overlooked by most scholars of Islamic political thought and institutions. The findings arrived at by the author are true not only of Pakistan but may also be true of other Islamic movements in general. A comparative study of various Islamic movements might have put the findings on a firmer ground and might have indicated the nature and direction of change that the author has analysed. In this sense, this study may be considered within the framework of a hypothesis generating type.

The book is not a philosophical analysis of the wider question of religion as a factor in Pakistani politics before and since independence. The author's contribution lies in giving us an objective account of various transformations that have taken place in the Jamāᶜat-e-Islāmī since its inception in 1941 and linking it with the changes that have taken place in the elite structure of the organization. To that extent the author has been fairly successful in bringing out what may be regarded as a pioneering work on this subject. It is hoped that this book will not only fill an important gap in the literature on Islamic movements but will also generate interest in more sophisticated studies on this and other Islamic movements and organizations. *Wa'Llāhu aᶜlam.*

M. Kamal Hassan
Kuala Lumpur
1 Ramaḍān 1422/17 November 2001

PREFACE

The purpose of this study is to pinpoint various milestones in the transformation of the Jamā'at-e-Islāmī from a quietist movement with the objective of Islamic revival to an active political party and a mass revolutionary movement bent upon wresting power from "the leadership of the wayward and of those gone astray." It enquires into the value and validity of this transformation and assesses its impact upon the organization and upon the society as a whole. Rather than studying the impact of Islamization on politics, this study reverses the sequence and evaluates the consequences of "politicizing" an Islamic movement. It attempts to answer the following questions: What is the balance sheet of the Jamā'at-e-Islāmī movement in terms of its achievements? Why has it failed to achieve what it wanted to achieve? What suggestions can be proffered to help it and similar other movements sustain the tempo that they have generated?

This study offers a micro-view of the experiences and attitudes of the rank and file of the Jamā'at-e-Islāmī at certain points in time and over a period of time. Based upon the elite approach, it emphasizes not merely interactions among elite members but also considers the general context within which they operate, emphasizes interactions between the elite and their social and physical environment and finally, highlights the outcomes or effects of elite action.

The study found that the transformation of the Jamā'at has been piecemeal and evolutionary. It began as a revivalist movement and gradually changed first to a pressure group, then to a cadre party, a mass party and eventually to a mass revolutionary movement. The transformations took place during the civilian era and the military regimes assisted in radicalizing the party. This transformation is associated with both the leadership and elite structure of the Jamā'at. Despite the transformation, the party has not been able to capture power. It needs to take *da'wah* and welfare activities seriously to alleviate material and spiritual poverty, cultivate grass-root networks, attract followers to the cause, and challenge the inefficient, competing institutions of the political system of Pakistan.

The study is organized into five chapters. Chapter one after discussing the reaction of Muslims to the challenge of the West, defines the research problem, provides a background to the research questions, a context literature review and the design of the research. Chapter two serves as an introduction to the complex socio-economic environment in which the Jamāʿat operated both before and after the independence of Pakistan. It briefly analyses the nature and direction of the successive political regimes in Pakistan from 1947 to 1999 and highlights the governmental structures and the policies pursued by various regimes vis-a-vis Islam and their consequences for the forces seeking Islamization of Pakistan. Chapter three examines the policies and strategies adopted by Jamāʿat-e-Islāmī of Pakistan under the leadership of Sayyid Abul A'la Mawdudi. It also analyzes the transformation of the Jamāʿat from a quietist revivalist movement to an interest group and eventually into a cadre-based political party aimed at capturing decision-making power, alone or in coalition. It examines this evolution by referring to the social and intellectual base of its leadership structure as reflected in the changing composition of the working committee of the Jamāʿat-e-Islāmī. Chapter four evaluates the performance of the Jamāʿat under the leadership of Qazi Hussain Ahmad, and its transformation into a mass revolutionary movement. The final chapter summarizes the findings of this study and explores their implications for the future of Islam in the politics of Pakistan.

While all references have been given in the relevant notes, the references to the Qur'ān have been given within parentheses immediately after the citation. In translating the Qur'ān, the study has benefited from the translations of Abdullah Yusuf Ali and T. B. Irving. In transliterating the Arabic words, the study has followed the Library of Congress transliteration system.

Abdul Rashid Moten
Department of Political Science
International Islamic University Malaysia

ACKNOWLEDGEMENTS

All praise be to Allah (s.w.t), the Creator, Cherisher and Sustainer of the Universe, and may He shower peace and blessings upon His last Prophet Muhammad (s.a.w). This book had its origin in a paper presented at an international conference on Islamic political movements. My colleagues and friends persuaded me to expand it into a monograph that eventually matured into its current form. Professor Abdullah Hassan provided the original impetus and encouragement for this book. He was equally instrumental in getting the work finished on time for the Isma'il al-Faruqi award for academic excellence. Alḥamdulillāh, the manuscript did win an award. Professor Zafar Afaq Ansari has been wonderfully supportive throughout this project, exchanging ideas and information, opening his private collections on Jamā'at, and helping to give an overall shape to the work. Professor A. Khaleq Kazi and my colleague, Dr. Noor-e-Alam Siddiqui carefully read and reviewed the first draft and provided the kind of ongoing stimulation, serious criticism, and friendship that help to make intellectual life so deeply satisfying. Professor Syed Nasir Reza Kazmi has been extremely generous with his time and helped greatly in revising and editing it. His rigorous reading of the text has lightened my load tremendously. Professor Kamal Hasan, Dato' Dr. Jamil Hj. Osman, Professors Aris Hj. Othman, Mohd. Yusof Hussain, Hassan Ahmad Ibrahim, Abdullahil Ahsan, Dato' Dr. Syed Arabi Idid, Dr. G. Subramaniam, Dr. Khaliq Ahmad and colleagues at the Kulliyyah (faculty) and the Department provided valuable encouragement and sympathetic support. I am particularly grateful to Professor M. Kamal Hasan, Rector of the International Islamic University Malaysia, who despite his extremely busy schedule, provided the foreword to this book. The University Librarian, Syed Salim Agha, and the two information librarians, Abd. Rashid Abd. Rahman and Rosmawati Mohd. Akhiar have rendered invaluable assistance and always with a smile. Sisters Rofeah bt. Ishaque, Roseniza bt. Talib, Mohana Nambiar and Farikah bt. Mohd. Yusof were readily available to share their knowledge and skill. Finally, I want to thank most heartily my publisher Islamic Book Trust for their dedication and hard work throughout the revision process. My thanks to all those people does not implicate them for any inaccuracies that have inadvertently crept into the text.

My wife, Ramizah Wan Muhammad, has provided support and understood the reasons for my being less sociable than usual. Our sons, Ahmed Zaki, Ahmed Wafi and Ahmed Lutfi, have displayed some understanding of the time I needed to work on this project and have now and then politely enquired: "What takes you that long" to complete the book? This book is dedicated to the youngest member of our family, Ahmed Lutfi Rashid, whose silent smiles provided a wonderful escape from books, files, and statistics and in that process provided further impetus to complete the project. May Allah, *subḥānahū wa taʿālā,* reward them all and forgive me for all errors and shortcomings.

1

INTRODUCTION: A FRAMEWORK
FOR ANALYSIS

Despite half-a-century of its existence, the Jamā'at-e-Islāmī of Pakistan is at bay. Its mixed record includes survival in the face of state repression and some impact on political decision making, but a general failure in the attempt to capture power avowedly for the Islamization of Pakistan. This failure is all the more glaring because it happens in Pakistan, a country where Islam provides guidance for and regulates every aspect of life and occupies centre stage in the social, economic and political life of all Pakistanis. Admittedly, though the vague but tenaciously held beliefs of the inarticulate, illiterate average Muslim differs from the Islam of the educated, urban and non-practising Muslims, the imprint of Islam nonetheless is clearly visible.[1] Why has the Jamā'at reached this impasse? What strategy did it follow in its aim of Islamizing the government and politics of Pakistan? Has it been consistent in pursuing the strategy it adopted to transform Pakistan into an Islamic political system? How did the Jamā'at interact with successive regimes in Pakistan and with what results?

ISLAM AND POLITICS
Islam is not a religion in the sense commonly understood, that is, as being no more than the sum of several beliefs, rituals and sentiments, but rather a system that deals with all aspects of human existence and performance. It is a well-ordered system, a consistent whole, comprising a set of universal principles and pan-cultural values for the socio-economic, political and moral guidance of humanity.

The Qur'ān condemns anarchy and disorder (*al-Baqarah*, 2:205), and the Prophet (s.a.w) stressed the need for organisation and authority in society. Similarly, ᶜUmar, the second Caliph, considered an organised society impossible without an *imām* (the leader), and added that there could be no *imām* without obedience.[2] The first four rightly guided caliphs (*khulafā' al-rāshidūn*) and their companions recognised that the divinely mandated vocation to realise the will of Allah (s.w.t) in history was communal as well as individual. They held an organic, holistic approach to life in which religion was intimately intertwined with politics, law and society. This is well expressed by Ka'ab as quoted by Ibn Qutaybah:

> Islam, the government and the people are like the tent, the
> pole, the ropes and the pegs. The tent is Islam; the pole is
> the government, the ropes and pegs are the people. None
> will do without the others.[3]

Thus the fusion of religion and politics is the dictate of Islam and cannot be disregarded. The choice between the Creator and Caesar does not *simply* arise. For Islam, there is no Caesar, there is only Allah (s.w.t) and His Messenger. The sharīᶜah (the Islamic law) incorporates the temporal with the spiritual. In Islam, ethics sets the tone for politics and the rules of political behaviour are derived from the ethical norms of Islam. Thus the major concerns of politics namely, striving to control the state-structure, to wrest power for the righteous, to root out evil and bring about the good life are all relevant to and encouraged by Islam. Islam accords centrality to these activities with the difference that the political life has to be situated within the larger frame of the religious and spiritual life. Religion and politics, as such, are not "two sides of a single coin in Islam."[4] Neither can they be rank-ordered, making one the independent and the other the dependent variable in the relationship. The truth, as Muhammad Iqbal puts it, is that "Islam is a single, unanalysable reality which is one or the other, as your point of view varies."[5]

This interlocking of the spiritual and the temporal was exemplified in the roles donned by the Prophet (s.a.w) and by his successors - the *rāshidūn* caliphs. This Madinah model exemplifies the principles of an Islamic polity in its pure and perfect form. Since then, as ibn Khaldun argues on the basis of historical evidence, a radical change took place which caused a deviation from the true Islamic governance decreed by the Qur'ān and the Prophet (s.a.w). Starting with the Umayyads, there ensued a new variant in Muslim history – dynastic rule that sometimes degenerated into unbridled monarchy.[6] The Umayyad caliphate was for all practical purposes a secular empire. The same could be said more or less about the Abbasids. In the case of Muslim rule in India, the Delhi Sultanate (1206-1398), its successor regional states and the Mughal Empire ran the administration, except the judicial administration, almost on secular patterns.[7] Yet the dynastic rulers publicly recognized the supremacy of the sharīʿah and sought the legitimacy of their political rule in the doctrines of Islam. During those turbulent years, the Muslim thinkers grappled with the onerous task of fostering in the believers an authentic religious spirit and in conjunction with this an insistence on the implementation of all the injunctions of the sharīʿah. Their lives exuded a mutually enriching togetherness of spiritual striving and effective socio-political reform activity.

During the nineteenth century, Islam experienced a particularly grave crisis. The Muslim world succumbed militarily, economically and politically to Western Christendom that shook the confidence of Muslims in their own civilization. Their analyses of historical reverses and their prescription for remedial action produced three different perspectives referred to by Khurshid Ahmad as traditionalism, modernism and *tajdīd*.[8] The traditionalists advocated holding fast to Islamic tradition and its legacy and a total withdrawal from the processes of Westernization. The Westernizing Muslim modernists, like Sir Sayyid Ahmad Khan of India, even if they meant well in their desire to defend Islam, in effect presented a truncated and deformed Islam. The interaction between the two viewpoints has given rise to a vibrant and modern interpretation of Islam, known as *tajdīd*, which emphasizes the totality of Islam as the divinely mandated alternative to the materialism and secularism of the West.[9] *Tajdīd* is a call for a return to the original message of Islam, to discover its relevance to the existing milieu and to strive to change the status quo to conform to the tenets and principles of Islam. The call of the *tajdīd*, which is integral to the Jamāᶜat-e-Islāmī of Pakistan, the Muslim Brotherhood of Egypt and other Islamic movements, is for a comprehensive reform along Islamic lines in all aspects of life including politics. Religion, which under the impact of secularism lay dormant for a while, had re-emerged in Muslim politics and society.

Such was the strength of this aspiration that it destabilized the governments of Muhammad Raza Shah of Iran and Z.A. Bhutto of Pakistan. Subsequently, it is Islam that gave legitimacy to their successors, the Ayatullah Khomeini and General Ziaul Haq. Under Zia, Pakistan came to be regarded by the Muslim world as the most Islamic-oriented polity after Iran. Brunei, attaining independence in 1984, proclaimed itself as the Sultanate of Brunei Darussalam, declaring thereby its identity as part of the Muslim ummah in its official designation. Even Turkey, which drastically broke its spiritual bond with the Islamic world in 1924, evidenced a reawakening of Muslim identity and elected the Muslim Refah Party to power.

ISLAM AND THE WEST

The resurgence of Islam in contemporary Muslim societies has increased attention by the West to an alleged Islamic threat. The collapse of communism has left a threat vacuum and led to clamorous fears of militant Islam in the media and scholarly work. Leslie Gelb wrote in 1992 that "Islam doesn't recognize coexistence as a basic doctrine. Coexistence goes against Islam's sense of world order."[10] Amos Perlmutter wrote in 1995 that in the post-Cold-War world, one form of totalitarianism has been replaced with another; "the soviet model with an Islamic one."[11]

Bernard Lewis places the Gulf War and rise of Islamic radicalism within the context of a centuries-long struggle between Christendom and Islam, an antagonism that he calls a "clash of civilizations."[12] Lewis views Islamic revivalism and its rejection of both the West's secularism and its modernism as being rooted in the corruption and impoverishment of the Muslim way of life as a result of Western domination and influence. He argues that "since the United States is the legitimate heir of European civilization and the recognized and unchallenged leader of the West, the United States has inherited the resulting grievances and become the focus for the pent-up hate and anger."[13] Lewis's discussion, though lacking in depth and analysis, received national and international coverage. Judith Miller argues that virtually all militant Islamists oppose democracy and pluralism. They are, "and are likely to remain, anti-Western, anti-American and anti-Israeli."[14]

Samuel Huntington, taking the title for his controversial article "The Clash of Civilizations?" from Bernard Lewis, argues that with the end of the Cold War, ideological conflicts will be replaced by wars between nations and groups of different civilizations.[15] "The fault line between civilizations will be the battle lines of the future."[16] Rather than one global world order emerging from the collapse of the Soviet Union and the end of the Cold War, nations will gradually coalesce into civilizational blocs. They will do so in order to defend themselves against the West's efforts to promote its own values of democracy and liberalism as universal values, maintain its military predominance and advance its economic interests. Like Lewis, Huntington believes that this struggle for a New World Order is taking place in the long boundary separating the West and Islam. Huntington, furthermore, identifies a Confucian/Islamic connection that has emerged to challenge Western interests and power.

Huntington's perception that the danger mainly comes from the Islamic world is biased in favour of the Western trend that considers Islam the new threat, without giving the evidence to that or even without discussing the other alternative Western trend expressed by John Esposito. For Esposito, considering Islam as an enemy to the West that threatens its interests is an exaggeration and a distortion of the nature of Islam. In addition, this viewpoint belies the basic realities of the Islamic world and its different relationships with the West.[17] Nevertheless, Huntington has been

very influential and has provided Western policy makers and
geostrategists an intellectual paradigm for their post-Cold War
policies towards China and an assertive Islam.

WESTERN STRATEGIES TO DEAL WITH ISLAM

Experts disagree on how governments should respond to the
religious upsurge. Some think that repression works and they cite
the decisive action that Syria took against the Muslim Brotherhood
in the mass slaughter at Hama in 1982. Others argue that militants
thrive on martyrdom and that the best way to deal with them is to
co-opt, or allow, them into power.

Peter Rodman, a former member of the National Security
Council in the Reagan and Bush administrations, advised American
foreign policy makers to take serious note of the fact that the
fundamental principle of Islamic fundamentalism is resentment of
the West and hence it should be treated as an adversary of "our
most basic principles."[18] Judith Miller argues that Islam is
fundamentally incompatible with values and truths Americans and
most Westerners hold as self-evident. She concludes that an
American dialogue with such Islamic forces is a waste of time.
Trying to distinguish good from bad fundamentalism, as the U.S.
did in the "Meridian House declaration," will only lead to victories
by Islamist parties who will violate democratic principles once in
power.[19] Indeed, Samuel Huntington did argue that the West will
"have to accommodate" civilizations whose values and interests
differ significantly from its own. His accommodation, however,
was to prepare for conflict by maintaining "American military
superiority" in the heartland of Islam, i.e., in East and Southwest
Asia.[20] Daniel Pipes has suggested that the West should combat
Islamic fundamentalism the way it did communism. This includes:
opposing all forms of Islamic fundamentalism; utilizing the many
instruments of leverage to press fundamentalist states to reduce
their aggressiveness; supporting Muslim individuals and
institutions confronting fundamentalist "scourge"; and, providing
assistance to those Muslim governments, like Algeria, which are
combating the fundamentalists.[21]

The American government did take the above policy proposals seriously. Consequently the cornerstone of U.S. policy is to weaken the influence of Islamic forces in the Muslim world. The U.S. does this by draining the financial and political resources of Islamic fundamentalism, by erecting rigid military security measures, by positioning of massive U.S. troops in the Gulf and the Horn, and by bombing the "so-called" suspected Muslim extremist areas. The last strategy was exemplified, among others, by the U.S. bombing of Iraq in January and June 1993 and December 1998, of Sudan and Afghanistan in August 1998, and of Taliban-ruled Afghanistan in October-November 2001. Dual containment of Iran and Iraq, which is central to U.S. strategy in the Middle East, has been reinforced with the extension of sanctions against Iraq and the complete trade embargo on Iran announced on April 30, 1995. The U.S. has signed counterterrorism treaties with Israel and Egypt and promoted security conferences between states threatened by Islamic fundamentalism. The U.S. by giving its uncritical support to regimes that practice mass arrest, torture, and other extralegal procedures is guilty of the worst of human rights abuses.

President Clinton found it useful when visiting Indonesia to declare that "even though we have had problems with terrorism coming out of the Middle East, it is not inherently related to Islam – not to the religion, not to the culture." Earlier in Jordan, he had said, "America refuses to accept that our civilizations must collide. We respect Islam."[22] These fine sentiments are not backed by any positive action in this regard. The intimidation of Islamic forces by America has not grown any weaker. The U.S. list of terrorism sponsors is dominated by Muslim states such as Libya, Iran, Sudan, Syria, and Iraq. Apparently, the U.S. equates Islam with terrorism. The two bomb blasts which occurred in Nairobi and Dar es Salam on August 7, 1998 were blamed upon the Muslims and a global witch-hunt started, resulting in the firing of some missiles into Afghanistan and Sudan. Yet when terrorists blew up the small Northern Ireland town of Omagh, killing 28 and injuring 220, on August 15, 1998, the fact that religion was at the center of that despicable act was hardly spoken about.

The most convincing voices countering the generalizations

and over-simplifications about modern Islamic movements belong
to academics who themselves have criticized many aspects of Islam
over the years. They include John Voll, John Esposito, James Bill,
John Entelis, Richard Bulliet, Charles Butterworth and Augustus
Richard Norton. They assert that the failure to make distinctions
among the many Islamic movements and the stereotyping of
Muslims as violence-prone radicals will strengthen the extremists
at the expense of the vast majority of moderate and responsible
Muslims. Robin Wright argues that Islam should not be seen as a
replacement for communism and an ideological rival of the West.
Islamic parties are not necessarily anti-democratic and hence should
not be demonized wholesale.[23] The crusade against political Islam,
writes Leon Hadar, is in danger of becoming a "self-fulfilling
prophecy" and a vicious circle.[24] Continued support for repressive
regimes, exacerbated by America's alliance with Israel, only fans
resentment toward the United States. And the existence of that
resentment makes it more difficult for Washington to tolerate the
idea of democratization and reform in the region.

John Esposito criticizes the media for too often placing Muslim-
Western relations in a context of confrontation, wherein Islam is
pitted against "our Judeo-Christian and secular West."[25] While
attempts are made to portray assaults on the West by irrational
Arab masses, no mention is made that cancelling elections and
repressing populist movements can indeed create conditions that
lead to political violence. Esposito argues that political Islam did
not begin with the Iranian revolution but is the result of the failure
of secular nationalist governments to halt widespread corruption,
stem the widening gap between rich and poor, achieve economic
self-sufficiency, and resist Western political and cultural hegemony.
These failures, exacerbated by the disastrous defeat by Israel in
the 1967 war, have triggered soul-searching in the Muslim world
and the quest for an Islamic solution. These diverse Islamic
movements are being led by a developing alternative elite made
up of university graduates and professionals and they seek the
gradual Islamization of society through words, preaching and social
and political activity.

Esposito, Wright, Hadar and others advocate moderation and advise Washington to work with all governments, gauging the depth of its relationship on shared values of democracy, tolerance, and economic and political justice. They argue that the West should initiate direct dialogue with Muslim theologians and activists. They should display more sensitivity in distinguishing between Islam and terrorism. The West and particularly the U.S., should recognize that there are various models of Islamic empowerment. Muslim activists in countries like Malaysia, Pakistan, Jordan, Turkey and the like have participated in parliaments and coalition governments and have shown a great deal of moderation and tolerance. The West should support and encourage these Islamic forces and work with democratic openings and influence their development. As pointed out by Robin Wright, Algeria provided an opportunity for the West to work with a fundamentalist movement. Such opportunities should be fully utilised to promote civil society in the Muslim world.

THE MUSLIM RESPONSE
The suggested strategy for the Islamic movements to work within the democratic framework has been opposed on various grounds. First, it is argued that the democratic method will not stop society's drift towards Westernization and secularism, let alone help bring about the desired Islamic system. Second, participation in the secular, democratic processes may adversely affect the idealism and probity of the movement and tarnish its image as an organization of selfless people working for the pleasure of Allah (s.w.t). Third, the Muslim authoritarian regimes will either not allow the Islamic movements to participate in the democratic game, or if allowed, it will be under their terms and conditions which will reduce the Islamic movements to play a second fiddle. They will be given minor ministries as junior partners in the coalition without the possibility of exerting any influence on public policy as was the case with the Jamāᶜat-e-Islāmī in the government of Nawaz Sharif. Fourth, no Islamic movement or Islamic party has ever won power through the ballot; elections are rigged almost

everywhere. The Islamic movements have been a victim of suppression and oppression in many countries for a long time. In most of the countries doors for a peaceful change are totally closed. Wherever there are so-called openings, different types of methods are applied to crush the Islamic movements. Egypt, Turkey, Algeria, Pakistan and Sudan are some of the examples. In Sudan and Egypt, the effort towards a peaceful transfer was and is being physically obstructed. Turkey is a country where a popular Muslim party partially succeeded but the further progress was blocked. In Pakistan, opportunities exist but effort, so far have been unsuccessful. Finally, even if an Islamic party or movement somehow succeeds in coming close to capturing power, the results would be annulled one way or the other as happened in the case of the Islamic Salvation Front of Algeria. Muslim rulers sheepishly follow steps of their Western masters to fulfil their political and economic interests. In retaliation if some people were to resort to force, they are branded as terrorists. These rulers are promoting non-Islamic culture and crushing Islamic forces in their own, as well as their masters' interests.

Nevertheless there are many Islamic movements that insist on the evolutionary approach for carrying out social change. They believe in the affinity between democracy and Islamic governmental system, even though they reject the philosophical assumptions of Western democracy. They are opposed to all unlawful, unconstitutional and subversive acts and distrust political radicalism of any kind. They argue that the Islamic movement is for the cause of Allah (s.w.t) and it should be conducted openly and peacefully even at the risk of courting hardship and miseries.[26] Sayyid Abul A'la Mawdudi and others like him justify their predilection for non-violent approach on theoretical as well as practical grounds. Thus one argument is that it is against the natural order of things to force change as all stable and far-reaching changes in the collective life of people come about gradually. From the practical point of view, if change was to be lasting, it had to be carried out slowly; for, "the more sudden a change, the more short-lived it generally turns out to be."[27] In the specific case of Pakistan, it is argued that the government permits freedom to preach Islam and that change of government is possible through peaceful means of elections. In this respect, Sayyid Mawdudi has clearly stated:

> In the country you are living in, there exists a legal and constitutional system. For a change in its leadership there is only one lawful way: elections. While living within a legal and constitutional system, adoption of any unlawful means for changing its leadership is not just according to sharīᶜah. On this basis the constitution of your Jamāᶜat has bound you to follow only legal and constitutional ways for the reformation and the revolution that you have in view.[28]

STUDYING THE JAMĀᶜAT

The Jamāᶜat-e-Islāmī of Pakistan under the leadership of Sayyid Mawdudi has taken an active part in the politics of Pakistan. The model of the political system discernible in Mawdudi's later writings, approaches the institution of Western parliamentary democracy, with a chief executive elected on the basis of universal adult franchise and with state power distributed among judicial, executive and legislative branches of government. The Jamāᶜat's prime objective is to reform the existing set-up of government and to establish the Islamic system through constitutional means. In operational terms, the objective of the Jamāᶜat is to render sound counsel to the government and to participate in elections with all its concomitants of campaigning and alliance formations to change the political leadership of the country. This, however, was not the Jamāᶜat's objective at the time of its formation in 1942. In other words, the Jamāᶜat's strategy changed with the change in the environment.

The purpose of this study is to point out various milestones in the transformation of the Jamāᶜat-e-Islāmī from a quietist movement with the objective of Islamic revival to an active political party bent upon wresting power from "the leadership of the wayward and of those gone astray."[29] It examines this organizational evolution by referring to the social and intellectual base of its

leadership structure. It enquires into the value and validity of this
transformation and assesses its impact upon the organization and
upon the society as a whole. Rather than studying the impact of
Islamization on politics, this study reverses the sequence and
evaluates the consequences of "politicizing" an Islamic movement.
It attempts to answer the following questions: What is the balance
sheet of the Jamāᶜat-e-Islāmī movement in terms of its
achievements? Why has it failed to achieve what it wanted to
achieve? What suggestions can be proffered to help it and similar
movements sustain the tempo that they have generated?

This study offers a micro-view of the experiences and attitudes
of the rank and file of the Jamāᶜat-e-Islāmī at certain points in time
and over a period of time. The choices made by the leadership of
the Jamāᶜat are determined, like all human decisions, by a wide
range of factors and not simply by their religious predisposition.
They are guided, in their decisions, often by desire for social status
and prestige, as well as cultural and spiritual concerns that go
beyond short-term maximization of material gains. This study
considers some of these factors in its explanation of what is termed
as the politicization of an Islamic movement. The study, it must be
noted, is not about Islam per se, but Islam did act as a major driving
force behind the thoughts and actions of the elite of the Jamāᶜat-e-
Islāmī in Pakistan.

THE APPROACH
This study considers the elite approach as the most appropriate
starting point for an understanding of the transformation of the
Jamāᶜat-e-Islāmī movement in Pakistan. Elite studies were
developed in early twentieth century European scholarship as an
alternative to the Marxist emphasis on class and as a corrective to
the egalitarianism of democratic philosophy. Originating in the
writings of Vilfred Pareto, Gaetano Mosca, and Robert Michels,
elite analysis was further pursued, toward the middle of the century,
by others; notably by Lasswell and Lerner, C. Wright Mills and
Robert Dahl.[30] In much the same way as Marx had viewed class
conflict as endemic in all societies, so the elite theorists saw elite

groups as endemic in all societies, as perpetual elements of social organization. The basic premise of the earlier elite theory is that all of humanity can be divided into two groups: the elite and the masses. This premise finds its elaboration in the writings of Pareto and Mosca. Elites not only exist, Michels argued, but they are inevitable. Whatever the form of organization, an oligarchy will emerge to occupy the positions of authority. To Michels, "organization" is simply another way of spelling "oligarchy."[31] To this doctrine he attached the label, "iron law of oligarchy" - a law which received a succinct restatement at the hands of Lasswell; "Government is always governed by the few, whether in the name of the few, the one, or the many."[32] From here it was just a small step for C. Wright Mills to propound his "power elite model" - an interlocking power elite consisting of a political directorate of politicians and bureaucrats, high corporate executives, and prominent military figures.[33]

The elite approach adopted in this study also has its root in Islamic scholarship. Abu Nasr Muhammad al-Farabi (259-339 AH/ 870-950 CE), the Muslim philosopher, who sought to harmonize classical philosophy with Islam, bases his theory of an ideal state on elite rule. He rested his case on the argument that "there are some who have the intellect to draw conclusion better than others, while some can convey their deduction to others with greater facility."[34] Those who can deduce conclusions from given facts lead those who cannot. Those who guide are known in modern political science terminology as the elite. Al-Farabi influenced later writers profoundly. Among them, Ibn Sina (Avicenna, 370-427 AH /980-1037 CE) also links the ideal state of Islam with that of philosopher king and Fakhr al-Din al-Razi (543-606 AH/1149-1209 CE) who adapted the theory of the philosopher king to the Ideal Islamic rule.

Among the jurists, Abu al-Hasan al-Mawardi (364-450 AH/ 974-1058 CE) adopted an elite approach in his exposition of the ideal Islamic government. In an age in which the prestige of the caliphate had fallen to its lowest ebb, Al-Mawardi strains himself to propound a theory of the caliphate in which everything depends

on the authority of the caliph. The caliph or the *imām*, to al-
Mawardi, is the defender of the faith, the chief administrator, the
dispenser of justice, and the leader in prayer and in war. Hence he
gave a detailed exposition of the conditions required of the caliph,
the manner of his election, of his functions and those of the officers
under his authority. He has also discussed the qualifications of
those entrusted with the task of electing the *imām*, the *ahl al ḥal
wa al ᶜaqd* (those who loosen and bind).[35] The *imām* and the
qualified electors together constitute the elite. The emphasis on
elite is also found in the "theory of Islamic government" given by
Abu Hamid Muhammad al-Ghazali (450-505 AH/1058-1111 CE)
that contained three elements, the caliph, the sultan and the
ᶜulamā'.[36]

Among the contemporary Muslim thinkers and that with whom
this study is largely concerned, Sayyid Abul Aᶜla Mawdudi (1322-
1399 AH/1903-1979 CE) has argued for an elite approach. He
believed that the essence of politics in Pakistan, as elsewhere, is to
be discerned in the nature and behaviour of political elite. It is
within a numerically miniscule percentage of the population that
differences over the allocation of values, the policies and the
mission of the nation are worked out. This fact, to Sayyid Mawdudi,
was so obvious that it could be seen "even with little insight," that
"human civilization travels in the direction determined by the
people who control the centres of power."[37] Mawdudi refers to
the Prophet (s.a.w) saying: "There are two classes in my ummah -
if they are right the ummah is set right, if they go wrong the ummah
goes wrong: they are rulers and scholars."[38]

In colonial and post-colonial societies, the elite has played
significant roles as leaders of protest and reform, as opposition to
the governing elite, as allies of a "power elite" and sometimes, as
seekers of power through revolution or election.[39] However, it
would be inaccurate to refer to the elite as a single class or a group.
The Jamāᶜat-e-Islāmī elite, for instance, is not a homogeneous
group. It spans a wide range of incomes, diverse and differing
levels of educational attainments and varying status and power in
society. Nor is it a static category: its composition changes by

recruitment into or slippage out of the category. Elite analysis to be meaningful should not merely emphasize interactions among elite members but also consider the general context within which they operate, stress interactions between the elite and their social and physical environment and finally, highlight the outcomes or effects of elite action. This study is an attempt in that direction.

DEFINING THE POLITICAL ELITE

Who are the political elites? Scholars using an elite approach vary considerably in their definitions. Some define them very narrowly to consider only the "men at the top."[40] Others define them broadly to include all "those who get most of what there is to get,"[41] or all "those persons in a society with power - individually, regularly and seriously - to affect political outcomes."[42] Thus authors employing the elite approach vary in their definition of elites. In this study, the term political elite is used to refer to small active minorities who play an important role in the "authoritative allocation of values" and are directly engaged in the struggle for political leadership.

To be useful however, the concept has to be operationalized and the elites identified. Identifying the political elites and attributing degrees of influence is an undertaking fraught with methodological problems and pitfalls. Broadly speaking, empirical efforts to identify elites have tended to center on one of three fundamental questions: Who occupies the formal positions of power? Who is reputed to possess the most power? Who actually makes decisions? These methods are labelled respectively as the positional, the reputational, and the decision-making method of elite identification.[43] The political elites of the Jamāᶜat-e-Islāmī movement in Pakistan are identified by using the positional approach. The most important positions in the Jamāᶜat are the office of the Amir or President, the Deputy presidents, the Secretary General and the members of the Consultative Assembly or Majlis-e-Shura. Outside the Jamāᶜat, elite occupying such strategic positions as President of the republic, central ministers, members of the national and provincial assemblies and top ranking civil servants and military officers are identified as political elites.

DATA BASE
The data for this analysis came from the usual major sources of
non-survey data, namely the press reports, party publications, and
other government and nongovernment sources of aggregate data
on elections and other variables. The newspapers served as a
valuable source of information. They indicated periodic changes
in the Pakistani political scene, chronicled events, and reflected
elite views on important issues in the country. The study also
benefited immensely from various scholarly publications dealing
with the Jamāᶜat-e-Islāmī movement in particular and the
government and politics in Pakistan in general.

2

SOCIO-POLITICAL ENVIRONMENT AND THE JAMĀᶜAT

The Jamāᶜat-e-Islāmī (Jamāᶜat), Party or Association of Islam, was founded in 1941 in Lahore, British India, by Sayyid Abul Aᶜla Mawdudi with the aim of assuring a healthy religious environment in India for Muslims. The socio-political environment, however, changed in 1947 with the withdrawal of the British and the emergence of two independent dominions: India and Pakistan. The Jamāᶜat moved to Pakistan and has since been playing an active role in shaping the nature and content of Islamic political discourse in Pakistan.[1] Depending upon the circumstances, the Jamāᶜat played either a confrontational or an associational role vis-a-vis the government and other contending political groups.

This chapter, after introducing Sayyid Mawdudi, analyses the complex socio-political environment in which the Jamāᶜat operated, both before and after the independence of Pakistan. It also highlights the governmental structures and the policies pursued by the governing elite in promoting or containing the influence of the Jamāᶜat in the politics of Pakistan. This chapter should serve as a backdrop to the discussion on the transition of the Jamāᶜat from a revivalist movement to a political party.

SAYYID ABUL AᶜLA MAWDUDI
Sayyid Abul Aᶜla Mawdudi was born on September 25, 1903 into a respectable family of strong religious traditions at Aurangabad, Deccan, India. He claimed direct descent from a renowned leader of the Chishti Sufi order, Khwaja Qutub al-Din Mawdud Chishti (430-527 AH/1038-1132 CE) and traced his lineage, on the paternal side, to Prophet Muhammad (s.a.w). His ancestors had, for a long

time, lived in Chishti, Iran, from where they migrated to the Indo-Pakistan subcontinent towards the end of the ninth century.[2] They held prestigious positions in social hierarchy and managed to rise in social status.

Mawdudi's grandfather was a religious scholar and his grand mother was closely related to Sir Sayyid Ahmad Khan (1232-1316 AH/1817-1898 CE) who belonged to the nobility and was close to the court at Delhi. Mawdudi's father, Sayyid Ahmad Hassan, was a lawyer by profession. He was educated mainly at Aligarh (Mohammedan Anglo-Oriental College founded by Sir Sayyid Ahmad Khan) but obtained his law degree from Allahabad. He was very much influenced by Western culture and civilization. Later in his life, however, he grew incessantly disenchanted with the British rule and the culture it imported. He became so devoted to his faith that he gave up his legal profession as he found it discordant with Islamic ideals.[3] In any case, Sayyid Mawdudi was born to a privileged family that had enough connections at higher levels of society, which would help any young man at that time to be drawn into politics and lead him to an important position in society.

The young Mawdudi possessed some other personal qualities that enabled him to rise in status and assume a leadership role. He possessed charm, a receptive mind, native intellect and an inquisitive nature, which delved into very serious and searching questions. He took keen interest in learning and had memorized "30 verses of the Qur'ān with meaning" at the age of five. He inherited this religious devotion from his mother. She was deeply religious, reciting the Qur'ān aloud every morning and fasting regularly.[4]

Mawdudi's education was short and unsystematic. Having acquired early education at home under close supervision of his father, he joined a high school (Madrasah Furqaniyah Mashraqiyah) and passed the "moulvi" (equivalent to secondary school certificate) examination in religious studies in 1916. He obtained sixth position in order of merit and excelled in subjects like *fiqh* (jurisprudence), *ḥadīth* (prophetic traditions) and *mantiq* (logic). Thereafter, he was admitted to Darul Uloom College,

Hyderabad, for a "Moulvi ᶜĀlim" course (graduate studies) which was disrupted by the death of his father.

Mawdudi left school and took up journalism for a livelihood. He joined the weekly *Madīnah* of Bijnore (Uttar Pradesh), India, and later became the editor of the daily *Tāj* published from Jabbalpore (Madhya Pradesh) India. In 1920, Mawdudi shifted to Delhi, edited the weekly *Muslim* and *al-Jamᶜīyat* and eventually started his own journal *Tarjumān al-Qur'ān* from Hyderabad. Despite working, he continued his studies outside the regular educational institutions but always maintained close contact with and took regular lessons from religious scholars. By the year 1928, he had successfully completed several courses in Islamic Sciences and had obtained certificates from three famous teachers of Madrasah Aliyah Arabiyah Fatehpuri, Delhi.[5]

Mawdudi started learning English at the age of 16 and in about six years he was in a position to read, digest and assimilate English works dealing with history, philosophy, economics, political science and other subjects with ease.[6] The influence of traditional and Western knowledge is discernible upon careful reading of his essays that cover a wide spectrum of subjects: from a critique of Hegel and Marx to the religious injunctions concerning meat and establishing an Islamic political system.

However, Mawdudi received most of his training for academic and public life from his father. It was his father who taught him the reality of belief, which lay behind the holy books and doctrine; the language in which to express his feelings; and the manners for interacting with others. In a fragment from his autobiography, Sayyid Mawdudi revealed something of what he owed his father and the affection in which he held his memory. "My father groomed me well. He spoke the language of Delhi notables." And Hassan made sure that his son, Mawdudi, did the same. He would talk to him, tell him stories about prophets and other historic figures, and would take him on small outings. Remarks about men and public affairs opened Mawdudi's eyes, and he began to mature early in life. He learned the manners of great men from association with "gentle, educated and civilized" friends of his father with whom he was a great favourite. From this association, Mawdudi learned patience, self-possession and the ability to know "things."[7] From early childhood, Mawdudi combined an appreciation of Islamic values of uprightness, propriety and righteousness and a sense of reality about human affairs - all because of his parent's close supervision and direct guidance.

Inspired by his parents, Mawdudi read the Qur'ān and studied the life of Prophet Muhammad (s.a.w), both of which left a marked impact on his thoughts. In the "life of the Prophet" essayed at the age of twelve, Mawdudi extolled the greatness of the Prophet (s.a.w) and suggested a close study of his life in order to understand the humanity. "This," he wrote, "would be much better than researching the rest of the world's books."[8] In his later life, he reiterated the same message and tried his best to follow the footsteps of the Prophet (s.a.w) in chalking out the strategy for Islamic revival.

As for the influence of the Qur'ān, it is better to quote Mawdudi verbatim:

> But when I was awakened and studied the Holy Qur'ān, I felt that I had now laid hands on the very root of knowledge. The greatest thinkers of the West like Kant, Hegel, Marx and others were reduced to dwarfs. The book alone is my guide and philosopher - my real benefactor. It has transformed me. It has elevated me from the animal to human level. It is like the master key that can open every lock. I have no words to express my sense of gratitude to the Lord who has bestowed upon us such a Book.[9]

Sayyid Mawdudi saw in Islam a body of intellectual ideas and a programme of action for a "return to Islam," to the pure sources of the sharīʿah. This idea is the direct product of the historicist thinking which claims the necessity of referring to the Prophetic era. For Mawdudi, the time of the Prophet (s.a.w) and his immediate successors to the caliphate (khulafā' al-rāshidūn) approximate the ideal - the embodiment and epitome of the Islamic way of life. The structure of state and society that developed during the formative phase provide the paradigm or ideal to be emulated.

Consequently, he preached a return to the Qur'ān and the Sunnah, sidestepping but not denouncing *fiqh*, and stressed the importance of reasoning (*ijtihād*) in jurisprudence. Khurshid Ahmad calls him a "practical idealist" who approached "a complex problem with a high degree of realism," analyzed its different elements and used "the tools of deductive as well as inductive reasoning."[10] Mawdudi used contemporary idiom in his exposition of doctrine and as his instrument for Islamic revival.

The task, which Sayyid Mawdudi set for himself, required an organized movement. On the advise of Sir Muhammad Iqbal, Mawdudi settled in Pathan Kot (Punjab) on an endowment of eighty acres of land and converted it into the "Dar al-Islam" academy. His intention was to collect capable young representatives of both the old and new traditions and to train them for providing a new moral and intellectual leadership for the process of Islamic revival. Unfortunately, as a center for the revivalist movement, Dar al-Islam was "considered to be absolutely insignificant."[11] Only four people joined him in that struggle. Hence he decided to organize a broad based movement to usher in the Islamic movement. He formed a well-knit, well-organized and well-disciplined organization, the Jamāᶜat e-Islāmī. Through it, he worked for the ousting of the British from India, for changing many practices that were hindering progress without being authentically Islamic, and for transforming a secular state into the Islamic Republic of Pakistan.[12]

BRITISH-INDIAN ENVIRONMENT

The pre-independent Indian environment had at least three characteristics. First, it was dominated by three major political forces: the British Raj, the Indian National Congress and the All-India Muslim League. While the British rule was steadily weakening in determination and effective powers, the Indian National Congress was concerned with uniting the Indians for independence. The British and the Congress were determined to preserve the unity of India (though for different reasons) while the All-India Muslim League was the sole champion of the Muslim cause struggling for a Muslim homeland. Second, the environment was characterized by the cultural onslaught of the West. Finally, there were two separate, radically different educational institutions in the country. The Congress tried to mobilize Muslims in the ethos of secular democracy, and to wean them away from the Muslim League on strictly economic issues. They called for Hindu-Muslim unity based "composite nationalism" which Mawdudi felt was impossible to achieve. He argued that if the Muslims accept this type of nationalism and join the Congress, they would be annihilated and absorbed into the Hindu majority. "What was uppermost in my mind," wrote Mawdudi, "was to keep alive in the Muslims a sense of their separate entity and prevent their absorption into a non-Muslim Community."[13] The articles he wrote to that effect were collected and published in his three-volume Urdu book, *Musalmān awr Mawjudah Siyāsī Kashmakash* (Muslims and the Current Political Crisis).[14] According to I.H. Qureshi, "Mawdudi's rejoinder was so logical, authoritative, polite and devastating that ... (it turned) sincere and intelligent Muslims away from the Congress who mostly swelled the ranks of the Muslim League as followers of the Quaid-e-Azam."[15]

The All-India Muslim League, however, was wedded to the concept of Muslim nationalism, seeking a homeland for the Muslims of the subcontinent. Indeed, the poet-philosopher of Islam, ʿAllamah Muhammad Iqbal (1876-1938), had made an earlier proposal for a separate Muslim homeland.[16] In 1930, he had stated: "Self-government within the British Empire or without the British Empire, the formation of a consolidated North-West Indian state appears to me to be the final destiny of the Muslims of at least North-West India."[17] Iqbal had a federated India in mind with a consolidated Muslim state as its constituent unit.[18] Ten years later Muhammad Ali Jinnah (1876 -1948), once hailed as the Ambassador of Hindu-Muslim Unity, took up Iqbal's notion of a separate Muslim homeland for the discovery of an Islamic identity.[19] He, however, went further and, speaking before the Muslim League at Lahore in March 1940, enunciated what became known as the "two-nation" theory. He talked of Islam and Hinduism as two "different and distinct social orders" whose adherents can never evolve a "common nationality." He added, "Musalmans are a nation according to any definition of a nation, and they must have their homelands, their territory and their state."[20] Accordingly, the Muslim League in its annual session at Lahore adopted on March 23, 1940 a resolution, subsequently known as "the Pakistan Resolution." It called for the creation of independent Muslim states in the Northwestern and Eastern zones of the subcontinent where the Muslims constituted the majority of the population.[21]

Mawdudi, however, argued that a national government based on secular or Muslim nationalism would not be qualitatively different from the imperial government of India. Nationalism was an alien concept imported by colonialism to break up the unity of the Muslim world. They likewise injected Western currencies, influence, thought and all sorts of heresies into the Islamic way of life. Being a divisive phenomenon, a nation state cannot be helpful in bringing about the Islamic socio-political system. Mawdudi, therefore, rejected the existence of Muslim nationalism as incompatible with Islam. He also mounted scathing criticism against the Muslim League for having accepted the West's supremacy in the realm of knowledge, culture and philosophy. Contrary to the prevailing view, Mawdudi did not oppose Pakistan. He, however, opposed the Muslim League and its leadership. "Our concern then was Islam, and the ability of those who sought to represent it."[22]

Mawdudi was approached twice, in 1937 and in 1945, but both times he refused to work with or for Jinnah's Muslim League.[23] Jinnah, however, succeeded in securing the adherence of some ᶜulamā' when the *Jamīᶜat-al-ᶜUlemā-i-Islām*, organized in 1945, allied with the League. Several prominent ᶜulamā' including Mawlana Akram Khan, the Pir of Manki Sharif, Mawlana Shabbir Ahmad ᶜUsmani and others joined ranks with the League. To make up for the lack of support from eminent religious elite, the Muslim League bestowed religious titles upon ordinary politicians and upon some members of the landowning elite:

Khan Iftikhar Hussain Khan of Mamdot was described as
pir Mamdot Sharif, Sirdar Shaukat Hayat Khan as sajjada
nashin of Wah Sharif, Malik Feroz Khan Noon of Darbar
Sargodha Sharif and nawab Mohammad Hayat Qureshi as
sajjada nashin of Sargodha Sharif and to top it all, the
secretary of this committee, Mr. Ibrahim Ali Chishti, was
designated Fazil-I-Hind sajjada nashin of Paisa Akhbar
Sharif.[24]

Reportedly 500 religious scholars including some pirs and
mashaikhs attended a conference in 1945 and passed a resolution
calling for the creation of Pakistan as the only means to save the
Muslims and the sharīᶜah from the domination of non-Muslims
and unbelievers.[25] The Muslim League and Jinnah went on to
gain in strength, forged links with many groups, and scored a
major victory in elections held in 1946. Congress, however, still
hoped to inherit an undivided India.

In meeting the problem of assuring a healthy religious
environment in India for Muslims, the Jamāᶜat embarked upon a
plan to break the hold which Western culture and ideas had over
the minds of Muslim intellectuals by a critical analysis of the
Western system showing its weaknesses and shortcomings. This
also necessitated showing that Islam has "its own code of life, its
own culture, its own politico-economic system and a philosophy"
and that these are superior to the Western system and hence the
Muslims need not borrow from others in cultural matters.[26]
Mawdudi appealed to Muslims to strengthen and restore their
spiritual and national life and presented Islam as progressive and
culturally advanced.[27]

The final feature of the environment was the existence of two
different and conflicting systems of education: the old religious
schools and the new Westernized schools. The former suffered
from stagnation and imitation (taqlīd), the characteristic ills of
conservative Muslims, and the latter from excessive dependence
on foreign culture and total estrangement from Islamic orientation.
One failed to prepare people to shoulder practical responsibilities
of worldly life and administration of state, while the other failed to

provide any religious guidance and moral orientation. The two systems, therefore, produced two different spirits and outlooks, which resulted in dangerous internal conflict in society.[28] The Jamā‘at felt the need for integrating the healthy elements of both, leading to the emergence of a unified system of education. Its aim was to bridge the gulf between the two strata of the society, and in so doing, to strengthen its moral roots.

The period between the founding of the Jamā‘at in 1941 and the advent of Pakistan in 1947 was spent in molding the character of members of the movement. The Jamā‘at also tried to mobilize public opinion for the propagation and adoption of an Islamic ideological concept with a view to transforming India into Dār al-Islām. With the partition of India, the Jamā‘at had to split into two organizations: an Indian and a Pakistani, each working within its respective political environment.

THE PAKISTANI ENVIRONMENT

Pakistan emerged as an Independent Dominion within the British Commonwealth on August 14, 1947. Pakistan was demanded, achieved and introduced in the name of Islam in order to establish an Islamic way of life. The British-trained rulers of Pakistan were unable or unwilling to enforce the much-promised Islamic system in the country. Most of the Muslim League leaders including Liaquat Ali Khan, the first Prime minister of Pakistan, who ruled the country and dominated the first Constituent Assembly, maintained what has been called a "modernist Islamic" position.[29] Their desire to build "a truly Islamic society" was expressed in their speeches on the Objectives Resolution passed by the first Constituent Assembly of Pakistan in 1949. Little equipped to provide effective leadership, they did not "lead Pakistan aspiration towards an Islamic quality for the state."[30]

The evasive attitude of the leaders in power caused unrest among Muslims and gave fillip to the efforts of the orthodox religious groups who demanded a traditional Islamic set-up for the country. The traditional stand-point found expression in the views of the "Board of Ta‘līmāt-e-Islāmīyah" (the Board of Islamic Teachings) appointed by the Government in 1948 to advise the

Constituent Assembly on the requirements of an Islamic constitution.[31] In the opinion of the Board, the Islamic government is a consultative government based upon *shūrā* as required by the sharī‘ah. The purpose of the state is the implementation of the commands of Allah (s.w.t) and not the will of the people. The executive powers should be vested in the head of the state (the President) who may hire and fire his Ministers at will. The Ministers may not challenge the decisions of the President except on grounds of religious law, in which case the question was to be referred to the Committee of Experts on Sharī‘ah. The head of state should be a Muslim, a male and should be elected by the learned and pious representatives of the people. In a sense, they advocated the reproduction of Islamic system as practised in the days of the *khilāfat-e-rāshidah* (rightly guided caliphs). In addition to being oblivious to the ever-changing nature of the society, they were not well versed in the socio-economic and political problems of the day. Consequently, they were handicapped to take the lead in the new ideological situation. But, as Khurshid Ahmad points out, they "did realise their weaknesses and tried to adapt themselves to the movement" led by Mawdudi.[32]

The ideological schism between the above two groups was fully exploited by the secularists, primarily the civil-military bureaucracy, the landed interests, and some politicians working in the opposition. They tried to play down the religious content of the Pakistan movement. Their views found expression in the Report of the Court of Inquiry presided over by Justice M. Munir, who later became the Chief Justice of Pakistan, which commented:

> The present argument that Pakistan was demanded in order to enable or compel the Muslims to lead their lives in accordance with the injunctions of Islam was then in nobody's mind. The transcendental had not yet been lowered into a common place and the Holy Book and Tradition had not been converted into a potent weapon of the politicians, though implicit in the demand had been the hope that Pakistan would provide a favourable ground for experimentation in Muslim social and political doctrines.[33]

H.S. Suhrawardy, the leader of the Awami League party, also expressed the secularist position and opposed the Islamic provisions of the Constitutional Bill of 1956.[34] He argued that "the bond which is generally put forward - that Islam is the bond which unites one and the rest - is a very fatuous one" and that what keeps "the two wings together (is) the realization that neither part of Pakistan can live without the other."[35] In sum, the secular elite believed in a democratic, Westernized state. They held that the sharīᶜah is static while democracy ensures dynamism; that the sharīᶜah is archaic while democracy is progressive; that the sharīᶜah perpetuates old customs or beliefs while democracy assures economic and social progress of the nation, and hence sharīᶜah cannot be adequate for a complex modern society.

Thus the Pakistani environment was characterized by the dominance of three disparate theories of traditionalism, modernist Islam and secularism – all conflicting with each other and vying for the allegiance of the politically relevant strata of the Pakistani society. The role of the Jamāᶜat in this confused situation lay in winning or eliminating a good number of the Muslim secularists and in bridging the gulf between the traditionalists and the Muslim modérnists. To that end, Mawdudi formulated a blue print of an Islamic state relevant to contemporary times. He defined the Islamic state as "nothing more than a combination of men working together as servants of Allah to carry out His will and purpose."[36] The most distinguishing characteristic of the Islamic state is the concept of the sovereignty of Allah (tawḥīd). Sovereignty implies absolute overlordship or complete suzerainty that does not exist within the bounds of humanity. In Islam, the ultimate legal and constitutional sovereignty rests with none but Allah (s.w.t). No one, be it a human agency as with a Hobbesian Monarch or a legal fiction in the form of a state, as with John Austin, can have the right to order others in his own right. Even the Prophet (s.a.w) was subject to Allah's commands. The second fundamental basis of the Islamic order is the prophethood (risālah) that is the practical manifestation of tawḥīd. Risālah, in fact, is meant to concretize tawḥīd in life.

The third feature of the Islamic order is the vicegerency (khilāfah) of man on earth. It is through the concept of khilāfah

that Mawdudi resolved the conflict between Allah's sovereignty
and the need for human government. Allah (s.w.t) remains the
absolute sovereign but the exercise of that authority is delegated
to man, His *khalīfah* on earth. As vicegerent, his mission in life,
by virtue of powers delegated to him by Allah (s.w.t), is to exercise
the divine authority within the limits prescribed by Him. A measure
of freedom of choice strictly circumscribed by the sharīʿah is
allowed to man. The sharīʿah is an organic whole and cannot be
applied in bits and pieces. It is eternal and valid for all time. Since
the *khilāfah* has been promised to the whole community of
believers, everyone is the repository of caliphate, denoting thereby
a popular, and not a limited, vicegerency. The *khilāfah* therefore,
is a democracy "which in essence and fundamentals is the
antithesis of the Theocratic, the Monarchical and the Papal forms
of government."[37] It also contrasts sharply with secular Western
notion of democracy. Islam altogether repudiates the philosophy
of popular sovereignty and rears its polity on the foundations of
tawḥīd, *risālah* and *khilāfah*.

The structure of the Islamic state as envisaged by Mawdudi is
composed of the executive, legislature and judiciary. The executive
is headed by the *amīr* (the leader), a Muslim male, who will be
elected from among the "most respectable" and "most pious" men.
He will enforce the sharīʿah and "will bring about a society ready
to accept and adopt these directives for practical application in its
life."[38] He will enjoy full confidence, authority and obedience so
long as he follows the sharīʿah and avoids transgression and sin.
He can be sued in a court of law, is bereft of any special prerogative,
and is liable to deposition.

The *amīr* works in consultation with the legislature which
Mawdudi conceived of in terms of the *ahl al ḥal wa al ʿaqd*, the
"body which resolves and prescribes." The legislature is to advise
the *amīr* in matters of law, administration and state policy.
Additionally, it is to enact the explicit directives of the sharīʿah
and to formulate laws, where basic guidance is not available, in
conformity with the sharīʿah.[39] He maintained that only a pious,
deeply learned jurist could accomplish the task of legislation. The
judiciary called *qaḍā*, is independent of the executive and is to

adjudicate in strict accordance with the sharī‘ah.

The term used by Mawdudi to identify the Islamic state is "theo-democracy" which means "Kingdom of Allah" administered not by a priestly class - of which Europe had a bitter experience - but by the entire Muslim population in accordance with the sharī‘ah.[40] This divine democratic government (Mawdudi prefers the parliamentary system) has to be run not by atheists or polytheists "with a materialistic and utilitarian mentality" but by pious, selfless, committed, truthful, strictly conformist Muslims of impeccable character. Devoid of such men, it is impossible to establish and run an ideological state. Mawdudi's Jamā‘at was created with this programme in view.

The second important feature of the Pakistani environment was the plural nature of the society itself. Pakistan, with an area of 310,403 square miles, presented a unique example of a "fragmented state." The western wing of Pakistan was nearly six times the area of its (Bengali) eastern counterpart with 55,126 square miles. The two wings were separated by about one thousand miles of hostile Indian territory. Furthermore, its 93.8 million population was composed of distinct territorial, linguistic, ethnic, and cultural entities with little or no sense of mutual history.[41] The horizontal cleavages in Muslim India were temporarily suppressed by the Islamic fervor generated by the Pakistan movement. Then the Muslims agreed with Jinnah that "We shall have time to quarrel among ourselves and we shall have time when these differences will have to be settled ... but first get the government. This is a nation without territory or any government."[42] With Pakistan a reality and the Quaid-e-Azam (Great Leader) Mohammed Ali Jinnah dead, divisions were already in evidence, giving birth to sub-national tendencies in different parts of Pakistan. The Punjabis, Pathans, Sindhis, Baluchis and Bengalis have their own languages, literature and sense of identity. The smaller provinces of West Pakistan had a deep-seated fear of Punjabi domination. The Bengalis of the Eastern wing of Pakistan complained of "being neglected and treated merely as a 'colony' of Western Pakistan."[43]

The Muslim League leaders tried to solve the ethnic conflict through an indigenous lingua franca. The continued use of the

English language seemed to militate against the creation of a
sustained Pakistani nationalism, and it was hoped Urdu could be
substituted without great difficulty. The attempt to impose Urdu
as the sole state language of Pakistan aggravated the discontent in
East Bengal and gave fillip to the Bengali language movement
there. The strong regional feeling in East Pakistan was expressed
in the overwhelming defeat of the ruling Muslim League in the
provincial elections of March 1954. The League secured only 9
of the 237 Muslim seats in the East Pakistan assembly as against
212 seats won by the United Front of the East Pakistan based
parties.[44] Indeed, the success of East Pakistani regionalism spurred
the already existing Pathan and Sindhi regionalism. Successive
Pakistani governments also tried to shore up nationalist sentiment
by concentrating on external issues, namely the Indian and Soviet
threats. The militarization of Pakistan, the development of US-
Pakistan alliance, and the development of an anti-India and anti-
Soviet orientation in Pakistan's external policy reflected a strategy
to deflect attention from internal pressures to foreign and security
issues.

In short, the ruling elite emphasized the vague sense of
Pakistani nationalism, pressed the use of Urdu as a lingua franca,
and raised the fear of an external enemy (mainly India and
occasionally Soviet Union) as a means to maintain the solidarity
of Pakistan. The Jamāᶜat, however, repeatedly pointed at Islam as
the only factor binding the regions of Pakistan. It argued, first,
that Pakistan was demanded and achieved in the name of Islam.
Second, an overwhelming majority of the Pakistanis are Muslims.
Finally, there is a consensus among the Pakistanis that Islam should
play a dominant role in the economics and politics of Pakistan.
Consequently, the Jamāᶜat argued that sub-national tendencies can
be countered effectively only by laying due emphasis on Islam.
The downplaying of the Islamic factor eventually led to the break-
up of Pakistan and the creation of Bangladesh in 1971.

The last feature of the environment, noted by the Jamāᶜat, was
that the passion for and enthusiasm about Islam notwithstanding,
a great majority of Muslims in Pakistan knew very little about

Islam and had no proper training to be able to live up to the demands of Islam. According to Mawdudi's estimate, only five percent of the Muslim population of Pakistan was enlightened about Islam, 90 percent were illiterate with blind faith, and the remaining five percent were corrupted by Westernization.[45] The most dedicated followers of the Jamāᶜat, understandably, came from among the enlightened group.

THE GOVERNMENT OF PAKISTAN AND THE JAMĀᶜAT

Given the fact that Pakistan was demanded for the introduction and preservation of an Islamic order and given the supposed inability of the rulers to bring about the desired transformation of the society along Islamic lines, the Jamāᶜat decided to embark upon a comprehensive movement for the implementation of Islamic ideology. Such a movement should comprehend not merely the various aspects of individual and social life but also those of the state. In other words, given the change in the political environment, the Jamāᶜat thought it essential to be politically active and change the Pakistani leadership. Mawdudi provided the justification for the Jamāᶜat's involvement in politics:

> The fact of our being Muslims demands that we put an end
> to the leadership of the wayward and of those gone astray.
> The objective of Islamic *jihād* is to put an end to the
> dominance of the un-Islamic system of government and
> replace them with Islamic rule.[46]

The political activities of the Jamāᶜat brought it to a head-on clash with government authorities and it was frequently accused of fomenting trouble. Sayyid Mawdudi had to pay the price of spending a total of 45 months in Pakistani prisons: 20 months during 1948-1950 and 25 months during 1953-1955. In 1953, he was even awarded the death sentence, which under colossal pressure from within and outside the country, was commuted to 14 years' rigorous imprisonment.

The Period of "Modernist Islam" (1947-1954)

During the early years, the founder of the nation Quaid-e-Azam
Mohammad Ali Jinnah and his lieutenant, Liaquat Ali Khan, had
no doubt about the Islamic identity of Pakistan. Jinnah spoke of
the idea of Pakistan as a state "where principles of Islamic social
justice could find free play."[47] He emphasized that "We must work
our destiny in our own way and present to the world an economic
system based on true Islamic concept of equality of manhood and
social justice."[48] He talked of marching to the "renaissance of
Islamic culture," to "secure liberty, fraternity and equality as
enjoined upon us by Islam," to "take our inspirations and guidance
from the Holy Qur'ān" and to "stand guard over the development
and maintenance of Islamic democracy and Islamic social
justice."[49] He categorically stated that the future constitution of
Pakistan would be "of democratic type embodying the essential
principles of Islam."[50] It will be made "on the basis of Shariat."[51]
Even his presidential address to the Constituent Assembly of
Pakistan on August 11, 1947, in which Jinnah seemed to have
struck a secular note, was very much in line with Islam. In it his
emphasis was on universal Islamic principles of justice, equality,
morality, piety and human tolerance irrespective of colour, caste
or creed.[52] Yet, it must be pointed out that Jinnah categorically
asserted that "Pakistan is not going to be a theocratic state to be
ruled by priests with a divine mission."[53]

Like Jinnah, Liaquat emphasized repeatedly the Islamic basis
of Pakistan and successfully piloted the Objectives Resolution in
the Constituent Assembly of Pakistan on March 7, 1949. While
moving the Resolution, the Prime minister, Liaquat Ali Khan,
declared that Pakistan wanted to "demonstrate to the world that
Islam provides a panacea to the many diseases which have crept
into the life of humanity today."[54] Hence, he stated that the State
will play a positive part in creating "such conditions as are
conducive to the building up of a truly Islamic society...."[55]
Similarly, Sardar Abdur Rab Khan Nishtar declared that they were
trying to "put forward an alternative social system" based on Islam
as opposed to "capitalism as represented by certain countries of
the West and communism as represented by Russia."[56] The leaders

of the Muslim League sincerely believed in the application of Islamic principles, but they certainly did not want to create a theocratic state in Pakistan. Additionally, they were trying to build a national consensus on the issue of Islam in Pakistan. Hence, as early as 1948, the government, as a matter of compromise, agreed to the Islamist's demand and appointed the Board of Taʿlīmāt-e-Islamīyah to advise the government on the requirements of an Islamic Constitution.

The first concrete step in building the ideological consensus was the Objectives Resolution that the League leadership introduced in the Constituent Assembly in 1949. Subsequently, with some modifications, this became the preamble to the constitution and eventually was made a substantive part of the constitution. The Objectives Resolution affirmed that "sovereignty over the entire universe belongs to God Almighty alone" which He has delegated to the state of Pakistan through its people to be exercised within the limits prescribed by Him. This delegation of authority was in consonance with principles of representative democracy, freedom, equality, tolerance and social justice as enunciated by Islam. It also affirmed that Muslims shall be enabled to order their lives in accordance with the Qur'ān and the Sunnah.[57] The Resolution thus set the pattern for a compromise between the concepts of Divine sovereignty and popular sovereignty. The Jamāʿat was satisfied with the Resolution and considered it a milestone in that it has turned Pakistan into an Islamic state.

Not much, however, came out of these pious statements. By 1953, it became evident that the ruling elite had failed to "generate an interpretation of Islam that could serve as an effective, realistic, meaningful ideology" that "could fit a valid substance to the Islamic form of socio-political aspiration."[59] This failure was largely due to the fact that the institutionalization of Islam in Pakistan would have jeopardized the vested interests of the feudal and capitalist forces as well as the civil-military bureaucracy.[60] The members of the landowning elite held the key to politics in Pakistan and they acted in concert with the administrative, military, and industrial elite and resisted giving Islam a role in the politics of Pakistan.[61] Yet they continued to pay lip service to the ideal of an Islamic society.

The fact that successive regimes in Pakistan preferred to use Islam in the running of the administration encouraged, on the one hand, the expectations that sharīᶜah would eventually be implemented but it created, on the other hand, an atmosphere of frustration and extremism. This frustration of the Islamic forces found manifestation in the anti-Ahmadi agitation in the Punjab. This agitation aimed at forcing the government to declare the Ahmadis (known also as Qadianis) a non-Muslim minority, and to dismiss Sir Zafrullah Khan from the Foreign Ministry since he was an Ahmadi. The Ahmadis are the followers of Mirza Ghulam Ahmad who claimed to be the promised Messiah and Mahdi, arousing strong opposition among Muslim theologians.[62] Since the government had not acceded to the demands of the ᶜulamā', they decided upon direct action and demanded the resignation of the prime minister, Khwaja Nazimuddin. The direct action resulted in picketing by ᶜulamā' at the houses of the prime minister and the governor general. It also led to widespread violence in Punjab such that the army was called in and Lahore was placed under martial law on March 6, 1953.

The Jamāᶜat-e-Islāmī did neither initiate nor join the anti-Ahmadi agitation until its representatives were invited to the Muslim Parties Convention held on January 16, 1953. The Jamāᶜat, as a matter of fact, was not so much interested in the agitation as it was in framing an Islamic Constitution for Pakistan. But the Jamāᶜat's denunciation of the Ahmadis and its presence in the Muslim Parties Convention was taken as a pretext by the civil-military-bureaucratic complex to accuse the Jamāᶜat of fomenting the trouble. The Court of Inquiry, established to look into the causes of the agitation, concluded that the anti-Ahmadi agitation was the natural consequence of the Islamic constitution controversy created by Mawdudi and the Jamāᶜat. The agitation, according to the Report, was "a corollary from the Objectives Resolution passed by the Constituent Assembly of Pakistan on March 12, 1949, and from the religio-political system which they call Islam."[63]

The Secular Response to Islamization (1954-58)

One of the major consequences of the anti-Ahmadi agitation was that the prime minister, Khwaja Nazimuddin, who was sympathetic to the ᶜulamā', was dismissed by the governor general Ghulam Muhammad on April 17, 1953. Apparently, the ᶜulamā' had lost the constitutional battle to secularism. The governor general, a seasoned Bureaucrat, was a secularist as was the new prime minister, Muhammad Ali Bogra, who advocated the abolition of the board of ᶜulamā'. The new East Pakistan governor, Chaudhri Khaliquzzaman, considered the ᶜulamā' as the chief threat to Pakistan and advocated the subordination of religion to the state. Similarly, the chief minister of Punjab and other central ministers expressed themselves against the views of the ᶜulamā'.

However, given the fervent zeal for Islam expressed by the population, the secularist oriented ruling elite used Islam as a devise to mobilize the population for state building activities.[64] The Jamāᶜat knew that the people in power who talked about Islam were, in the words of Mawdudi, "simply paying lip-service to Islam" and hence intensified its activities for the Islamization of Pakistan.[65] The secular ruling elite on their part were impressed by the remarkable show of strength displayed by the ᶜulamā' during the anti-Ahmadi agitation, and hence adopted an Islamic formalism to assuage what they saw as potentially disruptive forces in society. They made it quite clear that they were willing to concede a role for Islamic forces in national politics but not surrender the power of legislation or decision-making, not even the power to interpret as to what was Islamic and what was not. H.S. Suhrawardy, the prime minister of Pakistan in 1956, stated:

> The National assembly, in our constitution occupies that
> place as interpreter of what is Islamic and what is not and no
> one can take away from it that right.[66]

They would endorse, as they did in the constitution of 1956, the concept of an Islamic state and Pakistan as an Islamic republic but not at the cost of secularism, modernization and development.[67] Consequently, the 1956 constitution envisioned the law and

administration of the state as "modern, even broadly secular."[68]
Its Islamic provisions were no more than high-sounding phrases
having no correspondence with the country's socio-political and
legal set-up. The constitution made provision for the setting up of
"an organization for Islamic research and instruction" to assist in
the reconstruction of Muslim society on a truly Islamic basis (Article
197). It also provided that a commission would be set up for
recommending measures for bringing the existing laws into
conformity with the injunctions of Islam. It, however, provided
that the recommendations would have to be laid before the national
assembly which alone had the power to enact laws in respect
thereof. Thus, the ultimate responsibility for the interpretation of
Islam was given to the representatives of the people. The
constitution stipulated that no laws could be enacted by the
legislature which were repugnant to the injunctions of Islam, but
it denied judicial intervention in case the legislature did enact such
laws.

At the same time, attempts were made for a more
institutionalized response to counter religious influences,
particularly that of Mawdudi and the Jamāʿat-e-Islāmī. For
instance, the Institute of Islamic Culture was set up in 1954 - a
year after the anti-Ahmadi agitation. It was headed by Khalifah
Abdul Hakim who considered Islam as "spirit and not body; it is
aspiration and not any temporal or rigid fulfillment." Islam, he
said, now lies buried under "heaps of retrograde legalism and life
thwarting practices" over centuries during which the West
progressed and began to describe Islam as "outworn creed
incapable of adaptation to changing circumstances."[69] Evidently,
Khalifah Abdul Hakim and his followers had held up the West as
a kind of model and shown themselves to be particularly concerned
about what the West thought of them. The negative reaction of the
ʿulamā' to such a scheme was understandable. There were also
attempts to provide a liberal interpretation of Islamic injunctions.
Thus, in 1955, a seven-member commission was appointed to study
the existing laws of marriage, divorce and family maintenance to
see if they could be modified to give women their proper status as

prescribed by Islam. The commission recommended liberal reforms in the existing laws, but its recommendations were ignored.

Meanwhile the Jamāᶜat exhibited the qualities of adjustment and accommodation. Despite its shortcomings, Mawdudi and the Jamāᶜat accepted the 1956 constitution as generally "Islamic." Yet, the constitution could not endure for longer than 30 months and 15 days. On October 7, 1958, Iskander Mirza abrogated the constitution, dissolved the political parties, abolished the legislatures and imposed martial law. General Mirza did not like the constitution. He stated:

> I was opposed to inserting Islamic provisions into the machinery of government. We have seen how Liaqat Ali Khan's "Objectives Resolution" gave a handle to the ᶜulamā', and allowed them to go and almost destroy Pakistan in 1953. But the Muslim League never learnt anything from past experience. Despite my repeated warnings, Muhammad Ali deliberately created an "Islamic Republic" for Pakistan, giving the ᶜulamā another invitation to interfere. Maulana Maudoodi and his party were given a heaven-sent opportunity to mess up the state.[70]

Three weeks later Iskander Mirza was sent packing to London by the chief martial law administrator and prime minister General Muhammad Ayub Khan who continued the ban and set himself to a decennial rule of personal, though benign, autocracy.[71]

Ayub Khan's "Tutorial State" (1958-1969)

The military regime that came to power in 1958 made the civil-military bureaucracy the dominant policy-making elite. In the initial period of martial law rule for forty-four months, political parties and political activities were banned throughout the country. During this period, General Ayub ruled by personal fiat. Legislation came in the form of executive orders and the bureaucrats came to have a dominating influence on Pakistan's politics. Ayub Khan was fully aware of various misdeeds perpetrated by the members of the Civil Service of Pakistan. He, therefore, carried out a cleaning up

operation in the bureaucracy by purging out some, demoting others
and reprimanding many more for having been in league with the
politicians. The civil servants, nevertheless, were "a steel frame of
greater strength," well trained, reasonably mature, and most of
the officers in the elite service came from families of social and
political influence. Consequently, Ayub Khan relied upon this elite
cadre to execute his directives. The system he built has been termed
"a co-dictatorship of the higher army officers and civil servants."[72]
With the withdrawal of martial law and the subsequent
promulgation of the constitution in 1962, political activities were
renewed. General Ayub Khan wanted to preside over a "tutorial
state" that would work to create statewide loyalties by mobilizing
efforts for social change and economic development. To Samuel
Huntington, "... more than any other political leaders in a
modernising country after World War II, Ayub Khan came closest
to filling the role of a Solomon or Lycurgus, or 'Great Legislator'
on the Platonic or Rousseauian model."[73]

Ayub Khan believed that Pakistan was not ready for democracy
but "the people must be involved in state affairs." Hence, he devised
a scheme of Basic Democracies (BD) wherein people were allowed
to choose an Electoral College that would elect legislatures, local
government councilors and Pakistan's president.[74] Ayub argued
that the Basic Democracies scheme was based upon Islamic
injunctions of conscience. Nevertheless, major emphasis was upon
economic development that bred economic inequality.[75] None of
these institutions changed the elitist approach to politics in Pakistan.
The policies and programmes adopted during the Ayub regime
had a particularly adverse effect on the growing middle classes of
East Pakistan. Their participation in the effective ruling institutions
of the government (i.e., the cabinet, the civil service, and the armed
forces) was much less than the Bengali numerical majority
deserved. They found the Ayub-led West Pakistani dominated
government of Pakistan unresponsive to their political and
economic hopes and aspirations. They came to perceive the Ayub
regime as a colonial dispensation imposed on them. Consequently,
the separatist tendencies in East Pakistan became stronger than

ever before during the decade of Ayub's rule.

General Ayub held the ʿulamā' in low esteem for they had petrified Islam. He was disdainful toward the ʿulamā' and in particular toward Mawdudi. He wrote:

> Some of the nationalist ulema ... hastened to Pakistan to lend a helping hand. If they had not been able to save the Muslims from Pakistan they must now save Pakistan from the Muslims. Among the migrants was Maulana Abul Aala Maudoodi, head of the Jamāʿat-e-Islāmī Party, who ... forthwith launched a campaign for the "Muslimization" of the hapless people of Pakistan. This venerable gentleman was appalled by what he saw in Pakistan: an un-Islamic country, un-Islamic government, and an un-Islamic people! How could any genuine Muslim owe allegiance to such a government! So he set about the task of convincing the people of their inadequacies, their failings, and their general unworthiness.[76]

Ayub also had misgivings about their demand for an Islamic constitution. He wrote:

> Since no one had defined the fundamental elements of an Islamic Constitution, no Constitution would be called Islamic unless it received the blessings of all the ʿulamā'. The only way of having an Islamic Constitution was to hand over the country to the ʿulamā' and beseech them, "lead kindly light." This is precisely what the ʿulamā' wanted. A Constitution would be regarded as Islamic only if it were drafted by the ʿulamā' and conceded them the authority to judge and govern the people. This was a position which neither the people nor I was prepared to accept, opposed as it was to the fundamental democratic principle that all authority must vest in the people.[77]

The regime publicly professed the importance of Islam to boost its legitimacy but reinterpreted it to serve modernization and social change. Ayub counseled the ʿulamā' to "comprehend the basic principles of Islam, ... and to discover fresh avenues for their

application in the present and the future."[78]   Soon the government
formulated a modernist view of Islam and enacted the Family Laws
Ordinance in 1961 which secularized the family law precipitating
confrontation with religious parties.[79] The constitution of 1962
removed the word "Islamic" from the official name and termed
the state as the "Republic of Pakistan." This was followed by a
host of other measures including organisation of religious training
courses for the ʿulamā' and writing of sermons for Friday prayers.
The regime also established the Central Islamic Research Institute
(1962-1968), under Dr. Fazlur Rahman, to promote a liberal
interpretation of Islam and to justify, among others, birth control,
family laws and bank interests.[80] All these measures were aimed
at banishing the religion-based parties, in particular the Jamāʿat-e-
Islāmī, from the political arena.[81] Instead, the regime strengthened
the Jamāʿat's resolve for active political participation.

Throughout the period, the Jamāʿat played the role of an
opposition. During the martial law period, it convened the meeting
of the religious elite to prepare a set of proposals for the constitution
in the making as well as to demand an end to the dictatorial rule.
Likewise, the Jamāʿat took the lead in organizing street
demonstrations and publishing the religious decrees of the leading
ʿulamā' denouncing the Family Laws Ordinance in 1961. The
government responded by imprisoning a number of Jamāʿat
workers including Mian Tufail Muhammad.

Seyyed Vali Raza Nasr reports that the ministry of Information
had presented a report to the cabinet in 1961-62 describing the
Jamāʿat as seditious. It recommended that the Jamāʿat be dealt in
the manner president Gamal Nasser dealt with the Muslim
Brotherhood in Egypt. The cabinet did not endorse the line of
action.[82] In any case, the Jamāʿat members realized the futility of
force when faced with the power of the military institution and
hence remained low-key. They intensified their activism only after
the government lifted the martial law. In August 1962, the shūrā
passed a resolution condemning the new constitution and calling
for the restoration of democracy in the country. This was followed
by the demand to add the word "Islamic" to the official name of

the country and to provide greater guarantees for fundamental rights. The Jamāʿat also opposed the Ayub regime's foreign policy towards communist China and accused it of undermining the Islamic basis of the country. The government responded by banning the party in January 1964 and imprisoning Mawdudi and 43 other leaders on charges of "subversive activities against the state" and of becoming a "danger to the public peace."[83] The Jamāʿat successfully challenged the government's action in the court which declared the banning of the Jamāʿat illegal and ordered the party restored.

The fact that the Ayub regime had preferred to pay lip-service to the ideal of an Islamic society encouraged, on the one hand, the expectations that sharīʿah would eventually be implemented but it created, on the other hand, an atmosphere of frustration and extremism. Ayub remained in power until a popular uprising forced him to step down in 1969 in favour of his army successor, General Yahya Khan.

Yahya Khan Interregnum (1969-1971)

Ayub Khan, in his own words, was not willing to preside over the break-up of Pakistan. His successor Yahya Khan could not avoid dealing with the problems of imminent break-up of Pakistan. The country was virtually in a state of anarchy without a leadership of national stature and national organization to fill the void. General Yahya Khan announced his first task was the establishment of sanity in the country. He declared that he would restore constitutionalism to Pakistan and that he was in a hurry to leave with no desire to perpetuate himself in office.[84] His advise to his country men was that:

> We have to unlearn and discard the sordid trend away from idealism and towards vicious and corrupting pre-occupation with selfish and base pursuit of material gain at the cost of the community and the larger interests of the nation.
>
> Our Struggle for independence did not end with the transfer of sovereignty and power from the British to our

people. Real and meaningful independence has many more
dimensions. The people must have the full right and
opportunity to exercise their sovereign power. They must
ensure for themselves freedom from ignorance, hunger and
disease. For this they must develop workable political
institutions, end all forms of exploitation, including
favouritism, shed parochial and sectarian attitudes and
firmly check the growth of all forms of intolerance.[85]

Yahya Khan followed the footsteps of Ayub Khan. Law and
order was restored through a series of Martial Law Regulations
that were rigorously enforced. Schools and colleges were reopened.
A total of 303 Class I gazetted officers were suspended from service
to face the charges of corruption, misuse of office and misconduct.
He however, made it clear that "the normal administration of the
country had to be run by normal functionaries."[86] The old
provinces of Sindh, Baluchistan, Punjab and the North West
Frontier which had been amalgamated into the One Unit in 1955,
were reconstituted. The parliamentary system was accepted in
principle, and a new constitution, drafted by the representatives
of the people of Pakistan, was promised. Yahya pledged that his
regime was transitional in nature. The ultimate aim of his regime
was to "create conditions conducive to the establishment of
constitutional government ... to establish constructive political life
in the country so that power is transferred to the elected
representatives of the people."[87]   In his first press conference on
April 10, 1969, Yahya announced that the elections would be held
"on the basis of one man one vote."
      The Yahya regime took the unusual step of setting a general
election date because the anti-Ayub movement indicated clearly
that the old ruling elite needed new allies in order to maintain its
power. The regime expected that the election would bring to power
the centre right parties like Pakistan Democratic Party or Islam-
based parties like the Jamā'at-e-Islāmī that would not threaten the
old elite fundamentally. At the least, the regime expected to see a
large number of parties sharing the parliamentary seats with no
one commanding an absolute majority. This would allow the

military to play the role of a mediator among the feuding parties and thus maintain its position as the key decision-maker in the country. To preserve their vested interests against a possible Bengali-dominated Assembly, Yahya Khan issued the Legal Framework Order (LFO) on March 31, 1970.

The LFO contained a Preamble, 27 Articles and two Schedules. Article 20 of the Order spelled out five "fundamental principles" to be followed by the representatives of the people in framing the future constitution of Pakistan. These principles were:

1. Pakistan shall be a Federal Republic to be known as the Islamic Republic of Pakistan in which the Provinces and other territories which are now and may hereinafter be included in Pakistan shall be so united in a Federation that the independence, the territorial integrity and the national solidarity of Pakistan are ensured and that the unity of the Federation is not in any manner impaired.

2. (a) Islamic ideology which is the basis for the creation of Pakistan shall be preserved; and
   (b) the Head of the State shall be a Muslim.

3. (a) Adherence to fundamental principles of democracy shall be ensured by providing direct and free periodical elections to the Federal and the Provincial legislatures on the basis of population and adult franchise;
   (b) the Fundamental Rights of the citizens shall be laid down and guaranteed;
   (c) the independence of the judiciary in the matter of dispensation of justice and enforcement of the fundamental rights shall be secured.

4. All powers including legislative, administrative and financial, shall be so distributed between the Federal Government and the Provinces that the Provinces shall have maximum autonomy, that is to say maximum legislative, administrative and financial powers but the Federal Government shall also have adequate powers

including legislative, administrative and financial
powers, to discharge its responsibilities in relation to
external and internal affairs and to preserve the
independence and territorial integrity of the country.

5. It shall be ensured that -

(a) the people of all areas in Pakistan shall be enabled
to participate fully in all forms of national activities;
and

(b) within a specified period, economic and all other
disparities between the Provinces and between
different areas in a Province are removed by the
adoption of statutory and other measures.[88]

Yahya Khan was emphatic in declaring that the elected National
Assembly would have to follow the principles laid down in the
LFO, and the representatives would have 120 days to complete
their work of writing the constitution. Given the failure to write a
constitution in this period, president Yahya Khan warned he would
dissolve the body and call another election. Hence, Yahya felt the
deliberations of the Assembly could be controlled. Thus Yahya
Khan's decision was to proceed with the elections to be held on
December 1970.

During the election campaign, both Shiekh Mujibur Rahman
and Zulfikar Ali Bhutto complained of the regime's active support
of Islam-based parties. The election results, however, caught the
ruling elite by surprise. Mujib's Awami League won a comfortable
majority in the National Assembly (167 out of 313 seats) followed
by Bhutto's People's Party with 81 seats. The military's expectations
proved ill founded. All their plans and calculations received a
serious jolt. The elections polarized Pakistani politics into a three-
way struggle between the Army, Bhutto and Mujib. Yahya Khan
drifted from democracy to ideological rhetoric and dithered on
the transfer of power to the majority party – the East Pakistan
based Awami League. The ensuing ethnic violence, followed by
Pakistani military action, Bengali guerilla resistance, and Indian
military intervention, resulted in the break-up of Pakistan and the

emergence of Bangladesh in 1971.

"With us Pakistan is as sacred as the mosque," said Mawdudi.[89] The Jamā°at, therefore, did not side with the liberation struggle of Bangladesh. It construed it as an Indian machination aided by imperialist powers, the Hindus, and "a particular section of the Bengali nationalists who had been taught and educated in the colleges and universities mostly by Hindu professors."[90] The Jamā°at supported the military actions of the government of Yahya Khan against Muslim Bengal through organisations like Al-Badr and Al-Shams which were heavily represented by the Biharis, the Urdu-speaking inhabitants of Bangladesh. The news of the break-up of Pakistan and the emergence of Bangladesh as an independent state was, therefore, shocking. To the Jamā°at, this was due to the fact that successive governments had not considered Islam as a basis for state building and national integration.[91]

The Pakistan of Mohammad Ali Jinnah had been reduced from a country of approximately 130 million to something closer to 65 million. The post-1971 Pakistanis were demoralized and openly disenchanted with their leadership. Of psychological importance was the weakening of Pakistan's "two nation theory" – the belief that the Muslims of South Asia were a separate and distinct community, entitled to a sovereign independent state "to develop to the fullest our spiritual, cultural, economic, social and political life in a way that we think best and in consonance with our own ideal and according to the genius of our people."[92] In terms of socio-economic stratification or class formation, Pakistan remained a predominantly agrarian, rural, and feudal society. Although it had been undergoing rapid urbanization, the land-based feudal structure remained all-powerful. The landed elites had built up trans-regional alliances through matrimonial, political, and financial associations.

Z.A. Bhutto and "Islamic Socialism" (1971-1977)
In the post-1971 Pakistan, the military was in shambles and, accordingly decided to hand over authority to Zulfiqar Ali Bhutto, the leader of the Pakistan People's Party (PPP).[93] Bhutto, through

his PPP, played a significant role in bringing about Ayub's fall. Later he led the party to victory in the 1970 general election, capturing the majority of national assembly seats reserved for West Pakistan, a majority in the Punjab provincial legislature, and a plurality in the provincial assembly of Sindh.

Bhutto's PPP was formed as a bridge between parties of the left and of the right. Hence, to aggregate the conflicting interests and demands of the diverse elements of Pakistani society, the PPP adopted four vaguely worded basic principles: Islam is our faith, democracy is our polity, socialism is our economy, and all power to the people. Ambiguity notwithstanding, the PPP was perceived as a party aimed at transforming Pakistan into a socialist country. The Foundation document declared in no uncertain terms that the PPP aimed at the attainment of an egalitarian democracy wherein all members of the nation would enjoy equal rights in every sphere of activity. It declared "socialism as the highest expression of democracy and its logical fulfillment."[94]

Bhutto initially governed under military-sponsored emergency legislation. Soon, he lifted martial law and governed within the context of an "interim constitution." The national assembly selected a constitutional committee, which was charged with the responsibility for drafting a new constitution with a target date of August 15, 1973. Despite considerable tension between the various parties in the assembly, particularly over Bhutto's desire to retain the presidential system of government, the opposition was successful in having the parliamentary system reinstated. They also succeeded in making Islam as a state religion and a provision for a Council of Islamic Ideology to advise the government on how to bring existing laws into conformity with Islamic sharīʿah. The new draft constitution was approved by the national assembly on April 10, 1973 and was promulgated on August 14, 1973.

The advent of a secular, populist Bhutto advocating a socialist economy in an Islamic Pakistan led to an intensification of opposition movement. The Jamāʿat's publicity machinery went into full swing against Bhutto's dictatorial rule and socialist policies. Against Bhutto's ideology of socialism, the Jamāʿat presented a strong case for Islam in Pakistan. Mawdudi warned his co-patriots that what happened to the pre-1971 Pakistan might happen to what remained of Pakistan if Islam was not given the urgency and attention denied it for so long. There was no reason to refuse a viable system such as Islam. The added factor was that it was never given a trial in Pakistan. The Islamic sentiment thus revived was reflected in the constitution of 1973, which for the first time declared Islam to be the state religion of Pakistan.[95] The polarization between the Jamāᶜat and the PPP continued. The Jamāᶜat leaders and workers were intimidated, threatened and imprisoned. Dr. Nazir Ahmad, one of the prominent leaders of the Jamāᶜat and a member of the National Assembly, was shot dead. The Jamāᶜat nevertheless remained steadfast and undaunted.

Faced with the opposition of the Islamic parties led by the Jamāᶜat and to undermine their influence, Bhutto aligned his socialism with Islamic beliefs and values and presented it as "Islamic socialism" and replaced social equality with "Musāwāt-i-Muḥammadī (Muhammadan equality). "If it is really based on Qur'ān and Sunnah," charged Mawdudi, "then what is the need for calling it socialism."[96] Unable to stem the tide, Bhutto made further conciliatory moves towards Islam. He banned gambling and racing, replaced Sunday with Friday as the weekly holiday; introduced Arabic language courses into the school curricula, inducted a former member of the Jamāᶜat, Kausar Niazi, into the cabinet, and declared, through legislation, the Ahmadi community as a non-Muslim minority. Apparently, Bhutto was using the Islamization programme as "a tool" to appease and undermine his enemies, and to ward off the imminent threat to his power which the Jamāᶜat and other parties had posed. The strategy failed and, freed of the restrictions of state control, the Jamāᶜat, as a leading component of the nine-party Pakistan National Alliance (PNA), mounted a fierce anti-Bhutto campaign. The government response was two fold. First, it imposed martial law on 21 April 1977, placed tighter censorship on the mass media and arrested hundreds of people who opposed the regime.[97] Among those arrested were the front ranking members of the Jamāᶜat, its secretary general, Mian Tufail Muhammad, and the then secretary general of the PNA, Abdul Ghafur Ahmad. Second, Bhutto, with the assistance

of top officials of Saudi Arabia, United Arab Emirate, Kuwait and
Libya, convened the "Islamic Solidarity Committee" to negotiate
the issue with PNA and other opposition party leaders.[98] The anti-
Bhuto movement, however, continued undeterred and culminated
with the military coup in July 1977. "I appointed a chief of army
staff belonging to Jamā'at-e-Islāmī," lamented Bhutto, "and the
result is before all of us."[99] The Chief of Army Staff, General
Mohammad Zia ul-Haq (1924-1988), led the coup.[100]

Zia ul-Haq's "Niẓām-e-Muṣtafā" (1977-1988)

General Zia maintained power for over eleven years. From 1977
to 1985 he ruled as chief martial law administrator and thereafter
till 1988 he governed as the President of Pakistan. Throughout
this period, Zia viewed his role as that of an Islamic head of state
and justified his rule as a matter of accommodating the necessities
of Islam.[101] He was impressed by the success of the Nizam-e-
Mustafa movement, and committed himself to work for the
realization of its objectives. In addressing the nation on the eve of
the coup, General Zia echoed Mawdudi's warning: "Pakistan, which
was created in the name of Islam, will continue to survive only if
it sticks to Islam."[102] To him, the Nifāz-e-Sharī'ah (implementation
of the sharī'ah) was "not only the basis of our existence but also
... a guarantee for our survival."[103] Thus committed, Zia went
ahead to co-opt the forces of the Islamic revival into a role
supportive of the regime and its policies. He offered "the Islamic
parties a power-sharing arrangement in which the state would act
as a senior partner, but the Islamic forces would gain from state
patronage and enjoy a modicum of political activity."[104] The
Jamā'at accepted the invitation and, during 1977-1979, became
part of the ruling establishment holding the portfolios of production
and industry; petroleum, minerals, water, and power; information
and broadcasting; and planning.[105] It continued to provide support
to the regime even after the dissolution of the PNA led government
in 1979. Furthermore, Zia staffed the reconstituted Council of
Islamic Ideology with a number of Jamā'at supporters and inducted
several others into the inner circle of his advisers. The Jamā'at
suffered a credibility gap among the public at large because of its

support for Zia and his policies. To the consternation of the Jamāᶜat, the regime simultaneously cultivated ties with a number of ᶜulamā' from the Jamīᶜat-e-ᶜUlamā-e-Pakistān, and other Islamic parties so as to create a manageable equilibrium in his vital "constituency" after the army. The critics viewed it as a crude manifestation of ad-hocism aimed at perpetuating his personal rule.

Furthermore, the regime co-opted hundreds of ᶜulamā' and those associated with traditional religious institutions into the newly created government structures effectively controlled by the civil servants. Thus, the government created more than 18,000 local Zakat Committes and co-opted into this structure about 126,000 mosque leaders and preachers. Likewise, through the Maktab Scheme under the education department, the government recruited about 3,000 village ᶜulamā' as part-time schoolteachers.[106] By offering them positions in these committees, the government effectively depoliticized a large segment of the ᶜulamā'. "The Federal Sharīᶜah Court, the Majlis-i-Shūrā and other Islamic institutions established under the ministries of religious affairs, education, information and law were similarly controlled by senior military and civilian officials and ᶜulamā' were only there in consultative capacities."[107]

Thus unlike earlier rulers, Zia did not keep the Islamic forces at bay. His stated "ambition in life" was "to complete the process of Islamization so that there will be no turning back."[108] He worked in tandem with them and carried the Islamization programme forward – in the realm of possibility. The Islamic provisions in the 1956, 1962, and 1973 constitutions were in the nature of an ideal attached as a preamble to the constitution. Zia provided the much-needed substance to these provisions through constitutional amendments of March 1985 and various other measures. He made the principles and provisions set out in the (1949) Objectives Resolution a substantive part of the Constitution, by inserting Article 2A through Presidential Order No. 14 of 1985, enforceable by the courts.[109] In the legal, economic and social spheres, Zia introduced several measures to provide substance to the Islamization process. Thus, he introduced Islamic banking system, eliminated *ribā* (interest) and imposed Islamic taxes (*zakāh* and *ushr*). Likewise, he promulgated the *ḥudūd* (Islamic penal law) Ordinance, established the sharī°ah bench in the high court and an Appellate Bench in the supreme court and, in June 1988, two months before he died in a mysterious plane crash, he promulgated the Shari°ah Ordinance. Interestingly, the jurisdiction of the sharī°ah courts excluded constitutional principles, fiscal matters, and martial law regulations.

As part of mainstream educational reforms, Zia called for revising the curriculum and textbooks from the primary to the university levels. The objective was to make students aware of the Islamic mainsprings of Pakistan's creation, its ideology and the history of Islam. In addition, an Islamic University was established at Islamabad with the objective of fusing "religious" and "secular" education. Its graduates were to staff the *qāḍi* courts that would eventually form a parallel Islamic - and supposedly more equitable - system of justice. Also official recognition was given to degrees from traditional theological schools and colleges (*dīnī madāris*). In the words of General Zia:

> There is hardly any walk of life where a beginning has not been made for its progress and reconstruction. The most important change that has taken place during this period of six years is that the Qibla (orientation of the people) has been set right. The process of the march towards an Islamic way of life, which had been deliberately neglected some time back, is now once again in evidence. People no longer feel ashamed of identifying themselves as Muslms and Pakistanis. They take pride in praying to God Almightly, and mosques now overflow with devotees. Now religious scholars, divines and thinkers of Islam are accorded a respect in our society.[110]

Nevertheless, these policies placed the Islamic parties in a very difficult situation and muted their resistance somewhat. In fact, Zia questioned "the need for the parliamentary opposition to challenge the government's programme, because the programme is based on the Qur'ān ... and the Holy Qur'ān is my manifesto, ... so what is there to oppose?"[111] Evidently, Zia, despite his piety and sincerity, was using Islam to disarm the Islamic forces active in the political arena.

Like his predecessors, General Zia distrusted politicians and hence placed severe restraints on political activities. He repeatedly postponed elections and when the call for elections became intense, the Jamāᶜat and other political parties, were legally outlawed on 16 October 1979. He believed in centralized, authoritarian government and, disregarding repeated calls from many quarters including the Jamāᶜat, did not hold national level elections until 1984. The Jamāᶜat gradually intensified its anti-Zia campaign which resulted in increased repression and banning of all student unions which were largely controlled by the Jamāᶜat and were considered to be its most active arm. In December 1984, Zia held a referendum and won a 97.7 percent approval vote endorsing his Islamization package that was interpreted as a mandate for Zia to remain as president for an additional five-year term ending in 1990. In February 1985, the president arranged for "party-less" elections for the national and provincial assemblies. General Zia seeing a discouraging performance of the Jamāᶜat in the elections replaced it with a secular Muslim League as the pillar of his regime. The Muslim League government led by Muhammad Khan Junejo was dissolved by presidential fiat in May 1988 as it tried to assert its independence from Zia.

The Post-Zia Governments (1988-1999)
The politics of Pakistan in the post-Zia period are characterized by a high incidence of political instability. Between 1988 and 1999, four elections were held, four national assemblies were dissolved, three prime ministers were dismissed, and in between the dismissals, three caretaker prime ministers were appointed by the President of Pakistan. The drama ended with the military coup d'etat of 12 October 1999 that toppled the government of Prime minister Nawaz Sharif. Nevertheless, the politics of Pakistan during this period revolved around the Western educated and secular Benazir Bhutto (1952 -) and the industrialist turned politician and moderate Islamist, Mian Nawaz Sharif (1948 -).

Benazir Bhutto, the leader of the Pakistan People's Party, had the honour of being the Muslim world's first elected female head of government.[112] She was elected the prime minister of Pakistan in 1988 but was dismissed, through a presidential order, after staying in power for 18 months. The sacking of the Benazir government was facilitated by her political opposition consisting of 'ulamā', the right wing parties, and the Islami Jamhoori Ittehad (IJI) led by Nawaz Sharif. These alliances started with street demonstrations, personal attacks on Bhutto and her family, *fatwā* (a legal opinion of a jurist) against the leadership of a woman, calls for mid-term elections and non-cooperation. Finally, they brought a no-confidence motion against the prime minister but it failed. Before the opposition could mount another no confidence motion against Benazir Bhutto, the president dismissed the government on August 6, 1990. She, however, managed to stage a comeback by winning a plurality in the 1993 national elections but was dismissed once again in 1996.

During the 1988 elections, Benazir campaigned throughout Pakistan and her speeches emphasised the urgent need to grant real economic and political freedom rather than the "vague Islamic doses" that were, according to her, "a hoax played by General Zia to fool the poor and the downtrodden."[113] She promised to dismantle Zia's Islamic policies, as they were barbaric, reactionary and undemocratic. Indeed, she was unable to deliver on this promise. A woman with Western education and an assertive temperament, Benazir did not find any favour among her well-entrenched opponents, including the army leadership.[114] Once in office, Benazir adopted a policy of appeasement towards religious groups by covering her head, wearing the *chadar*, visiting shrines, and avoiding handshakes with men. She visited Makkah frequently and was even shown in the national media rolling her beads. Thus, for Benazir, Islam was confined to her personal appearance and public display of piety. At the public decision making level, she would have nothing to do with Islamic forces except if it was dictated by power politics considerations. It must be noted that the first Benazir government was based on a shaky coalition and hence much of the energy of the PPP leadership was expended in the attempt to maintain power.

Though she failed in her attempts to get the cooperation of the Jamāᶜat against her opponents, Benazir nevertheless succeeded in making an ad hoc parliamentary alliance with Jamiᶜat-e-ᶜUlamā'-e-Islām and appointed its chief, Maulana Fazlur Rahman, as Chairman of the Parliamentary Foreign Affairs Committee. In general, she systematically avoided a formal power-sharing arrangement with Islamic forces. On the contrary, she apparently moved in the opposite direction. She claimed that hers was a moderate Muslim government and that she was determined, in cooperation with the United States' government, to fight radical Islamic activities in Pakistan. To her opponents, these manoeuvres appeared as attempts at silencing the Islamic voices or at least marginalizing Islamic parties from the national arena. Benazir appeared to be emphasizing human rights though the state structure over which she presided felt no qualms in violating them.

Mian Nawaz Sharif, the Lahore-based industrialist, had close ties with General Zia ul-Haq and hence enjoyed good relationship with Islamic forces including the Jamāᶜat. He, with the support of the army leadership, had masterminded an umbrella alliance called the Islamic Democratic Alliance (or Islami Jamhoori Ittehad, IJI) and won the elections in 1990. The Jamāᶜat was a component of the IJI and hence was a part of the government formed subsequently. The Jamāᶜat and other religio-political parties demanded the rapid Islamization of the country's institutions as promised during election campaigns. Sharif's own Muslim League, a combination of liberal and right wing politicians but largely dominated by landed groups and industrial elite felt uncomfortable with such pressures. Additionally, as an industrialist, Sharif was "working hard to burnish Pakistan's image as a stable and progressive place for foreign investors."[115] The state of Pakistan's economy gave him little choice but to woo foreign investors. He did not want his development projects to fall in the doldrums because of excess Islamization demanded by his partners. Nawaz Sharif consequently avoided carrying on Zia's policies of Islamization. Given the fact that the Jamāᶜat was a coalition partner, Nawaz Sharif's government could not simply ignore the question

of sharīᶜah as a non-issue. He, therefore, pre-empted the sharīᶜah
bill, waiting since Zia's time, by introducing his own form of the
sharīᶜah bill that was adopted by the National Assembly in mid-
May 1991 and approved by the Senate two weeks later. On most
issues the Sharī'ah Act remains vague. For instance, it commits
the state to take "steps" for "Islamization of the economy"
("Enforcement," 1991, clause 8), take "effective steps" to Islamize
education ("Enforcement," clause 7), and the like. Meanwhile,
Clauses 18 and 19 of the Act, however, exempt Pakistan's
international financial dealings from the constraints of the Sharīᶜah
Act until an "alternative economic system" is evolved. In other
words, Nawaz Sharif was willing to allow the Islamic parties and
particularly the Jamāᶜat to influence government policies only to
a certain extent and that too if they acted in accordance with the
wishes of the senior partner namely, the Muslim League. Nawaz
Sharif was following the footsteps of General Zia to work in tandem
with Islamic forces but always keeping the initiatives with him
rather than with the alliance partners. The Jamāᶜat wanted to change
its status in the cabinet and asked for the crucial ministries like
Finance and Foreign Affairs. On refusal, the alliance broke down
and in the 1993 elections, the Jamāᶜat and the Muslim League
fielded separate candidates and divided the votes to the advantage
of Benazir's Pakistan People's Party.

On his return to power in 1997 with an absolute majority of
134 out of 217 national assembly seats, Nawaz Sharif embarked
upon a series of populist measures like tax reductions, boosting
agricultural and textile productions, and the "qarz utaro, mulk
sanvaro" (repay the debt and develop the country) scheme in which
overseas Pakistanis were requested to deposit a minimum of US
$1,000 as an interest-free loan to help boost Pakistan's foreign
exchange funds. He also talked again about Islamizing Pakistan.
In late August 1998 Nawaz Sharif introduced the 15th
Constitutional Amendment Bill to the national assembly to replace
the country's legal code with the sharīᶜah. His decision to introduce
full sharīᶜah arose from his desperation to hold the nation together
at a time of crisis resulting from institutional collapse, corruption
and economic recession in the country. The bill also aimed at

placating the Islamic forces in the country that were angered by
his dictatorial style and his acquiescence to the United States' anti-
Muslim policies and actions. The Jamā°at-e-Islāmī and other
mainstream religious parties opposed the Bill for various reasons.
The Jamā°at doubted the sincerity of the prime minister. Others
thought that the Bill, if approved, would over expand the power
of the Prime minister at the expense of the judiciary and the
legislature.[116] The prime minister succeeded in having the 15th
Constitutional Amendment Bill passed in the national assembly,
by 151 to 16 votes. He, however, failed to get it ratified by the
senate. Nawaz Sharif and his government were overthrown by a
bloodless military coup in October 1999.

Politics during the post-Zia period was not much different from
the earlier days in that the ruling parties utilized state agencies and
private goons for their personal purposes. Operations against
dissenting politicians, intellectuals and other activists were carried
out through police-backed preemptive measures, systematic
harassment, wild accusations of corruption, smear campaigns, and
assassinations. Thus there are reports of Benazir having applied
coercion against her opponents and carried out Mafia-style
campaigns to eliminate her rivals. In June 1995, she instituted
160 court cases against Nawaz Sharif, including a more serious
charge of sedition. The Nawaz Sharif government, in turn,
reportedly arrested 15,000 people on "the pretext that they might
be travelling to Islamabad for the march" under the leadership of
Benazir Bhutto.[117] The Sharif government is also accused of having
been involved in smear campaigns against critics of his policies.
One incident involved Mawlana Sami ul-Haq, an °ālim and a
senator from the North West Frontier Province. He was alleged, as
per confession of Madame Tahira, to frequent a brothel in
Islamabad. "One theory is that the government "doctored" the
brothel keeper's confession because the Maulana had been
attacking the government for dragging its feet over implementing
Islamic laws."[118] The Mawlana claimed that "the campaign had
been begun by malicious elements and was baseless and
concocted." Subsequently, the Mawlana toned down his criticism
of the sharī°ah bill and the matter was hushed up.[119] Indeed, the

stories of corruption have received wide coverage in the media and one of the common reasons given for the dismissal of the two governments was their involvement in large scale corruption.

CONCLUSION

The Jamāʿat-e-Islāmī was born in India and struggled to generate Islamic consciousness among the Muslims. For the Jamāʿat, the socio-political environment changed in 1947 with the withdrawal of the British and the emergence of two independent states: India and Pakistan. Consequently, the Jamāʿat's perception was double: one which projected the large Indian environment under the political domination of the British, and the other of Pakistan with a different set of problems and religio-political values. The Jamāʿat's reactions to the two environments were equally different. In British India, it did not and could not take part in politics as it was under the domination of an unIslamic and secular government. With the establishment of Pakistan, the Jamāʿat found it imperative to strive for the implementation of an Islamic order in the country. It was the political activities of the Jamāʿat which brought it to a head-on clash with government authorities.

The Pakistani environment was not to the total liking of the Jamāʿat. During its formative phase, the Pakistani decision-making apparatus was small in size, elitist, and closed in nature. Following Jinnah's death, the ruling elite maintained a facade of parliamentary democracy; the trend nevertheless was one of a closed oligarchy. After the Ayub coup, the political system remained closed to the masses. Ayub's basic democracy system did not provide for popular politics. The Yahya era was a significant stage towards the development of democracy in Pakistan. The democratic idea then entrenched in Pakistani thinking was irreversible.

All the rulers except Jinnah and Liaquat have used Islam to legitimize their authority and to avoid electoral politics and accountability. The young state, while coopting the religious elite to build a consensus from above, adopted the Objectives Resolution in 1949 which was incorporated with minor modifications in the successive constitutions of 1956, 1962, and 1973. However, the ruling elite and the religious elite were not always mutually supportive.

Pakistani ruling elites have generally tried to pacify the elite through cooption, failing which they have resorted to coercion. Ayub Khan enjoyed a rapport with certain religious leaders and declared the Pir of Daiwal to be his personal spiritual guide. Yahya Khan, in his hour of trial, invoked Islam to crush Muslim Bengalis. Bhutto, heading an "authoritarian populist" regime declared Pakistan to be the Islamic Republic and held an international Islamic summit in Lahore the following year. Zia used Islam, the ᶜulamā' and others affiliated with religious institutions to his maximum benefit and consolidated his power in the country. The referendum of 1984 made Zia and Islam integral to each other in Pakistan's state structure and he took it as a vote for his presidency until 1991. Table 2.1 shows the composition of Pakistan's ruling elite, its constitutional shifts and the shifting Islamic content in its constitutional arrangements.

Looking back at these long decades of uncertainties in Pakistan, it is clear that the politics and administration of the country have revolved around personalities, so-called strong men, who by virtue of being non-representative and simply authoritarian refurbished governmental control over the country. The mutilation of political opponents, exploitation of Islamic symbols and institutions, muzzling of the press, and the manipulation of power have all combined to constrict the activities of Islamic political parties and hindered the evolution of Pakistani political culture supportive of a participatory political system. They have also produced persistent street agitation and violence to defy these regimes, given that no other politico-constitutional mechanism of change was available.

Period	Leader	Position	Leader's Orientation
1947-1948	M.A. Jinnah	GG	Modernist Islam
1947-1951	Liaquat A. Khan	PM	Modernist Islam; Objectives Resolution
1948-1951	K. Nazimuddin	GG	Modernist Islam
1951-1955	Ghulam Mohammad	GG	Secular
1951-1953	K. Nazimuddin	PM	Modernist Islam
1953-1955	Mohd. Ali Bogra	PM	Secular
1955-1958	Iskander Mirza	GG/Pr	Secular
1955-1956	Chy. Md. Ali	PM	Secular; 1956 Constt; Pakistan declared an Islamic Republic
1956-1957	H.S. Suhrawardy	PM	Secular
Oct-Dec 1957	I.I. Chundrigar	PM	Secular
1957-1958	Firoz Khan Noon	PM	Secular
1958-1969	Md. Ayub Khan	CMLA/Pr	Islamic Modernism; 1962 Constt; Islamic content was cosmetic & vague
1969-1971	Aga Md. Yahya Khan	CMLA/Pr	Secular, presided break-up of Pakistan
1971-1977	Zulfiqar Ali Bhutto	CMLA/Pr/PM	Islamic Socialism; 1973 Constt; Islamic content was cosmetic and vague, secular, left
1977-1988	Mohd. Zia ul-Haq	CMLA/Pr	Pious Muslim; Islamization
1985-1988	Mohd. Khan Junejo	PM	Moderate Islam
1988-1993	Ghulam Ishaq Khan	Pr	Moderate Islam
1988-1990	Benazir Bhutto	PM	Secular
Aug-Nov 1990	Ghulam Mustafa Jatoi	PM (CT)	Secular
1990-1993	Mian Nawaz Sharif	PM	Moderate Islam; Shari'at Bill
Apr-May 1993	Balakh Sher Mazari	PM (CT)	Secular
May-July 1993	Mian Nawaz Sharif	PM	Moderate Islam
July-Nov 1993	Wassim Sajjad	PM	Secular
July-Oct 1993	Moeen Qureshi	PM (CT)	Secular
1993-1996	Benazir Bhutto	PM	Secular
1993-1996	Farooq Leghari	Pr	Secular
1997-19971	Mian Nawaz Sharif	PM	Moderate Islam

Source: Peter R. Blood (ed.), *Pakistan: A Country Study* (Washington, D.C.: U.S. Government Printing, 1995), 328.

Notes: GG=Governor General; PM=Prime minister; Pr=President; CMLA=Chief Martial Law Administrator; CT=Care Taker

3

JAMĀʿAT-E-ISLĀMĪ: TRANSFORMATION OF A MOVEMENT

The Jamāʿat-e-Islāmī in Pakistan was credited to "have a well defined objective and work for it with single-mindedness of purpose and determination."[1] That objective, as stated by Sayyid Abul Aʿla Mawdudi, is Islam which is a universal and comprehensive way of life. It is a well-ordered system, a consistent whole with set answers to all problems. Its fundamental postulate is *tawḥīd,* the unity and sovereignty of Allah (s.w.t). The scheme of life envisaged by Islam is known as sharīʿah and is established on the bedrock of faith. It is on that foundation that the edifice of moral, social, political and economic system is created. The ideal Islamic society, to Mawdudi, consists of people who, through putting their faith in Islam, have liberated themselves from all allegiances except to Allah (s.w.t); such a society would be free and "theo-democratic" and its citizens would be as equal as the teeth of a comb.

Muslims, according to Mawdudi, belong to the *ummah wasaṭah* (just and balanced community), and, as such, are duty bound to enjoin what is right and forbid what is evil. The Qur'ān, he wrote, is not a book of abstract theories and religious enigmas to be unraveled in monasteries and universities; it is a book of movement and agitation revealed to invite the people to the one right way of Allah (s.w.t).[2] Consequently, Islam is the religion of revolutionary struggle and utmost exertion (*jihād*) aimed at shattering the myth of the divinity of demi-gods and promoting the cause of Allah (s.w.t) by establishing the Islamic political order. Islam, therefore, "is a dynamic force, a world-wide revolutionary movement bent upon transforming the world to be in accord with its tenets and principles to benefit mankind."[3] *Jihād* is but another name for the attempt to establish the Divine Order; the Qur'ān therefore declares it to be a touchstone of belief. In this struggle, there is no room for bystanders, spectators and backsliders and the venture is so crucial that, neglecting it, "one has no means left to please Allah."[4]

Initially, the Jamāᶜat tried to carry out this *jihād* by calling for a spiritual awakening based on the principles of Islam. With the advent of Pakistan, the Jamāᶜat decided to take an active part in politics and pursue the constitutional means to capture political power. This chapter pinpoints various milestones in the transformation of the Jamāᶜat from a quietist movement for an Islamic revival to an active political party bent upon wresting power from what Mawdudi called the "leadership of the wayward." It examines this evolution by referring to the social and intellectual base of its leadership structure as reflected in the changing composition of the working committee of the Jamāᶜat-e-Islāmī.

JAMĀᶜAT: THE MOVEMENT PHASE

The Jamāᶜat-e-Islāmī was formed on August 26, 1941 with an initial membership of 75 all of whom, according to Vali Reza Nasr, "... came from the ranks of the young ᶜulamā' and the religious literati of northern India."[5] Sayyid Mawdudi was elected its *amīr*. The initiation ceremony was very impressive, revealing the dedication and determination of those who resolved to change the world:

> The Mawlana, then rose and recited the *kalimah* [in Urdu, the testimony of faith] and asked the audience to bear witness that he has embraced Islam afresh and joined the Jamāᶜat-e-Islāmī. Next to profess his faith anew was Mawlana Mohammad Manzoor Nu'mani. All the people among the audience then followed suit one by one. Most of them did with tearful eyes, while a few were overwhelmed with emotion and wept excessively. Everyone was trembling with the sense of responsibility as he recited the *kalimah*. When everyone had finished bearing witness to the Unity of Allah and the Prophethood of Mohammed, Mawlana Mawdudi declared that the Jamāᶜat had been formed.[6]

The Jamā°at-e-Islāmī movement was not a chance occurrence but was conceived in its definite form in the period between 1938 and 1939. It was occasioned by the despicable servile attitude of Muslims facing a Hindu Congress leader, which Mawdudi witnessed while travelling on his way back to Hyderabad:

> I was in the same compartment with a Hindu Congress leader Dr. Khare and other Muslim fellow travelers. I saw that the Muslims were talking to Dr. Khare as if a conquered race was addressing the conquering ruler. Such an intolerable scene made me restless and wonder as to what was in store for the Muslims of India.[7]

The incident prompted him to write a series of articles and launch a collective struggle to awaken the Muslims. Soon other prominent °ulamā' joined the Jamā°at including six from Madrasatu'l Islah, four from Deoband, four Nadwis and two from the Ahl-i-Hadith. "By 1945, the Jamā°at boasted a membership of some 224 °ulamā', sixty of whom continued to teach at various dar al-°ulūms (religious seminaries)."[8] The °ulamā', then, constituted about 40% of its total membership. Some of these °ulamā' viewed themselves superior to Mawdudi in piety and scholarship and took on a leadership role in the organization.

The Jamā°at organization consisted of the office of the amīr, the central majlis-e-shūrā and arkān (full members). Supporters were divided into three categories, in ascending order: muta°arrifīn (those familiar with the Jamā°at's message), muta'aththirīn (those influenced by the Jamā°at's message), and hamdard (sympathizers). These supporters did not play any official role except to serve as a pool from which new workers could be drawn gradually.

The Jamā°at stood for Islam in its entirety and called for "nothing short of Islam, whose message is intended for the whole of mankind."[9] Mawdudi argued that an Islamic order without an Islamic revolution preceding it, is bound to falter on the moral infirmities of its adherents. The French, Russian and German revolutionary movements would not have succeeded, Mawdudi pointed out, without the backing of their appropriate social

consciousness and moral atmosphere. There was a sociological
reasoning as well. A socio-political order, he argued, is something
which is formed, not by artificial means, but as the natural
consequence of the interplay of certain moral, psychological,
cultural and historical factors, which pre-exist in a particular society
– a notion which can be traced back to Ibn Khaldun.[10] A revolution
is, therefore, a pre-requisite for an Islamic order.

Holding Prophet Muhammad (s.a.w) as the revolutionary
paradigm, Mawdudi discerned three phases in the prophetic
revolutionary movement. First, the Prophet (s.a.w) called to faith,
īmān, to build a strong structure on solid foundations. Second, he
organized all those who responded to the call of Islam on one
platform, training them to believe in and practise the Islamic way
of life, and prepare a strong public opinion which fosters good
and inhibits evil. The final stage of the movement began in
Madinah, where a mere 400 workers, fully trained in Islamic
principles and able to act as true Muslims, were called upon to
take the responsibility of administering an Islamic political system
and organize various aspects of social life on Islamic principles.
They presented such a shining example of Islamic government
that within a span of eight years the whole of Arabia heartily
responded to the revolutionary call of Islam.[11] This according to
Mawdudi was the right way of doing the work and "if we work in
this manner today the same result will appear."[12] Mawdudi followed
this model and chalked out the strategy of the Islamic revolution
which included the following four major elements.[13]

The first element of the programme was to plunge straight
into the revolutionary task with an uncompromising declaration
that "there is none worthy of worship but Allah" and to present
Islamic beliefs and injunctions in their right perspective and with
their true import. In preaching this message, the Prophet (s.a.w)
did not go about in a roundabout manner nor did he make any
preparatory attempts to impress people by some other activities.
The call was direct and straightforward, inviting mankind to accept
the faith with full understanding and consciousness and to fulfill
its obligations consciously. This step was necessary for it would

help weed out the people of weak character and irresolute determination and would enroll only the clear-minded, those who are willing to give up all prospects of worldly success for the sake of truth and righteousness.[14]

The recent attempts then to revive Islam, Mawdudi lamented, were centered on piecemeal modifications of Islamic law and compromises between Islamic and un-Islamic principles that resulted in the dominance of Western ideas. It is the apologetic approach of Sir Sayyid Ahmed Khan and others in India which made Western civlization "the judge of the merits and faults of Islam.... In Egypt, Sheikh Muhammad Abduh adopted a similar line of compromise and thus opened the door wide for the Westernizers in the Arab speaking world who came after him."[15] The correct approach, according to Mawdudi was to re-establish pure Islam in the world.

The preaching of the unity and sovereignty of Allah (s.w.t) entailed many activities: one, a searching criticism of other ideologies and philosophies and exposing their fallacies and weaknesses; two, a critical examination of all kinds of innovations in religion and a careful delineation of the boundaries between Islam and un-Islam; and three, revitalization of the spirit of *ijtihād*, i.e., exerting one's utmost to show how Islamic principles can be applied to new circumstances. Mawdudi would not permit the slightest deviation from the path of true Islam, which he considered as resting upon the Qur'ān and the teachings of the Prophet (s.a.w). Even *ṣūfī* (mystic) ideas and practices had to conform to sharī°ah.

The second step in the movement was to identify, select and organize those who responded to the revolutionary call on one common platform, and to devise a program for their moral, intellectual and social upliftment in such a way that they become permeated with the true spirit of Islam. The movement needed people of this type. Without them the movement could neither gain in strength nor grow in size. Mawdudi, therefore, emphasized the need for creating "a small, informed, dedicated and disciplined group" who would provide the leadership to the community through precepts and examples and achieve the objectives of the

Islamic revolution.[16]

The third element was to start an all-out campaign for the regeneration and the reconstruction of the collective life of the community along Islamic concepts of life. This programme of social reconstruction is a comprehensive one and consists of environmental change and change within the heart and soul of man – his attitudes, motivations, commitment and his resolve to moblize all that is within him and around him for the fulfillment of his objectives. The order of precedence in an Islamic system is, first, to acquaint the masses all over the country, in cities, towns and villages, with Islam and reform their minds through education and preaching so that their outlook is changed. This would require propaganda through verbal preaching and by distribution of tracts and pamphlets, operating reading rooms and establishing educational institutions with Islamic curricula. Then a gigantic propaganda effort has to be made, through "wisdom, excellent admonition and best manners," to create an Islamic character in them. This campaign has to be so tactfully arranged that it develops a group of good, pious men in every locality who are in a position to suppress the bad elements of the society and can strive to make the people of their own area religious and honest. In this way a popular opinion will emerge in the country which will suppress all kinds of evil and allow a just, balanced society to emerge and prosper.[17]

The final element of the movement called for a change of social, economic and political leadership of the country so that the resources of the state are harnessed to the service of Islam. The revolutionary movement, Mawdūdī contended, has no choice but to capture state authority, for without it the pious order that Islam envisages can never be established.

The Jamāᶜat was thus organized along the lines adopted by Prophet Muhammad (s.a.w). Its activities were not confined to the Muslims of India but transcended all geographical boundaries and encompassed the welfare of the whole world and all mankind. The Jamāᶜat was not a political organization seeking representation in parliament and government but an instrument which would bring a total transformation of society along Islamic lines. The membership of the party was restricted to men of sterling qualities – righteous, honest, moral, incorruptible and strong personal character that would inspire confidence in others. The emphasis of the Jamāʿat was not on numbers but on character, ideological commitment, discipline, spirit of sacrifice for fellow members, and dedication to the cause.[18] The Jamāʿat stood for the truth even if it went against public opinion. It gave priority to mental, educational and intellectual revolution, to the purification and reconstruction of thought, and to social reform.[19] Politics did form a part of the Jamāʿat programme but it received the least priority. Thus the Jamāʿat, at its inception, conceived of itself as a virtuous community (ummah) and a daʿwah (religious propagation) movement aiming at changing the society along Islamic lines. "It provided Indian Muslims with an organization to work out their religious, cultural and political demands."[20]

As mentioned above, the emphasis of the Jamāʿat was not on number but on character, ideological commitment, and dedication to the cause. It took Prophet Muhammad (s.a.w), Mawdudi pointed out, over thirteen years to organize and train, for the cause, about 400 dedicated and conspicuously upright men who within a short period established Islam in the whole of Arabia. Mawdudi therefore, emphasized the need for creating "a small, informed, dedicated and disciplined group" who would provide leadership to the community through precepts and examples and achieve the objectives of the Islamic revolution.[21] Sayyid Mawdūdī therefore, devoted his attention to organizational consolidation and character building of the members.

The character development programme was based on three elements. First, to inspire them to preach truth not in fragments commingled with elements of untruth, but truth as a whole and to cultivate the virtues: (a) of patience proportional to the persistence of opposing forces; (b) of sacrifice of time, energy and property; (c) of whole-hearted devotion to the cause; and (d) of persistent efforts and working in a systematic and methodic way.[22] Second, to cultivate a sense of loyalty to the organization, to have the interests of the organization at heart and to be a sincere well-wisher of co-members. The best way to promote the interests of the Jamāᶜat would be:

> ... to see that it does not swerve from the right path; that no wrong ideas and evil practices creep into it; that nobody in the organization is allowed to be high-handed; that no worldly object is cherished; that no personality is idolized and that its constitution is not vitiated by alterations.[23]

The final element of the character development programme was to emphasize the necessity of mutual consultation and constructive criticism as the essence of collective life and of the Jamāᶜat.

> Members should abstain from forming a party within the party. Intrigues, factionalism, canvassing, aspiration to offices, false sense of honor and personal rivalries constitute a serious danger to the very existence of organization and are repugnant to the genius of Islamic policy.[24]

Thus the plan of action, spelled out in 1951 by the Jamāᶜat, but pursued since its formation, was:

1. Purification and reconstruction of thought through personal contact, lectures, seminars and the use of mass media.
2. Search for training and organization of righteous people.
3. Social reforms including provision of free or cheap medical services, constructing rural roads, and bridges, establishment of schools for adults and children, organizing free public reading rooms, and helping the poor and needy.
4. Reform of the existing set-up of government and establishing the Islamic system through constitutional means i.e., rendering sound counsel to the government and participating in elections with all its concomitants of campaigning and alliance formations.[25]

Politics certainly formed a part of the Jamāᶜat's programme but it received the least priority. It "is a pity," said Mawdudi, "that Muslims see their objectives in purely political terms and are hence, oblivious to the role of religion in this world."[26] Earlier in 1941, Mawdudi had told the *majlis-e-shūrā* of the Jamāᶜat that:

> demonstrations or agitation, flag waving, slogans, uniforms and petitions, resolutions and addresses, impassioned speeches and emotional writings, and similar things, which are the heart and soul of nationalist or other movements, will prove deadly for the Islamic movement. You do not need to capture your audience through impassioned speeches, writings and demonstrations ... but you must kindle the light of Islam in your hearts, and as such, change those around you.[27]

The report presented to the general meeting of the Jamāᶜat-e-Islāmī, Pakistan, on Novemeber 20, 1955, categorically asserted that the first phase of the Jamāᶜat was one of "*daᶜwat wa tablīgh awr tarbiyat wa taᶜmīr sīrat*" (of religious propagation and of moral and spiritual training and character building) and hence from 1941 to 1947, the Jamāᶜat published more literature on basic religious education.[28]

JAMĀᶜAT AS A PRESSURE GROUP

Following the partition of India in 1947, Mawdudi, along with many party leaders, moved to Pakistan and established the headquarters of the Jamāᶜat-e-Islāmī of Pakistan in Lahore. The multiple reinforcing cleavages, elite incoherence, and tortuous and complicated political maneuverings during the formative phase of Pakistan, perhaps, influenced the Jamāᶜat leaders to become active in Pakistani politics.

The Jamāᶜat, according to Israr Ahmad, adopted the following two-point programme:

1. To embark upon a comprehensive movement for the implementation of Islamic ideology in order to convert to Islam the newly established state of Pakistan.

2. To bring about a revolutionary change in the political leadership of the country so that the resources of the state are harnessed in the service of Islam.[29]

Israr Ahmad blames Mawdudi for restricting the scope of Jamāᶜat's activities by its exclusive concern for the Muslims to the exclusion of non-Muslims and for transforming the Jamāᶜat into a nationalist organization serving the cause of Islam in Pakistan.[30] Mawdūdī's reasons for subscribing to an "Islam in Pakistan" thesis were two-fold. First, for an ideology to be useful, it must have an empirical import and make reference to particular cases or examples because it is impossible to build a pattern of life merely in the abstract. Second, for an ideology to attract worldwide attention, it must demonstrate its worth by evolving a happy and successful system of life and must present its theories and fundamental principles in operation. Consequently, Mawdudi thought it essential to have the Islamic state established in one country first so as to be emulated worldwide later.[31]

The Jamāᶜat started an organized campaign to realize the first of the two objectives. On January 6 and February 19, 1948, Mawdudi delivered two lectures at the Law College in Lahore in which he demanded the Constituent Assembly of Pakistan to accept the following four demands:

1. That the sovereignty belongs to Allah alone and that the state shall exercise its authority as His agent.
2. That sharīᶜah will be the basic law of the land.
3. That the laws in conflict with the sharīᶜah will gradually be repealed and that no such laws shall be enacted in future.
4. That the state in exercising its powers shall not transgress the limits prescribed by Islam.[32]

The Lahore lectures were followed by a tour of Pakistan in April and May 1948, extensive lobbying with the members of the Constituent Assembly and concerted public campaign to press upon the leaders to incorporate the above points into the constitution of Pakistan. On March 7, 1949 the Constituent Assembly passed the Objectives Resolution embodying the four-point demand. The Resolution, setting forth the ideals and values, acted as a guide for constitution makers in Pakistan in 1956, 1962, 1972 and 1973 in devising an Islamic order for the country. It was incorporated, with minor modifications, in all the constitutions of Pakistan. The Objectives Resolution was made a substantive part of the constitution by President General Zia-ul Haq through a constitutional amendment that was promulgated on March 2, 1985. Given the far-reaching implications for the future of Islam, the Resolution demands a full length quotation:

> Whereas sovereignty over the entire Universe belongs to Allah Almighty alone, and the authority which He has delegated to the State of Pakistan through its people for being exercised within the limits prescribed is a sacred trust;

> Whereas the founder of Pakistan, Quaid-i-Azam Muhammad Ali Jinnah, declared that Pakistan would be a democratic state based on Islamic principles of social justice;

> And whereas the Constituent Assembly, representing the people of Pakistan, have resolved to frame for the sovereign independent State of Pakistan a Constitution;

> Wherein the State should exercise its powers and authority through the chosen representatives of the people;

> Wherein the principles of democracy, freedom, equality, tolerance and social justice as enunciated by Islam, should be fully observed;

> Wherein the Muslims of Pakistan would be enabled individually and collectively to order their lives in accordance with the teachings and requirements of Islam, as set out in the Holy Qur'ān and Sunnah.[33]

With the passage of the Resolution, Pakistan, according to Mawdudi, in principle took the shape of an Islamic state. It is not the Resolution per se but the fact of it being adopted by the government in response to the unanimous demand of the people to lead an Islamic way of life that made it an Islamic state.[34] It would be an exaggeration to credit Mawdudi and his organization exclusively for the success. However, the organized strength of the Jamāᶜat under Mawdudi's leadership did play a major role. It may thus be construed as a triumph of Mawdudi and the Jamāᶜat-e-Islāmī of Pakistan.

The Objectives Resolution did not produce the desired result. Understandably, the institutionalization of Islam in Pakistan would have jeopardized the vested interests of the feudal and capitalist forces as well as that the of civil-military bureaucracy. The Jamāᶜat consequently intensified its efforts through public meetings, contacting members of parliament, and mobilizing strong public pressure to make Pakistan a truly Islamic republic. These efforts for the Islamic system involved Mawdudi and his colleagues in intense conflict with the authorities. The Jamāᶜat continued its efforts and Mawdudi produced several treatises on Islamic political theory, Islamic law and constitution, Islamic judicial and legal structures and the modalities for ushering in the Islamic political system in Pakistan. It is to the credit of the Jamāᶜat-e-Islāmī that it introduced Islamic idioms and concepts into the unfolding national political discourse and launched a vigorous campaign for the Islamization of Pakistan. The government responded by banning some of the Jamāᶜat publications and jailing its top ranking leaders including Mawlana Mawdudi.

THE JAMĀᶜAT AND ELECTORAL POLITICS

The Jamāᶜat, however, had tasted victory in the passage of the Objectives Resolution and considered it prudent to strive to realise the second objective of capturing political power and taking a more active part in the politics of Pakistan. The secretary general's report of November 10, 1951 states that the Jamāᶜat had resolved in April 1949 that it is permissible to take part in elections and to seek the membership of legislative assemblies.[35] The political environment seemed conducive to political participation since the ruling elite was involved in experimenting with parliamentary democratic system. However, it was the Punjab provincial assembly elections of March 1951 which acted as a catalyst to set off new trains of thought ushering the Jamāᶜat into electoral politics.[36]

The Jamāᶜat, however, made it clear that it did not approve of the prevalent party system and its method of nominating candidates for elections. According to Mawdudi, the lust for power and craving for office had reduced the elections to a mere farce. Consequently, the Jamāᶜat adopted a novel method of recruiting candidates for elections.[37] It did not field any candidate of its own. Instead, it formed panchayats (voters' councils), each consisting of 53 members in 1390 localities, and assigned them the responsibility of nominating those candidates whom they judged virtuous (ṣālih) and favourably disposed towards the Objectives Resolution passed by the Constituent Assembly of Pakistan. The Jamāᶜat then carried out a campaign on behalf of the virtuous candidates.

The Jamāᶜat made it clear that it was not participating in the elections for any political gain but to use the occasion to disseminate its ideas and to galvanize public opinion to help Islamize Pakistan.[38] The Jamāᶜat ran a pure, ethical election campaign devoid of all malpractices including intimidation, character assassination and falsification of information. It commenced its election campaign in July 1950 under the direction of Abdul Jabbar Ghazi.[39] It formulated the election manifesto, supported 53 candidates in the race for the 192 Punjab assembly seats, and campaigned vigorously for eight months.[40]

The results of the elections were disappointing. The Jamāᶜat-backed candidates won about 217,859 votes and succeeded in getting only one of its virtuous candidates, Mawlana Muhyuddin Lakhavi, elected.[41] This electoral defeat was attributed to various causes ranging from the media animosity and the banning of the Jamāᶜat newspapers *Kawthar, Tasnīm* and *Qāṣid* to the rigging of the election by the party in power.[42] Sayyid Mawdudi, however, considered it a success even though only one of its supported candidates had been elected to the Punjab assembly. The reasons were many. First, the system devised by the Jamāᶜat for candidate selection in Punjab election was novel and "was the first electoral experience in the history of democracy." Second, for the first time the general public was introduced to an electoral practice that was based upon pure ethical and moral code. Third, the people were informed about the nature of the Islamic system and the type of people required to run such a system. Finally, the Jamāᶜat gained the support of about 400,000 people in Punjab.[43] Nevertheless, the electoral experience did cause much soul-searching among some of the rank and file of the Jamāᶜat. Given the malpractices indulged in by the political parties, some members felt that they could never win an election through peaceful and ethical means. They also noted that some Jamāᶜat workers were swayed by the demands of the electoral campaign and hence transgressed the moral and ethical code of the organization. This ethical misconduct by the workers became glaring in the subsequent electoral campaigns in the Frontier Provinces. These members, therefore, argued for eschewing electoral politics and to continue working in the educational and religious fields.[44]

The campaign against electoral participation and consequent ethical misconduct became so vehement that Sayyid Mawdudi was forced to appoint an investigation committee, in 1954, to look into these allegations.[45] The committee submitted its report to the *shūrā* during its session in November 1956. The committee's report, according to Israr Ahmad, was a "top level secret" and hence was not released to the public.[46] All available information indicated that the committee was highly critical of the Jamāᶜat's activities and that its report can be summarised in the following three points:

1. Jamāᶜat had veered away from its "true" path by jettisoning its original mission and strategy of working in the religious and educational fields.
2. Jamāᶜat rank and file had shown laxity in their moral and ethical conduct and were involved in political activities to the detriment of religious studies and even worship.

3. Jamā'at's increased earning, largely from outside sources, was adversely affecting the thinking of the members and the decisions of the organization.[47]

The report concluded by suggesting that the Jamā'at should desist from political activities, refrain from taking part in future elections, and revert to the four-point plan introduced in 1951.

The fifteen-day *shūrā* session did endorse the recommendations of the Review Committee and it agreed to form a committee, under Mawlana Amin Ahsan Islahi, to ensure the implementation of its resolutions. However, the *shūrā* resolution did not have the blessings of Sayyid Mawdudi and attempts were made to reverse the decision. The matter dragged on for another two years and was hotly debated in the now famous Machi Goth, Bhawalpur State, session of the Jamā'at held in February 1957. This time Mawlana Islahi took the lead, arguing that election campaigns were not necessary to bring about the desired reform of the society; rather it would force the organization to compromise on principles.[48] Mawlana Islahi's arguments have been well summarized by Kalim Bahadur as follows:

> Islahi claimed that he neither considered the slogan of the change of leadership as the means to an Islamic revolution nor did he consider election campaigns as leading to reform of society. Constructive work, according to Islahi, would also prepare the ground for future elections. The people were not so eager to change the leadership of the country that if the Jamā'at did not participate in the election, Islam would be defeated.

> Contesting the elections would not be possible without compromises on principles, Islahi asserted. He alleged that candidature which had been condemned on the basis of the Qur'ān and Hadith, was now being justified without any reference to the Book and the Sunnah. This was the beginning of compromises the Jamā'at would be compelled to make.[49]

Mawdudi, in an equally famous six-hour long speech, countered and argued for giving primacy to politics as it was the only way to establish the Islamic way of life (*iqāmat-e-dīn*) and a government based on divine pattern (*ḥukūmat-e-ilāhīyah*).[50] Mawdudi conceded that there were problems in the organization but insisted that the Jamā°at had strictly followed its principles though tactics, of necessity, had changed.[51] In the end, Mawdudi won and all but 15 members (out of a total of 935 attendants) voted in favour of the Jamā°at taking part in electoral and political activities in future; "the fifteen handed in their resignations then and there."[52] There followed expulsions, defections and further resignations. According to Vali Reza Nasr, altogether 56 members left the Jamā°at; "most were °ulamā' and represented the party's religious weight and intellect. They were replaced by lay activists and functionaries."[53]

JAMĀ°AT AS A CADRE PARTY

The Machi Goth affair and the subsequent purge of the Jamā°at members reoriented the movement, giving primacy to politics to be followed by activities aimed at cultural and religious rejuvenation. In other words, the Jamā°at abandoned the 1951 strategy of "bottom-up" approach of converting first the individual to the true faith who then would act as a catalyst for social change and political reform. Instead, it would follow the "top-down" approach of Islamizing the society and the individual by first capturing the state machinery. In practice, it meant that the Jamā°at would struggle to: (1) ensure that the Constitution declared the sovereignty of Allah (s.w.t) and that the laws in conflict with the sharī°ah were repealed and that no such laws are enacted in future; (2) establish and sustain a democratic framework of government; and (3) take part in all elections so that the legislative bodies were dominated by pious, selfless, and committed Muslims of impeccable character who would frame laws in accordance with the sharī°ah.[54]

Mawdūdī contended that the Jamā°at had no choice but to capture the state authority for without it, the pious order which

Islam envisages could never be established. The struggle for obtaining control over the organs of the state, for the sole purpose of establishing Islam, is not only desirable but in the light of the Qur'ānic verse XVII:80, obligatory.[55] However, Mawdudi declared that the capturing of the state power must be accomplished through constitutional means i.e., elections, since sharī°ah forbids resorting to unconstitutional means for the transformation of the political system.[56]

Consequent upon the decision, the constitution of the Jamā°at was revised, in 1957, to provide for greater organizational unity and efficiency. The *amīr*, henceforth, would be elected directly by the members of the Jamā°at and not by the *shūrā*. The *shūrā*, in turn, was expanded to fifty members with a power to veto the decisions of the *amīr*. The *amīr* nevertheless controlled the agenda and discussions of the *shūrā*. Finally, a new organ was created, called *majlis-e-°āmilah* (executive council), to be composed of members appointed by the *amīr* from among the members of the *shūra*. The *majlis-e-°āmilah* "was formed to serve as the ultimate arbiter between the *amīr* and the *shūrā*."[57] Needless to say, the elected *amīr* was Sayyid Mawdudi.

Though Mawdudi decided to let the Jamā°at enter politics and win the support of the masses, he had no intention of turning the Jamā°at into a mass party. Mawdudi argued that the passion for and enthusiasm about Islam notwithstanding, a great majority of Muslims in Pakistan knew very little about Islam and had no proper training to be able to live up to Islam. According to Mawdudi's estimate, only 5 percent of the Muslim population of Pakistan were enlightened about Islam, 90 percent of them were illiterate with blind faith and the remaining 5 percent had been corrupted by Westernization.[58] The most dedicated followers of the Jamā°at came from among the enlightened group. The replacement of the *muta°ārif* and *muta'aththir* categories with that of a new category called *muttafiq* (affiliate), in 1951, which though it broadened the base, did not alter the organization much. Thus, Mawdudi's strategy for winning political power would be similar to Lenin's strategy of vanguardism. All along he stressed the need for awakening the Islamic consciousness of the masses from without through a tightly

organized cadre party. The party, therefore, continued to demand
the strictest discipline and loyalty from members and would not
permit the slightest deviation from its doctrines. Recruitment was
selective. The prospective member had to demonstrate his capacity
to live a life according to the tenets of Islam and his willingness to
carry out faithfully the duties assigned to him, involving a sacrifice
of both time and money.

Thus armed, the Jamāᶜat entered the Karachi Municipal
Corporation election of 1958 with full vigour. It nominated 23
candidates, spent a total of about Rs.40,000 on the campaign, and
won nineteen seats.[59] It was a sufficiently encouraging
performance for the party which emboldened it further to bid for
representation in the legislature as a step towards the acquisition
of state power. To that end, the Jamāᶜat published its election
manifesto and forged an electoral alliance with the Nizam-e-Islam
Party.[60]

Its election manifesto was a document expressing its social,
economic, political and religious ideas in a concise and readable
form for the information of the general public.[61] The party stressed
the need for modern techniques and methods of production to
develop the economy and pledged their application in agriculture
and industry. It attached the highest importance to the sanctity of
private property provided it was acquired in accordance with the
sharīᶜah. It promised to institute an inquiry committee to ascertain
the legitimacy or otherwise of the acquisitions and to take action
accordingly. Likewise in industry, it was against state enterprise.
It visualised partnership between tenants and landlords, workers
and capitalists as a new basis for economic and social organization.
Overall, the manifesto promised a welfare state capable of ensuring
the necessities of life for all its citizens. However, it was in the
moral and spiritual realm more than in the economic domain that
the party was an ardent advocate of state intervention. The
government under its control would have become the custodian
of people's morals, employing all the means at its command,
persuasive as well as coercive, to enforce compliance with religious
injunctions.

The Jamā°at's efforts were abruptly ended on October 7, 1958. The president, in response to a call from the army "to save the country from disintegration and total ruination," dismissed the civilian government and put the country under Martial Law.[62] The Jamā°at interpreted the coup as a conspiracy to foil the elections, which the Jamā°at was sure to win, and to deny the Jamā°at access to power positions.[63] The Jamā°at became all the more determined to fight for the restoration of the constitution and a democratic political set-up which would permit it to gain public office by winning elections in future.[64] This meant that the Jamā°at would continue to move in the political direction charted at Machi Goth.

During the period 1958-1969, the Jamā°at kept the Ayub regime under constant pressure to reassert the Islamic principles which had been diluted in the constitution of 1962. When the regime decided to go for an election in 1965, the Jamā°at decided to join the Combined Opposition Parties (C.O.P), an opposition electoral alliance for the forthcoming presidential election of 1965.[65] The C.O.P had agreed on a nine-point election manifesto that contained only one Islamic reference and that too a minor one, viz., amendment of the Muslim Family Laws Ordinance in accordance with Islamic provisions. In the negotiation for the formation of the opposition alliance, the Jamā°at was represented by Khurram Murad. Under his leadership, the Jamā°at compromised on several principles and not merely adopted the nine-point manifesto but also endorsed the candidacy of Miss Fatima Jinnah, the sister of the founder of Pakistan, Mohammad Ali Jinnah.

A majority of the °ulamā' were against the candidature of a female, Miss Fatima Jinnah; their opposition was based on a *ḥadīth* that a "nation that appoints a woman as its ruler shall never prosper." Maulana Abul Barkat Sayyid Ahmad Qadri and others of the Jam°iyyat al-°Ulamā-e-Pakistan issued a *fatwā* against Miss Jinnah. They went to the other extreme and lauded Ayub Khan's services for the prosperity and solidarity of Pakistan and for his promises to amend the Muslim Family Laws Ordinance in accordance with the Qur'ān and Sunnah. They even endorsed the candidacy of President Ayub and appealed to the members of the Electoral

College to vote for him overwhelmingly.

On December 6, 1964, an All Pakistan Sunni and Tablighi Conference was held in Lahore. The Conference, attended by more than 600 ᶜulamā', passed a resolution declaring that "to assign the office of the Head of the State to a female was un-Islamic and *harām* (prohibited) besides being destructive of the country and the nation."[66] Some of the ᶜulamā' even objected to calling Miss Jinnah "Mādar-e-Millat" (mother of the nation) because, according to them, such a title was reserved for the wives of the Prophet (s.a.w). Pir Abdul Majid of Dewal Sharif stated categorically that "it is *harām* to even vote for a woman."[67] Mawdudi and others, however, rationalized it by stating that in the "unusual situation" that existed in the country, the "candidature of a woman as Head of State is not against the sharīᶜah."[68] To Mawdudi the only way to dismantle the exploitative and oppressive system headed by Ayub Khan was to support the candidacy of Miss Jinnah in the presidential poll. He argued that the Jamāᶜat by endorsing the candidacy of a female had in fact adopted the policy of alleviating people's sufferings from an oppressive system.[69] Mawdudi ran a strong campaign and was even convinced that Miss Jinnah might defeat President Ayub Khan. This gamble, however, did not pay off. When the results were tabulated, Ayub Khan emerged the victor by polling 63.3 percent of the votes cast.

President Ayub interpreted the vote as an endorsement of his policies and a mandate to govern the country for five more years. Whatever opposition remained vanished with the outbreak of the Indo-Pakistan war of 1965. On the president's initiative, the Jamāᶜat agreed to support the war effort under his leadership and sink all its differences in the face of the challenge. It was a God-sent opportunity for Ayub to rally the nation round him. Instead, he used the emergency even after the war was over as a pretext for assuming more and more powers and pushed the opposition to the extreme. The Jamāᶜat joined the Pakistan Democratic Movement in 1967 and later on took part in the Democratic Action Committee activities for overthrowing the Ayub government in concert with all other components of the alliances regardless of its ideological differences with them. In opposition, the Jamā‘at did enjoy mass support and did succeed in mobilising them against the autocratic rule. Unable to stem the tide, Ayub Khan decided to "step aside" and asked the army to restore order on March 25, 1969.

The fall of Ayub Khan in the face of street violence and political agitation assured the masses of the power inherent in mass action. The mass movement radicalized Pakistani public opinion and it gravitated towards political parties, in particular towards Zulfikar Ali Bhutto and his Pakistan People's Party. The emergence of mass politics and party politics was irreversible after 1969. These events also radicalized the Jamā‘at and transformed it into a consummate political party.

JAMĀ‘AT AND THE FIRST NATIONAL ELECTIONS IN PAKISTAN

General Agha Muhammad Yahya Khan was forced by the prevailing circumstances to chart a new course in the development of the Pakistani political system. Yahya suspended the 1962 constitution, ended the electoral role of the basic democracy system, and re-imposed martial law. Most significantly, he acceded to popular demand and held Pakistan's first free and fair national elections, in December 1970, on the basis of adult franchise. Though Yahya Khan finally chose not to implement the electoral verdict, his actions did entrench the democratic idea in Pakistani thinking and gave a mass base to Pakistani politics.

By the time Yahya assumed power, the Jamā‘at had come to be controlled by those who had received modern education, those who maintained only informal ties with Islamic modalities and were not bound by their norms and discipline. The strength of the ‘ulamā' had dwindled to the mere 26 percent of the Jamā‘at's central shūrā.[70] It had also developed a women's wing, peasant unions, and a host of student unions to extend the purview of its activities. Mawlana Mawdudi, however, retained the leadership of the party. The emergence of a large number of lower middle class young men who were educated in the western tradition had, to a great extent, laicized the party, which may partly explain the weakening of its ideological zeal vis-a-vis a pragmatic approach to political activism.

Encouraged by the response it received during the anti-Ayub agitation, the Jamāᶜat decided to take part in the elections to capture power. It announced that it would contest all the seats of the national assembly. "This declaration was made in view of the growing popularity which Jamāᶜat-e-Islāmī had gained during the Democratic Movement as the most active party...."[71] To that effect, the Party issued an election manifesto in January 1970 which promised to reorder the society and the polity on the principles of probity and equity laid down by Islam. The party, it declared, would eradicate all forms of tyranny, exploitation and corruption; would establish justice in all spheres of life and would usher in a system that would follow the example set by the first four caliphs of the Prophet (s.a.w).

The manifesto issued by the Jamāᶜat is a historic document in that it provided a detailed and specific reform programme for the development of the country along Islamic lines. It is imperative, therefore, to discuss the manifesto at some length. The manifesto began with the constitutional issue and suggested that it would be difficult for the National Assembly to write a new constitution for Pakistan within 120 days as stipulated in the Legal Framework Order. It should instead adopt the 1956 constitution with four amendments. These amendments concerned the representation on the basis of population, the dissolution of one unit, full integration of the Frontier areas of West Pakistan with the rest of the country, and full regional autonomy consistent with the requirements of the preservation of national integrity.

To solve East Pakistan's economic backwardness, it pledged to give East Pakistan special preference in the allocation of foreign debts and aids and to manage currency, foreign exchange, central banking, and foreign trade through a board consisting of an equal number of members from the east and west wings of the country. It also promised special arrangements for flood control, construction of barrages over major rivers, transfer of naval headquarters to East Pakistan and self sufficiency in all respects in matters of defence.

For the first time in recent Islamic discourse, the manifesto expressed Islamic egalitarianism in specific terms. It said it would reduce the existing 1:100 ratio of disparities in remuneration for various posts in the country initially to a ratio of 1:20 and eventually to that of 1:10. It would fix the minimum wage at a figure between 150 to 200 rupees per month, which, according to its estimates at the time, was the amount a family needed to meet the basic needs. It promised proper residential and medical facilities as well as the facilities of education for the children of low-paid employees. The party offered workers a 42-hour week, and just unemployment, disability, and retirement benefits. The party promised food, clothing, housing, education and medical care for all citizens.

The section on economic reforms opened with a categorical statement opposing both landlordism and modern western capitalism. The manifesto promised, among others, a just distribution of wealth, the prevention of the concentration of wealth in a few hands, and an end to oppression and exploitation in their various forms, equality of opportunity for all citizens, the elimination of poverty, and the assurance of a minimum standard of living for all. The manifesto rejected the idea of nationalized economy as a principle. However, it would allow nationalization of industries if a representative assembly deems it necessary and only after the payment of due compensation. Within a private enterprise system, the party would dissolve monopolies and cartels, outlaw price fixing, extend corporate ownership to the general public, and fix ceilings beyond which individuals or families could not hold stock in a corporation. It would break the capitalists' hold on banks, insurance companies, public lending institutions, and stock exchanges. It would devise means to limit industrial and commercial profits; prohibit interest, speculation, hoarding, and all other means of acquiring wealth that are forbidden by the sharī°ah. It would take necessary measures to recover black money; terminate the managing-agency system; provide credit to small businessmen; and reorganize banking and insurance along Islamic lines. It would subject the landholding, as a temporary measure, to a fixed ceiling; and ensure a minimum wage for workers. It would enforce a moral order and mould social environment in accordance with the tenets of Islam.[72]

The party promised to enact Islamic principles and injunctions into law. It would forbid extramarital sex, drinking, gambling, obscenity, and pornography. It would repeal the existing laws relating to polygamy, divorce and inheritance. It would adopt all possible means of encouraging prayer, fasting, and other Islamic rituals. Friday, not Sunday, would be the weekly holiday. Education would be reorganized to ensure that the Islamic outlook permeated all levels and fields of study. Co-education would be abolished and separate institutions of higher education established for women, according to their needs.

The party's programme regarding national health comprised eight suggestions including the provisions of medicines at cheap rates and slashing down of expenses on medical treatment. It promised to expand hospitals, dispensaries and maternity homes; prevention of epidemics and contagious diseases, moral reform of hospital staff, end of adulteration in food and drugs, and sanitary arrangement on a very large scale.

In foreign relations, the manifesto pledged to adopt the policy of friendship with all the people of the world based upon right and justice. It would pursue an independent foreign policy and keep Pakistan aloof from the struggles of super power blocs. It, however, would oppose all forms of tyranny, aggression, imperialism and colonialism and would promote closer relations with the Muslim world. The manifesto pledged to maintain unity and to consolidate the ideological basis of Pakistan.

In the final analysis, the Jamāᶜat fielded 151 candidates for the national assembly and 331 candidates for the provincial assembly seats. The vast majority (70 per cent) of the total Jamāᶜat nominees for the national assembly seats were highly educated. Of these only 21 (or 19.81 per cent) were ᶜulamā', the rest came from the legal, medical and other professions.[73] All its nominees belonged to the middle class and none of them applied for nomination on their own accord. The Jamāᶜat organized mass rallies, street marches and political meetings to popularize the party manifesto and the "winning team."

On the eve of the general election, Sayyid Mawdudi expressed the confidence that the Jamā°at nominees would sweep the polls while the socialists and regionalists would be defeated. But the national assembly elections resulted in a near total victory for the Awami League in East Pakistan which captured 160 of its 162 National Assembly seats. In West Pakistan, the Pakistan People's Party (PPP) captured 82 of the 138 seats allocated to West Pakistan. The Jamā°at-e-Islāmī won only 4 national assembly seats in West Pakistan and 4 provincial assembly seats, one each in East Pakistan, Punjab, Sindh, and the Northwest Frontier Province. What is surprising is that two other religious parties, the Jami°at-e-°Ulamā-e-Islām (JUI) and the Jami°at-e-°Ulamā-e-Pakistan (JUP), humbled the Jamā°at by capturing 7 seats each in the national assembly and 9 and 11 seats respectively in the provincial assemblies.[74] Sharif al Mujahid has observed that the Islam-based parties divided the Islamic vote among themselves often to the advantage of secular parties.[75] Two further observations need to be made. First, the Islam-based parties combined did not win more than 15 per cent of the votes cast in the national or in the provincial assembly elections. Two, the non-revivalist groups like the JUI and JUP, performed better than the revivalist Jamā°at-e-Islāmī in the elections. Finally, the political parties in Pakistan took note of the potential of an Islamic platform in the elections and incorporated in their manifestos an appeal to the religiously conscious electorate. As observed by Sharif al Mujahid, four of the parties pledged to promulgate an Islamic constitution and four more favoured such a constitution.[76] Even the PPP, which stood for socialistic reforms, advocated an Islamic nationalism and "a thousand years war with India."

The defeat in the elections not withstanding, the central working committee of the Jamā°at congratulated President Yahya Khan for redeeming his pledge to hold the general elections and thus completed the first phase of the revival of democracy. The committee appreciated the arrangements made by the election commission. However, the resolution lamented that at many places in both wings of the country, large scale irregularities were committed by the administration as well as the voters themselves. It was most essential, it said, that an inquiry into these irregularities be made. These irregularities notwithstanding, the working committee accepted that those who had been elected to the national assembly had the support of the majority of the Pakistanis. The resolution asked the leaders of the two parties, Awami League and Pakistan Peoples Party, and the President of Pakistan to provide the country with a constitution that would safeguard her Islamic ideology, unity and solidarity and ensure the survival of democracy.

The election results dealt a severe blow to the morale and confidence of the rank and file of the Jamāᶜat. This was the first time that the Jamāᶜat experienced the psychology of the masses. They realised that piety, honesty, and sincerity were appreciable things, "but the support of the masses could not be enlisted only by dint of these qualities."[77] As pointed out by Khurram Murad, there were several flaws in the way the Jamāᶜat ran the election. First, In West Pakistan, the Jamāᶜat leaders were campaigning on the themes of "Islam and Pakistan in danger" and "1956 constitution as the solution to constitutional problems besetting the country." The ordinary voters were not so much interested in the above two themes. They were looking for the solution to their economic woes which the Jamāᶜat leaders were not stressing in their campaign activities. Second, while the East Pakistani voters were bitterly complaining about the ill treatment meted out to them by the central government, the Jamāᶜat was giving them lectures about how Islam would solve their problems. The East Pakistani leader Sheikh Mujib succeeded in selling his six-point programme as the panacea to all ills afflicting the Bengalis in East Pakistan. The Jamāᶜat sympathised with the plight of the Bengalis and did suggest some remedies but was vehemently opposing the six point programme of the Awami League.[78] Third, the Jamāᶜat leaders were not adept at communicating the message in a simple language to the masses. Their electioneering speeches were not comprehensible to the masses. Sheikh Mujib and Z.A. Bhutto were hammering the slogan respectively of "6 point programme" and "Food, Clothing and

Housing for all," and conveying their messages in ten to fifteen minutes; while the Jamā°at leaders were talking about an Islamic republic which the masses had no notion about and were not able to complete their speeches in less than an hour. Fourth, the Jamā°at leaders could not resort to lies, character assassinations, and rabble rousing, whereas the secular parties did indulge in all excesses with no holds barred.[79] Finally, the Jamā°at could have entered into an alliance with like-minded parties, at least with those working for the enforcement of sharī°ah but the Jamā°at ruled out any possibility of cooperation. It was reported that Mawlana Ehtishamul Haq Thanvi of Jam°iyat al-Islam did initiate a move for alliance of Islamic parties but it could not materialize as the Jamā°at wanted to go it alone. The Jamā°at organized the *shaukat-e-Islām* (glory of Islam) day on May 31, 1970 with great success. They erroneously concluded that the masses would respond in like manner in the elections and hence thwarted all attempts at forging an electoral alliance.

The Jamā°at members, blamed Sayyid Mawdudi for the electoral debacle. Several members observed that Sayyid Mawdudi, because of his old age and ill health, could not project his personality and disseminate the Jamā°at's message among the masses. Implicit in these observations was a demand for the change of leadership and a change in the electoral strategy of the Jamā°at. In 1972, Sayyid Mawdudi suffered a mild heart attack and stepped down as the *amīr* of the Jamā°at. Mian Tufail Muhammad replaced him as the *amīr* on November 2, 1972.

THE CHANGE OF GUARDS: POLITICS OF AGITATION AND ELECTIONS

Born in Kapurthalla (India) in 1914, Mian Tufail Muhammad earned his B.A. (Hons) degree in Physics and Mathematics in 1935 and two years later he completed his L.L.B. degree. He started his career as a lawyer but soon joined a relative in business in Lahore. A founding member of the Jamā'at, he was appointed the first secretary general (*Qayyim*) of the organization in 1944. "From that moment on, he was always in [the] company of Sayyid Mawdudi – attached to him physically and emotionally."[80] For his religious orientation, he owes much to Sayyid Mawdudi and Maulana Amin Ahsan Islahi from whom he took lessons in Qur'ān and ḥadīth.[81] A loyal lieutenant of Sayyid Mawdudi, Mian Tufail followed the policy laid down by his mentor.

The qualification, which elevated Mian Tufail to the position of the *amīr*, was his loyalty to Sayyid Mawdudi. He was not a charismatic leader nor was he known as an effective political leader. Unlike Mawdudi, he could neither command nor assert the power vested in the office of the *amīr*. Consequently, he felt obliged to delegate some of the powers to his lieutenants and ultimately to the *shūrā*. The office of *nāib amīr* created in 1941, which remained moribund during the period of Sayyid Mawdudi's leadership, was revived in 1976. Three *nā'ib amīrs*, Abdul Ghafur Ahmad, Chaudhri Rahmat Ilahi and Khurshid Ahmad, were nominated by the *amīr* and approved by the central *shūrā*. These *nā'ib amīrs* were given powers to oversee specific activities of the Jamāᶜat. In other words, the Jamaᶜat was effectively decentralized.

Mian Tufail's assumption of the office of the *amīr* coincided with the heralding of the Zulfikar Ali Bhutto era (1972-1977) in the politics of Pakistan. The Bhutto era is a story of fundamental infrastructural changes in Pakistani politics. Bhutto had increased mass consciousness in Pakistan. Large numbers of Pakistanis had rallied to his cause. His speeches raised popular issues such as the *rotī, kapdā awr makān* (food, clothing and housing) to the masses. By tapping into the public consciousness, and by creating a public identification with his cause, Bhutto made mass politics a new element in post-1971 Pakistan. This era is also remarkable for a total shift in the attitude of the governing elite vis-a-vis the place of Islam in the polity of Pakistan. The pre-1970 elite were either interested in evolving a polity that synthesized the secular and Islamic elements or they were less enthusiastic about Islamization per se. However after 1970 Islam came to be marginalised somewhat as new political parties with socialist orientations gained electoral support. They shifted public attention from Islam to socialism and some of their ideologues evolved what came to be known as "Islamic socialism."

The Jamāᶜat did notice the emergence of the socialist forces, for in 1969 some of its leaders were reported to have threatened to "crush the socialists."[82] With mounting dismay, the Jamāᶜat witnessed Bhutto's ascent to power and the subtle way in which he was trying to usher in what they regarded as socialism and secularism. Consequently, his policies and pronouncements were kept under very close surveillance by the Jamāᶜat rank and file. As discussed in chapter two, Bhutto's strategy was both to placate and to outwit the religious and conservative opposition. His insertion of Islamic provisions in the 1973 Constitution which he piloted, his frequenting of popular shrines, and adoption of a number of Islamic measures were meant to appease the Islamic forces. Even his declaration, in September 1974 through legislation, of the Ahmadi community to be a minority and a non-Muslim community because they did not believe in the finality of the Prophet Muhammad (s.a.w) was out of fear "that opposition politicians and extremist Muslim religious leaders would use the issue against him."[83] His manifesto prepared for the 1977 elections promised to "hold high the banner of Islam," declare Friday a holiday, establish a Federal ᶜUlamā' Academy, and make Qur'ānic instruction compulsory.[84] As observed in a local newspaper editorial, the major emphasis in the People's Party Programme for the future was on Islam. This was in sharp contrast to the concept of trinity, socialism, Islam and democracy, propounded in the last election.[85] Despite all these measures his credibility remained dubious. During the entire Bhutto period, the Jamāᶜat-e-Islāmī and other religion based parties continued to act as agents of political pressure for retaining Islamic ideology.

In the March 1977 elections, Bhutto's socialist policies and repression had united the religious and center-right parties into the Pakistan National Alliance (PNA).[86] It was a coalition of political parties with diverse interests but bound together by a common enemy in Bhutto, particularly to abort Bhutto's plans to introduce the presidential system and turn Pakistan into a one-party state. The thrust of the PNA manifesto, according to Sharif al-Mujahid's content analysis, was on the dismantling of the democratic institutions, the distortion of the 1973 constitution, the denial of civil rights, and the socioeconomic problems. The "civil rights" and socioeconomic issues as themes had a frequency of 25.46 and 46.37 respectively. On the other hand, "Islamic ideology" as a theme received a frequency mention of only 8.18 (see Table 3.1). The PNA movement's original plank, when it was launched on March 14, had only two aims – the restoration of civic freedoms and free and fair elections under neutral agencies (i.e., under the army and the judiciary). It expressed dissatisfaction with the PPP government's policies, and also the amendments made in the constitution. The Alliance promised to eliminate all amendments that injured the fundamental rights, and curbed freedom of the press.[87] Religious issues got incorporated into the PNA charter of demands much later.

Table 3.1
Main Political Themes and Their Relative Frequency in the Manifestoes and Major Addresses of the PPP and PNA Leaders (in percentage)

No.	Themes	PPP Manifesto	PNA Manifesto
1	Democratic Institution; Constitution	4.91	5.0
2	Civic Rights	4.31	25.46
3	Inherited Political Problems	6.10	—
4	Socioeconomic problems	61.06	46.37
5	Islamic Ideology	4.46	8.18
6	Foreign Policy and Defence	15.92	10.45
7	Miscellaneous	3.14	1.82
8	Negative Approach	—	2.72

Source: Adapted from Sharif al Mujahid, "The 1977 Pakistani Elections: An Analysis" in Manzooruddin Ahmed (ed.), *Contemporary Pakistan: Politics, Economy, and Society* (Karachi: Royal Book Company, 1982), 76.

The PNA was sure of winning the election and replacing the Bhutto government. The government was alarmed and hence resorted to manipulation and massive rigging of elections. The

PNA won 36 seats of which nine belonged to the Jamāʿat-e-Islāmī. To Mawdudi, "Bhutto won the elections but at the cost of his honour."[88] The election results produced a nation-wide agitation. The opposition boycotted the provincial assembly elections on March 10 and observed a complete strike the following day. On March 11, 1977, the Central Council of the PNA met again in Lahore and decided that the PNA would start protest demonstrations from March 14, 1977 unless: (1) elections were annulled; (2) the chief election commissioner was removed and a new election commissioner appointed; and (3) the prime minister resigned.[89]

Bhutto sensed the popular sentiment and hence in a hastily convened press conference announced a ban on drinking, night clubs and gambling, and invited Mawlana Mawdudi, Mufti Mahmud and Mawlana Noorani to join his Advisory Council for the implementation of the sharīʿah. As "the implementation of the sharīʿah was not one of the demands made by the PNA on the government, ... no one took the Prime Minister's offer seriously."[90] The PNA called for a general strike on April 20, 1977. In this strike, 25 people were killed in different parts of the country and the government responded by imposing curfew and martial law in Karachi, Hyderabad and Lahore. However, the PNA leadership decided to continue their struggle until the PPP government was removed. Bhutto tried once again to defuse the situation by bringing the PNA leadership to the conference table at Sihala Rest House near Rawalpindi. It was in Sihala that the ambassadors and foreign ministers of some Arab countries met the PNA leaders and tried in vain to mediate a settlement between the PNA and Bhutto.

Although the PNA movement was initially a protest against the rigging of the elections, it was gradually transformed into a movement for the establishment of a just socio-political order in Pakistan. From March to July 1977, the PNA rocked the country through *hartāls* (strikes) and *paiyah-jām* (wheel jam), bombings and processions. They were successful in mobilizing mass support for Islamic ideology. The slogan which PNA adopted and which inspired the demonstrators to withstand the police brutalities was the establishment of what is popularly called *niẓām-e-muṣṭafā*

(Prophetic Order).[91] Bhutto added fuel to the fire by publicly declaring, out of rage, that he drank liquor, not the blood of the poor masses. Alcohol is prohibited in Islam and the idea of the head of an Islamic state drinking liquor was abominable. Soon, the antigovernment movement took on the spirit of a *jihād*. Their aim was to displace the "Whiskey party leader" under whom "Islam was in danger."[92] The prominence of the Islamic issue indicated the ascendancy within the PNA of the Jamāʿat over the more secular National Democratic Party and Tehrik-e-Istiqlal. In class terms, it meant the ascendancy of a middle-class dominated, urban-based Jamāʿat over the more elitist Pakistan Muslim League. In fact, the hard-core organization of the movement came from the Jamāʿat which acted through organisational units and cells like the *madrasah*s (religious schools) and mosques, commercial associations or federations, and some trade unions. Led by a middle class organization, the anti-Bhutto movement was exclusively a middle-class phenomenon. It drew most of its inspiration and sustenance from middle and lower middle classes consisting of small merchants, traders, and professional groups like lawyers (see Table 3.2). During March – July 1977, Pakistan witnessed a total of 5,017 processions. The largest number of processions were carried out by the "public" which perhaps included labour demonstrations and also those by smaller organizations. Student demonstration was next in importance, followed by women's rallies.

Table 3.2
PNA Processions – March –July 1977

Province	Public	Women	Lawyers	Ulama	Students	Children
Punjab	2,537	105	71	12	92	17
NWFP	870	14	20	3	70	2
Sind	338	140	3	4	93	38
Baluchistan	575	3	1	—	28	11
Total	4,290	262	95	19	283	68

Source: Mr. A. K. Brohi, Counsel for Federation, *Statement in the Supreme Court of Pakistan* (Islamabad: Government of Pakistan, 1977), 65.

The ferocity and tenacity of the mass urban protest weakened the governmental authority. In desperation, Bhutto imposed martial law on 21 April 1977, jailed his opponents and finally sought the assistance of the diplomats from the Gulf States to resolve the issue.[93] The opposition movement continued unabated and ended only when the military staged a coup and imposed martial law throughout the country on 5 July 1977. Interestingly, though the Jamā'at had not mustered enough votes to form an elected government, it had the street power to displace the incumbent ruler and dismantle the structure of power.

The coup was led by General Zia-ul Haq, the Army Chief of Staff, "a true soldier of Islam."[94] He was a devout and pious Muslim and a close relative of the amīr of Jamā'at-e-Islāmī, Mian Tufail Muhammad.[95] Likewise, a new generation of officers with a religious bias had emerged in the top hierarchy. Coming from the relatively conservative urban middle class, and being educated entirely in Pakistani schools, they had a genuine reverence for Islamic principles. Thus there was an identity of outlook, behaviour, and policy orientation among the Zia-led military elite and the main protagonists within the PNA movement.

Although the praetorian military coup ran against the tenets of an Islamic political system as well as the democratic political order which Mawdudi and the Jamā'at had advocated in the past, the Jamā'at was prepared to cooperate with General Zia to help him Islamize Pakistan. In other words, confronted with the choice between democracy and Islamization, the Jamā'at chose the latter, hoping to get the former through working from within the system. Sayyid Mawdudi welcomed the military rule arguing that the objectives of Islamization and restoration of democracy were synonymous. In an interview with Nawā-e-Waqt, Mawdudi said that "there was no likelihood of free and fair elections in spite of an agreement between the PPP and the PNA over basic issues...."[96] Zia's assurance of power transfer, argued Mawdudi, dispelled apprehensions about permanent military rule in the country. To Mian Tufail, Zia provided "a golden opportunity for the establishment of an Islamic system which should never be allowed to go unavailed of."[97] Additionally, Zia declared that he was heading a "caretaker regime" and was dedicated to engage in "Operation Fair Play" and hold free and fair elections. The PNA delegation headed by Ghafoor Ahmad met General Zia and got an assurance for the transfer of power to the elected representatives after holding polls within eight months of the completion of the "accountability process" initiated in October 1977.[98] The coup, it was argued, was essential, "to provide a bridge to enable the country to return to the path of constitutional rule."[99]

Understandably, the Jamāᶜat as part of the PNA welcomed the offer made by General Zia to join him in helping to form a civilian government at Islamabad. For the first time in its history, the Jamāᶜat became part of the ruling establishment. Four Jamāᶜat leaders assumed ministerial positions in the 1977-1979 period.[100] Another Jamāᶜat leader was nominated as a judge of the Federal Sharīᶜah Court, an appellate bench with the power of judicial review. Additionally, two of its supporters were appointed as members of the Council of Islamic Ideology, a constitutional body that formulated recommendations that culminated in the package of Islamic penal and economic reforms announced by Zia on 10 February 1979. According to their own pronouncements, the Jamāᶜat had joined the government with the specific purpose of ensuring an early introduction of *niẓām-e-muṣṭafā* in the country, as well as for securing a final but firm date for holding the general elections. Immediately after General Zia had announced the introduction of Islamic measures and declared November 17, 1979 as the date for holding general elections, the PNA left the government on 21 April 1979. General Zia appealed the Jamāᶜat to continue in the government and forced the Jamāᶜat to choose between elections and Islamization. This time the Jamāᶜat chose the former as a means to bring about the latter subsequently. Consequently, the Jamāᶜat withdrew from the government to prepare for the promised elections which would usher in an Islamic state.

The Jamāᶜat apparently was too preoccupied with taking part in elections and capturing power to implement the sharīᶜah. Thus the Jamāᶜat was pleased when the Zia government decided to hold local-level elections on a non-party basis. The elections were boycotted by some of the components of the PNA. As shown in Table 3.3, the Jamā⁼at contested and won a good number of seats in the Karachi municipal elections and succeeded in getting its candidate elected as the mayor of Karachi. This victory made it all the more sanguine about its success in the upcoming national elections.

Table 3.3
Jamā⁼at's Fortunes in District Council Elections, 1979

Council	No. of seats	Seats won by JI
Karachi Municipal	160	57
Punjab District	500	35
NWFP District	360	32
Sind District	13	1

Source: Adapted from Seyyed Vali Reza Nasr, *The Vanguard of the Islamic Revolution: Jamā⁼at-i-Islāmī of Pakistan* (London: I.B. Tauris, 1994), 193-94.

General Zia, however, had gained legitimacy through his patronage of Islamization. The fact that the state was so openly Islamic placed the Jamā⁼at in a very difficult position. It could no longer join the government for fear of losing mass appeal. Furthermore, the military regime was still pursuing Islamization. Mian Tufail, the *amīr* of the Jamā⁼at, believed in gradual Islamization. He would let the Jamā'at try to wrest the control of the national leadership from secular forces. He, however, would not upset the status quo if it were sympathetic, as Zia was, to the cause of Islamization.

From 1979 to 1984, the Jamā⁼at remained in an uneasy opposition to the policies of the military regime of General Zia. It warned the government of dire consequences of further delay in honouring the promised elections. It repeatedly asked the regime to lift the martial law and restore an elected civilian government but it refrained from mounting or joining the opposition movement to restore democracy. On the contrary, the Jamā⁼at endorsed Zia's

decision to hold the referendum of 1984. According to Mumtaz
Ahmad, the Jamāᶜat's decision to support Zia was based upon the
President's promise "to make the Sharia the supreme law of the
land, to restore the 1973 Constitution, and to lift martial law without
delay."[101]

The Referendum Order issued in 1984 stipulated its objective
as one of assessing public opinion on the military regime's policy
of Islamization. It stipulated further that an affirmative vote was
also to serve as a vote of confidence in General Zia by electing
him President for the next five years.[102] The Referendum Order
was beyond the scope of judicial review. The referendum, held on
19 December 1984, went in favour of General Zia extending his
Presidential tenure till 1990. According to the election
commission's office, out of a total of 21,750,901 votes cast, 97.71
percent favoured continuing Islamic policies.[103] The voter turnout
was reported to be 62 percent. According to non-governmental
sources, however, the voter turnout ranged between 5 and 25
percent.

The next stage in the gradual unfolding of the constitutional
order prescribed by the military was parliamentary and provincial
elections in 1985. As announced, for the first time in the history of
Pakistan, the February polls were conducted on a "non-party" basis.
The rationale as advanced by Zia was that Islam did not approve
of the concept of political parties. As he explained:

> ... Islam does not prescribe a particular form of government
> or method of action. The only condition is that whichever
> way a government comes to power, it should be based on
> justice and benevolence; the ruler should be pious, just and
> a God-fearing person and should consult the people in the
> affairs of the state, because Islam attaches great importance
> to mutual consultation. Similarly, it is also essential that
> the people in key posts should have unblemished reputation
> and are God-fearing and pious people.[104]

For the 207-seat national assembly seats, 1291 candidates
contested as independents. The non-party polls, however, could

not remain unaffected by partisan interests. The nine party opposition coalition, the Movement for the Restoration of Democracy (MRD), formally boycotted the polls, so did some of the members of the PNA. However, the Jamāᶜat, Muslim League and some other parties did participate in the elections; they sponsored and supported candidates. The Jamāᶜat nominated 63 candidates and the Muslim League extended support to over ninety candidates. According to one estimate, approximately 120 candidates were associated with the parties belonging to the MRD, 70 of whom were known for their affiliation with Pakistan People's Party.[105] Candidates were not permitted to hold public meetings, organize processions or use public address systems.

The election results caused serious setback to the establishment as well as to the Jamāᶜat. The voters rejected six ministers, three city mayors and prominent men closely identified with the regime.[106] Zia interpreted voter rejections of people associated with the martial law regime as "a reflection of the government's impartiality and fairness."[107] The Jamāᶜat campaigned vigorously during the elections, promising an end to the martial law regime and speeding up the process of Islamization in Pakistan. Apparently the strategy failed. Out of nearly 63 seats it contested indirectly, the Jamāᶜat won only eight, two in Karachi, two in Lahore and four in the NWFP.[108] The election results clearly showed that the Jamāᶜat lacked a mass support base in Pakistan. However, the *nāib amīr* of the Jamāᶜat, Ghafoor Ahmad, expressed satisfaction over the achievements in the February polls as, to him, the Jamāᶜat improved upon its earlier electoral performance. In the 1970 elections, the Jamāᶜat had fielded 200 candidates but won only 4 seats and about 7 percent of the votes cast. In the 1985 elections the Jamāᶜat had secured about 20 percent of the total votes cast with 8 seats.[109]

The dismal performance of the Jamāᶜat in the elections caused a serious soul searching among a section of the Jamāᶜat leadership. Mian Tufail's conciliatory approach vis-a-vis the military did not command unanimous support from the Jamāᶜat. Not only had president Zia betrayed the expectations of the Jamāᶜat by coming

hard on its student and labour wings but had even cultivated
alliance with the non-Jamāᶜat ᶜulamā' to bolster his Islamic
legitimacy. Additionally, the 1985 election results showed beyond
doubt Zia's success in effectively constricting the popular base of
the Jamāᶜat. The opposition to Mian Tufail became more intense
when President Zia installed Mohammed Khan Junejo, a former
Muslim Leaguer with moderate to conservative views, as Prime
Minister of Pakistan on March 23, 1985.

Mumtaz Ahmad argues that, by 1984, Zia himself became
estranged from the Jamāᶜat for many reasons. First, he had
effectively suppressed the possibility of antigovernment
demonstration from pro-Bhutto forces. Second, the war in
Afghanistan and the resultant US-Pakistan relations had given the
army the much-needed self-confidence. Third, Zia had found new
nonpolitical allies capable of conferring Islamic legitimacy on his
regime. Finally, Zia wanted to weaken the political parties so that
independent candidates could win the ensuing elections and act
as his support base in parliament.[110]

The Jamāᶜat, in consequence, was forced to part company with
Zia and re-examine its strategy and to capture political power.
Unlike Mian Tufail and others who accepted a policy of
accommodation with the armed forces, the opposition group in
the party favoured taking the army head-on. This strategic rethinking
and the resultant changes in the organization had the impact of
transforming the Jamāᶜat into a mass party. The Jamāᶜat's political
activities in the post-Zia period and its metamorphosis into a mass
party are explored fully in the next chapter.

4

QAZI HUSSAIN AHMAD AND THE JAMĀᶜAT
AS A MASS PARTY

The dissension within the Jamāᶜat resulting from its poor performance in the elections became intense. Mian Tufail, apparently, gave priority to Islamization while waiting for an opportune moment to capture political power. Others in the party, however, were interested more in power and not happy with Islam alone. They argued for distancing themselves from the Zia regime and for joining the national chorus for free and fair elections. In one stroke, they obliterated the dichotomy between Islamization and democracy by arguing that Islamization could not be complete without democracy.[1] In response to the growing dissension, Mian Tufail Muhammad decided not to seek re-election as the president, paving way for a new generation to lead. The shūrā suggested Professor Khurshid Ahmad (deputy *amīr*), Maulana Jan Mohammed Abbasi (Sindh *amīr*), and Qazi Hussain Ahmad (secretary general) for the post. Qazi Hussain Ahmad was elected to the office on October 15, 1987. This chapter considers and evaluates the political performance of the Jamāᶜat under his leadership.

QAZI HUSSAIN AHMAD AND THE POLITICS
OF ALLIANCE

Qazi Hussain Ahmad was born at Ziarat Kaka Sahib, district Nowshera, NWFP, Pakistan, in 1938. His father Qazi Muhammad Abdul Rab was a respected religious scholar and a farmer by profession. His family had a close connection with famous religious institution in Deoband, India. Two of his elder brothers graduated from Dar al-ᶜUlūm Deoband.

Qazi Hussain Ahmad, however, attended a modern secular school and earned a Master of Science degree in Geography from Peshawar University. He first lectured for three years, teaching at the graduate level, and then ventured into a successful business in the pharmaceutical industry. He was elected the Vice President of the NWFP (Provincial) Chamber of Commerce and Industry.

Qazi Hussain became acquainted with the Jamāʿat through the Islāmī Jamīʿat-e-Ṭulabah, Pakistan. He became a member of Jamāʿat-e-Islāmī in 1970 and was elected to the office of the president of its Peshawar branch. He served Jamāʿat-e-Islāmī as secretary and then *amīr* of NWFP province. For a long time, Qazi Husain had been in charge of the Jamāʿat's propaganda work in Afghanistan and had developed ties with prominent Afghan leaders.[2] He assumed the office of the secretary general, Jamāʿat-e-Islāmī Pakistan, in 1978 and continued in that capacity till he was elected as *amīr* of the Jamāʿat-e-Islāmī, Pakistan, in 1987. He was first elected as member of the Senate of Pakistan in 1986 for a term of six years. He is the first *amīr* of the Jamāʿat to be elected as a member of the senate of Pakistan for two consecutive terms: 1985-91 and 1991-96. He is well versed in English, Arabic, Persian, Urdu and Pushto. "He is an eloquent orator, seasoned parliamentarian and respected politician."[3]

By the time Qazi Hussain took over, the leadership structure of the Jamāʿat had totally changed. This transformation was visible in 1983. According to Mumtaz Ahmad's survey, in 1983, a majority of the Jamāʿat's leadership at the district and provincial levels and in the consultative committee were businessmen, mostly in small-scale trade and industry. Professionals with secular education accounted for 32 percent and businessmen 57 percent. A similar pattern can be seen in the candidates of the Jamāʿat in the 1985 elections, with 44 percent businessmen and 31 percent professionals while the number of ʿulamā' and *pirs* accounted for about 4 percent.[4]

Since 1990, the leadership of the Jamāʿat has been almost entirely in the hands of modern educated laymen with some grounding in Islam but none of them are reputed ʿālim. As shown in Table 4.1, of the 15 top ranking office bearers of the Jamāᶜat in 1998, eight were professionals, four were businessmen, one a government employee, one a full time worker of the Jamāᶜat and only one a religious school teacher. Furthermore, the intellectual

Table 4.1
Educational and Occupational Background of the JI Leaders, 1998

Name	Position in JI	Education	Occupation
Q Hussain Ahmad	*Amīr*	Master of Science	Businessman
Khurshid Ahmad	Vice President	M.A.(Eco)	Former Professor
A. Ghafoor Ahmad	Vice-President	M.A. (Commerce)	Consultant
Khurram Murad	Vice-president	M.S. (Civil Engg)	Cons. Engineer
Jan Mohd. Abbasi	Vice-president	MadrasaGraduate	Former Teacher
Rahmat Ilahi	Vice-President	M.A. (Pol. Sc.)	Govt. employee
Aslam Saleemi	Secretary General	LL.B.	Former Attorney
Hafiz Mohd. Idris	Asst. Secy Genl.	M.A. (Humanities)	JI Worker
Liaqat Baloch	Asst. Secy. Genl.	M.A. (Journalism)	Businessman
Fateh Mohammad	*Amīr*, Punjab	M.A. (Humanities)	Former Professor
Munawwar Hasan	*Amīr*, Karachi	M.A. (Sociology)	Researcher
Asad Gilani	*Amīr*, Lahore	M.A. (Humanities)	Journalist
M. Azam Faruqi	Member EXCO	M.A. (Finance)	Publisher
Naeem Siddiqui	Member EXCO	Secondary	Journalist
Fazl Ilahi Qurashi	Secy, Baluchistan	M.S. (Food)	Food Technologist

Source: Mumtaz Ahmad, "Islamic Fundamentalism in South Asia: The Jam āᶜat-i-Islamī and the Tablighi Jamāᶜat of South Asia" in Martin E. Marty and R. Scott Appleby (eds.), *Fundamentalisms Observed* (Chicago: University of Chicago Press, 1991), 495.

and political leadership of the Jamā‘at "has passed from the Urdu-speaking refugees to the sons of the soil."[5]

Qazi Hussain is an assertive and populist figure. According to the Jamā‘at's web site:

> Qazi Hussain appealed to both conservatives and the liberal elements. ... His appeal has been viewed as more directed towards the Pakistani electorate than towards the rank and file of the Jamā‘at.[6]

It is perhaps no less important to note that Qazi Hussain's inclination towards populist politics had the active support of a person of high calibre such as Khurram Murad. Khurram studied civil engineering at the Universities of Karachi (BE 1952) and Minnesota, USA (MS 1958) and worked as a leading consulting engineer in Pakistan, Tehran and Riyadh. He had been actively involved in the Islamic movement since 1948 and served as the president of the Islāmī Jamī‘at-e-Ṭulabah, Pakistan, for two years, 1951-1952. He was a member of the central executive committee of the Jamā‘at from 1963 to 1977 and was the *amīr* of its Dhaka branch from 1963-1971. Khurram Murad all along believed in political activities to seize power "to make it serve Islamic purposes. If political power corrupts, this is the more reason for making it subject to God's law."[7] In his recorded memoirs, Khurram Murad defends Mawdudi's political campaign to Islamize Pakistan in 1948 "as timely and most appropriate."[8] He himself played a leading role in getting the Jamā‘at involved in the politics of Pakistan in the 1965 and 1970 elections. His populist inclinations were somewhat restrained during the period Sayyid Mawdudi dominated the party. It resurfaced with full force during the tenure of Qazi Hussain Ahmad and he came to be recognized as the brain behind Qazi Hussain's mass based activities. Qazi Hussain reorganized the office of *nā'ib amīr* in 1987 and increased its number from 3 to 5. Khurram Murad till his death was one of the five *nā'ib amīr*s of the Jamā‘at. Although he believed in them, Khurram Murad did concede that political activities might adversely affect individual

morality and spirituality. Yet he insisted on "taking the risk," as he
believed that a God-centered life possesses the possibility to escape
these perils and yet bring justice to mankind. He argued that the
moral laxity observed among the Jamāᶜat rank and file was due
not to their involvement in political activities but to the Jamāᶜat's
ineffectiveness in imparting moral training to its members.

Qazi Hussain's first priority in office was to provide the
organization with a mass base. Hence, he organized what is known
as the "Caravan of Invitation" and the "Caravan of Love and
Brotherhood" of cars and lorries loaded with Jamāᶜat members,
and toured the country for about 40 days inviting people to join
the organization.[9] In his speeches during the tour Qazi Hussain
laid strong emphasis on social justice that was very well accepted
in a country where extreme poverty and extravagant affluence sit
side by side. His vocabulary since then has been littered with
references to "feudals," "class," "masses" and "liberation" – words
usually associated with left leaning intellectuals.

Qazi Hussain also took the initiative to distance the Jamāᶜat
from the military regime. He was openly critical of President Zia
whom he accused of destroying the democratic fundamentals of
the country. To Qazi Hussain: "A man who dissolves a government
on charges of corruption and forms a new government with the
same faces cannot be regarded as a true Muslim... This is sheer
hypocrisy."[10] He even criticized the Islamization policies of
President Zia as merely cosmetic since they did not have any
bearing on the governing structures of Pakistan. To Qazi Hussain,
Islamization and democratization must go hand in hand; hence he
demanded that president Zia dismantle the military regime and
organize fresh elections to install a civilian government. He
threatened to mount an anti-government movement in cooperation
with all opposition forces, including the Pakistan People's Party. It
is reported that Qazi Hussain did encourage a dialogue with
Benazir's PPP to establish an alliance which did not materialize
because of active opposition from Mian Tufail and his followers.

On August 17, 1988, General Zia along with 29 others died
when the Pakistan Air Force C130 aircraft they were in crashed

near Bahawalpur in Punjab. Ghulam Ishaq Khan, chairman of the
senate and former minister of finance during a greater part of Zia's
rule, was sworn in as the acting president of Pakistan. One of the
first actions taken by Ghulam Ishaq Khan was to form an
Emergency Council comprising of chief ministers, senior ministers
from Zia's cabinet and the chiefs of the three wings of the armed
forces.[11]

The Emergency Council oversaw the elections on 16 November
1988 as announced by General Zia. Contrary to Zia's plans,
however, the elections were held on a party basis as decided by
the Pakistan Supreme Court on October 5, 1988. The main contest
occurred between the PPP, led by Benazir Bhutto, and the Islāmī
Jamhūrī Ittehād (Islamic Democratic Alliance, IDA or IJI) led by
Mian Nawaz Sharif. The army preferred Shariff to Bhutto since
the latter was interested in "teaching the military a lesson."[12] It is
alleged that the IJI was "put together by the military's Inter-Services
Intelligence (ISI), which brokered a deal between an array of right-
of-center and Islamic parties to prevent a PPP sweep at the polls."[13]

General Gul, the head of the ISI acknowledged that "the ISI
created the IDA to promote democracy after the August 1988 death
of president Zia ul-Haq in an air crash .... Without the IDA, Gul
claimed that Pakistan could not have returned to electoral
politics."[14] Thus, the IJI was crafted and sponsored by an
intelligence agency. The Jamāʿat, much to the dislike of Qazi
Hussain, joined the IJI with Ghafur Ahmad as the alliance's secretary
general.[15] It was given 26 seats to contest at the national level
elections.

The results of the November 1988 elections, however, favoured
the PPP (see Table 4.2). While unable to win a clear majority, the
PPP succeeded in securing 93 of the 205 contested seats in
parliament. The IJI, on the other hand, won 54 seats, emerging as
the second largest political group in the assembly.[16] The Jamāʿat
won eight of the 26 seats it contested. One of the seats was reserved
for women.

In December 1988, Benazir Bhutto was sworn in as the first
woman prime minister of Pakistan. The PPP had to form a coalition

'Table 4.2
Position of Political Parties in the National Assembly of
Pakistan, 1988

Party/Alliance	Seats Secured	% Seats Won	% Votes Polled (N= 19591265)
PPP	93	45.59	38.52
IJI	54	26.47	30.16
JUI(F)	7	3.43	1.84
PAI	3	1.47	4.39
Other Parties	7	3.43	5.59
Independents	40	19.61	19.50
Total:	204*	100.00	100.00

Notes:
* Excluding three constituencies declared void or terminated.
• PPP = Pakistan People's Party; IJI = Islami Jamhuri Ittehad;
JUI (F) = Jamiat-e-Ulama-e-Islam (Fazlur Rahman)
PAI = Pakistan Awami Ittehad
Source: Adapted from Election Commission of Pakistan, *1997
General Elections Report,* Vol. II (Islamabad: Printing Corporation
of Pakistan Press, 1997), vi.

with the Muhajir Qaumi Mahaz (Immigrant National Front, MQM)
which had emerged as the third largest political party in the
Assembly. Along with the IJI, the Jamāʿat had to sit in the
opposition.

The Jamāʿat tried, in vain, to remain influential in the alliance
and to help keep Benazir constantly under pressure. Extensive
propaganda was applied to discredit Benazir as a woman politician
lacking the essential religious credentials and legality to lead a
Muslim society. IJI and particularly the Jamāʿat blamed Benazir
for disowning the ideals and values of Islam. Soon the Jamāʿat
softened its criticism as it found the Muslim League, the major
component of the IJI, moving in another direction. Much to the
displeasure of the Jamāʿat, the Muslim League under Nawaz Sharif
was negotiating with and trying to buy the MQM away from the
PPP fold and thus destabilize her government. Benazir successfully
weathered a no-confidence motion in October 1989 but her

government lasted only 20 months. On August 6, 1990, President Ghulam Ishaq Khan accused Benazir, among other things, of corruption, political horse-trading and misuse of official machinery and resources. He "dissolved the National Assembly, dismissed the cabinet of prime minister Benazir Bhutto, and announced fresh elections to the assembly to be held in October this year."[17]

The 20-month rule of Benazir Bhutto was characterized by political horse-trading and the struggle to maintain power and hence inactivity in the social and economic arenas. Consequently, pre-election forecasts indicated that the PPP would not do as well in the contest for seats in the National Assembly as it did in 1988. Benazir made desperate attempts to win the people's mandate and with two other parties formed a front known as People's Democratic Alliance. The Jamā'at, expecting an electoral victory, competed as a component of the IJI. This time, however, the IJI was lukewarm about the Jamā'at and gave it 18 National Assembly seats, as against 26, to contest. The 1990 election results (see Table 4.3) showed that the number of seats for the PPP had reduced from 93 seats in the 1988 election to 44. The major winner was the IJI that captured 106 seats in 1990 compared to 54 in 1988. IJI's percentage of the vote rose from 30.6 in 1988 to 37.37 percent in 1990. The Jamā'at won eight out of 18 seats contested as against eight out of 26 in 1988. It won only 3 percent of the popular vote. In its strong base in Karachi, the Jamā'at was more or less eliminated by the MQM.

President Ghulam Ishaq Khan asked Nawaz Sharif to form the government and the latter took office on November 6, 1990. The Jamā'at neither joined the cabinet nor was it invited.[18] According to Khurram Murad, no one from the IJI invited them to join the cabinet and help run the government.[19] The relations between the two were strained for various reasons. First, the Jamā'at, from the beginning, did not like to associate with the Muslim League which was secular and whose chief, Nawaz Sharif, had "all along denied himself being a fundamentalist."[20] Second, the IJI was cultivating closer ties with the Jamā'at's arch-rival, MQM. Third, the government appeared to have neutralized the issue of Islamization. The *Sharī'at* bill became law but according to the Jamā'at, its symbolic value was greater than its practical effect. The bill consisted of promises to establish a number of commissions to recommend "measures and steps" to bring the social, economic, administrative and educational institutions in line with the teachings of the sharī°ah. Fourth, the Jamā°at requested that its parliamentary leader be made chairman of the Accounts Committee. Nawaz Sharif did promise but later on reneged. Finally, the Jamā°at demanded the formation of an 8-member committee (composed of 2 representatives from the Jamā°at and 6 from other components of IJI), to take decisions on domestic and international affairs. Nawaz

Table 4.3
Results of the 1990 elections and the position of Political Parties in the National Assembly of Pakistan, 1990

Party/Alliance	Seats Secured	% Seats Won	% Votes Polled (N= 21163911)
IJI	106	51.21	37.37
PDA	44	21.26	36.83
HPG	15	7.25	5.54
JUI(F)	6	2.90	0.29
ANP	6	2.90	1.68
JUP(N)	3	1.45	1.47
Other Parties	5	2.41	6.52
Independents	22	10.63	10.30
Total:	207	100.01	100.00

Notes:
- IJI = Islāmī Jamhurī Ittehād; PDA = Pakistan Democratic Alliance JUI(F) = Jamī°at-e-°Ulamā-e-Islām (Fazlur Rahman); HPG = Haq Prast Group; ANP = Awami National Party; JUP(N) = Jamī°atul °Ulamā-e-Pakistan (Noorani).

Source: Adapted from Election Commission of Pakistan, *1997 General Elections Report*, Vol. II (Islamabad: Printing Corporation of Pakistan Press, 1997), vi.

Sharif turned it down, as he wanted to centralize all powers in his own hands.[21]

The Jamāᶜat was better off under General Zia. Under Nawaz Sharif, it was not given the status it deserved in the coalition government and it felt compelled to do everything possible to stand on its own feet. Consequently, it embarked upon a mass mobilization programme extolling the virtues of the Islamic system and castigating capitalism, American hegemony, feudalism, exploitation, and corruption in the country. When the Persian Gulf war erupted in 1991, the Jamāᶜat, against the official policy of the government, took a highly popular pro-Iraqi stand. It dubbed the Gulf war as "the war between the Jews, the worst enemy of Islam, and the Muslims," and called upon the government to expel the US ambassador as a protest against the genocide of Iraqi Muslims by the United States' government.[22]

> The Jamāᶜat-e-Islāmī organized fifty-seven 'Jihad' rallies and two dozen "coffin clad" rallies to emphasize that its workers were ready for martyrdom in the jihad against the anti-Islamic forces of the West. Jamiyat-i-Tulaba (The Society of Students), the student wing of the Jamāᶜat-e-Islāmī, organized 338 rallies and public meetings throughout the various cities and towns of Pakistan.[23]

The government retaliated by accusing the Jamāᶜat of "exploiting the sentiments of the people" in order to boost their own political fortunes and to unseat the government of prime minister Nawaz Sharif.

The relations between the IJI and the Jamāᶜat reached a point of no return with the fall of the Najibullah government in Kabul. The proposed new government in Afghanistan, according to Jamāᶜat, must include the leaders of Jamīᶜat Islāmī and Ḥizb-e-Islāmī. "I had warned Nawaz Sharif" said Qazi Hussain, "that the exclusion of Jamāᶜat-e-Islāmī's Rabbani and Ḥizb-e-Islāmī's Gulbadan from the new government in Afghanistan would result in chaos and conflict."[24] But, the Qazi claimed, acting at the behest of the Jews and the U.S., Nawaz Sharif dropped both of them and agreed to recognize the Afghanistan government headed by Mujaddidi. At that point, the Jamā‘at announced that "we are no longer with the IJI."[25] The Jamā‘at formally broke away from the IJI on May 5,1992. Interestingly, four months later, Mian Tufail Mohammad resigned from the consultative assembly of the Jamā‘at in protest against the policies pursued by the Jamā‘at under the leadership of Qazi Hussain Ahmad.

Prime Minister Nawaz Sharif by then was already deep in conflict with the President because of his determination to move a constitutional amendment that would limit the powers of the President to control the political process, including the power to dissolve the National Assembly. The President had the upper hand. On April 18, 1993, president Ghulam Ishaq Khan "dismissed Prime Minister Nawaz Sharif accusing him of corruption and mismanagement, and dissolved the parliament."[26] These charges are similar to those the president leveled against Benazir Bhutto when he dismissed her government. He appointed a caretaker government and announced that new elections would be held on July 14, 1993. Indeed, in a rare display of courage, the supreme court declared the presidential action as unconstitutional and restored the Sharif government. The political stalemate resulting from the clash of personalities and interests was resolved on May 26, 1993 with the simultaneous resignations of both the president and prime minister, paving the way for the mid-term general elections to take place in October 1993.

THE JAMĀ‘AT AS A MASS PARTY: PAKISTAN ISLAMIC FRONT

Unlike those held in 1988 and 1990, the 1993 elections were held under a strictly neutral government comprising technocrats, backed by the military and headed by Moeen Qureshi, "the imported prime minister." The army was assigned the role of supervising the elections. Over 150,000 soldiers and officers were stationed at polling stations throughout the country. Again, unlike the two earlier elections, there were no major electoral alliances in the field. Although the main contenders were the two former prime ministers leading PML and PPP respectively, the Pakistan Islamic Front (PIF) under the leadership of Qazi Hussain Ahmad made its presence felt with its aggressive campaign highlighting economic issues and day to day problems.

The PIF may be considered as the electoral arm of the Jamāᶜat-e-Islāmī. Between 1988 and 1993 both the PPP and the Muslim League lost credibility with the masses as their leaders stood accused of corruption and mismanagement. Being discredited and exhausted, Qazi Hussain thought that the two parties would be vulnerable to a direct challenge from the Jamāᶜat. Earlier, the Jamāᶜat had decided against having any alliance with either the Muslim League or the People's Party.[27] Having decided to go it alone, the Jamāᶜat felt it necessary to widen its support base if it were to succeed in the forthcoming election. It was necessary to relax the membership criteria of the Jamāᶜat in order to accommodate all those people "who refrain from all major sins, fulfill obligatory rites, and are willing to sacrifice for the sake of Islam and for the domination of the Islamic way of life."[28] Such a drastic organizational restructuring of the Jamāᶜat was not looked upon with favour. A majority of members of the *shūrā* felt that "this might lead to the dilution and corruption of the nucleus of core workers that Jamāᶜat-e-Islāmī had so painstakingly built over the years. Hence the Pakistan Islamic Front."[29]

Mian Tufail Muhammad has accused the incumbent leadership of the Jamāᶜat of high handedness in forming the PIF. According to him, the leadership tried, first, to relax the conditions required for obtaining membership of the Jamāᶜat so as to enroll people from all walks of life like all other political parties. Failing in this, they proposed the formation of a parallel body, PIF, which also was not approved by the majority of the *shūrā*. The proposal was then sent to the executive committee of the Jamā'at and was approved. Later on, they succeeded in getting it endorsed by the *shūrā*.[30] To Mian Tufail, the existing leadership "has buried the Jamāᶜat, formed the Front, allowed the people to join en masse, flouted the religious and moral regulations, and tried to gain popularity by employing all those means used by parties like the PPP and Awami League."[31]

The formation of the PIF has been justified in many ways. First, such a drastic change was necessitated by the change in the environment in which the Jamāᶜat operated. Going back to history, Qazi Hussain argued that Mawlana Mawdudi formed the Jamāᶜat in 1941 with a definite plan in mind. He had to change the strategy immediately after the emergence of Pakistan. The famous Machi Goth meeting in 1957 that charted a new course for the Jamāᶜat was opposed by prominent members of the Jamāᶜat but Mawdudi did not budge. Qazi Hussain asked, "If there was a need to change the strategy of the Jamāᶜat 17 years after its formation, is it not essential to change it after 50 years?"[32] Second, change in the strategy is characteristic of a vibrant and lively movement. A movement that refuses to change its strategy with the change of time and which does not make use of new means and resources can never move forward to attain its objectives. Echoing Mawdudi, Qazi Hussain observed that although the Jamāᶜat had changed its strategy, its principles and objectives remained the same. Finally, he argued, it is the responsibility of the leader with a vision, a plan and a scheme to chart new ways and to guide the movement to its desired goal. As a leader, Qazi Hussain argued, it was his responsibility to chart new ways for the Jamāᶜat.[33] To Khurram Murad, formations of organizations like PIF with some limited objectives in specific areas,

> has always been a necessary part of JI's strategy in the past: e.g., Islami Jamiᶜat-e-Talaba, various trade unions and the National Labour Federation, Associations for Civil Liberty and Moral Reforms in early 50s. Even for elections, such structures as COP [Combined Opposition Party], PNA and IJI were raised, because the inherent logic of political change made them necessary. Indeed, since the experience of 1970, JI has never taken part in any election under its own banner, name, symbol, and manifesto, but always through a broad-based alliance between parties.[34]

As explained by Khurram Murad, the PIF was an autonomous organization. It held its first meeting on May 23, 1993, attended by 4,000 people from all over the country. Among the names of participants released to the press, there were as many as twenty retired senior officers of the armed forces. It was structurally different from the Jamāᶜat in two ways. First, it was an open organization. Any one who believed in its aims and sincerely stood for Islam and Pakistan (like *muttafiqs* in the Jamāᶜat) could become its member. Second, all the members of the Front had an equal voice in decision making.[35] The PIF had Qazi Hussain Ahmad as its president.

The Islamic Front announced a twenty-nine-point programme that included items appealing to every Pakistani. The PIF candidates, according to Qazi Hussain, "are men of caliber, character, and competence" determined to "create an altogether New World – honest, clean and God-fearing."[36] The manifesto promised to make Pakistan a "truly Islamic, democratic, welfare state" which will ensure rule of law, basic rights of citizens, independence of judiciary, minimum standard of living, and a just distribution of wealth. It promised provincial autonomy; elimination of ethnic, linguistic, provincial, and sectarian prejudices; an accountability system for president, prime minister, and all political leaders including members of the assembly; and working for the creation of an effective Islamic ummah. The economic charter included a pledge to launch an "industrialization model" which would ensure import substitution as much as export-promotion, strengthen the infrastructure, and create a network of industries "so that Pakistan can attain a competitive edge over other nations of the region."[37] The privatisation process was to be continued with proper planning and moderation. In the social sector, unemployment was to be overcome by creating new jobs and widening employment opportunities. A new labour policy was promised and proposed to link increase in wages with rise in prices "so that a worker's actual standard of living improved constantly."[38] It promised creation of an exploitation-free society, mass education, modern health and hygiene facilities, free and equitable prices for the farmer's produce and protection of the rights of the minorities. The manifesto promised to protect "personal, family, economic, social and political rights of women," to establish institutions of higher learning for women and to fully safeguard the rights of working women.[39]

The PIF manifesto, it may be noted, departed radically from the 1970s and 1980s by breaking away from the conservative approach to minorities and women. Its proposal for reserving some seats in the assemblies for party lists was equally novel. Accommodation of peasants and workers in the list system would have broadened the social base of legislative authority. Interestingly, the PIF manifesto shared many similarities with the manifestos of the PML and the PPP. They all accepted the market economy system; they were respectful of the defence lobby and they all took note of public interests in the controversies concerning the powers of the president and parliament. Likewise they were equally aware of the pressure for advances in social sectors, and the need to fight corruption.

The PIF fielded 103 candidates to contest national assembly seats and 237 for provincial seats. It launched a religiously charged and overtly anti-American campaign. Since the PIF had no electoral machinery of its own, its campaigning was carried out by the Jamāᶜat and its student and labour wings. Like other political parties, the Jamāᶜat made good use of posters, buntings, leaflets, and billboards, organized public rallies and mass processions, and its candidates visited houses and markets, soliciting votes. It also took part in other forms of campaigning, such as the incorporation of election based inspirational songs sung to the tunes of popular songs and satirical snippets on the various parties aired from various channels. These were exactly the things Sayyid Mawdudi disallowed in 1941 saying that these are "the heart and soul of nationalist or other movements ... [and that these] will prove deadly for the Islamic movement."[40]

The way the PIF handled the election campaigning created a good deal of furore among the rank and file of the Jamāᶜat. There was dissension within the Jamāᶜat. Some party leaders thought that Qazi Hussain Ahmad had gone too far beyond the original party mandate as approved by its central consultative committee. The party old guards feared that the new leadership of the Jamāᶜat was influenced more by the mob than by reason and logic. They thought that populism and demagogy were not befitting an Islamic movement. *Takbīr* and *Zindagī*, the two most popular pro- Jamāᶜat weekly newsmagazines, were highly critical of the Jamāᶜat's electioneering tactics. The most devastating public criticism of the Jamāᶜat's electoral activities came from its former leader, Mian Tufail, who described them as "unjustifiable." To Mian Tufail, the PIF flouted all the moral and ethical norms and adopted nefarious campaign tactics used by Z.A. Bhutto and Mujibur Rahman to popularize their Pakistan People's Party and Awami League respectively.[41]

Election Results
The elections "were remarkably free and fair."[42] According to the official results, a total of 20,449,700 votes were cast, which works out to 40.85 percent of the total registered votes. The PPP secured 90 seats and its leader Benazir Bhutto was invited to form the government. The PML led by Nawaz Sharif emerged as the major opposition with 73 seats. Yet, the voters apparently preferred the

Table 4.4
Results of 1993 elections and the position of political parties in
the National Assembly of Pakistan

Party/Alliance	Seats Secured	% Seats Won	% Votes Polled (N=20449700)
PPP	90	43.48	38.24
PML(N)	73	35.27	39.72
PML(J)	6	2.90	3.82
IJM	4	1.93	2.36
PIF	3	1.45	2.36
Other Parties	15	7.25	5.25
Independents	16	7.73	7.28
Total:	207	100.01	100.00

Notes:
- PPP = Pakistan People's Party; PML(N) = Pakistan Muslim League (Nawaz); PML(J) = Pakistan Muslim League (Junejo); IJM = Islami Jamhuri Mahaz; PIF = Pakistan Islamic Front.
Source: Adapted from Election Commission of Pakistan, 1997 General Elections Report, Vol. II (Islamabad: Printing Corporation of Pakistan Press, 1997).

PML which polled 39.72 percent of the total valid votes over the PPP which polled 38.24 percent of the votes (see Table 4.4). Many former ministers as well as other political luminaries lost their bid for seats in the national assembly. The PIF, despite assuming a populist stance, lost to the PPP and Muslim League. The much-expected "third force" did not materialize and the PIF received only three national assembly seats. Qazi Hussain Ahmad lost from the two prestigious constituencies of Karachi and Lahore and was not returned to parliament. Many observers of the politics in Pakistan hastily interpreted these as welcome developments for the evolution of a liberal democratic polity and as the beginning of a two-party system in the country.[43] In the same manner it was argued that religio-political parties do not convince Pakistani voters.

The Muslim League members actually blamed the Jamā'at for Benazir Bhutto's return to the office of prime minister. In ten constituencies, the Jamā'at, and the Muslim League together received more votes than the PPP (see Table 4.5) but the votes were split to PPP's advantage. The two together could have captured two additional seats won by minor parties. The twelve additional

Table 4.5
Constituencies vulnerable to possible PML+PIF alliance

Constituency	PML	PIF	PPP	PML+PIF
NA 61	60959	3025	63548	63984
NA 62	45298	4851	45457	50149
NA 80	74918	7228	79772	82146
NA 81	77365	4141	80759	81506
NA 84	47296	3420	47887	50716
NA 100	38361	11107	38433	49468
NA 102	56909	7062	61465	63971
NA 125	56079	4310	61015	60389
NA 140	46480	6296	51162	52776
NA 185	10218	7796	14866	18014

Source: Adapted from Election Commission of Pakistan, *1997 General Elections Report,* Vol. II (Islamabad: Printing Corporation of Pakistan Press, 1997), 1-162.

seats would have given the Muslim League the elections and denied
Benazir Bhutto the premiership.

As far as the Jamāᶜat leadership was concerned, there was not
much of a difference between the PPP and the PML. To them,
Nawaz Sharif, not unlike Benazir, was an evil, only if a lesser one.
According to Khurram Murad, Nawaz Sharif had repeatedly
refused to be identified as a "fundamentalist," had played foul
with Sharīᶜah Bill, appointed a die-hard secularist as minister of
education, and used the media to popularise non-Islamic culture
in the name of Islam.[44]   The Front leadership therefore argued
that choosing the lesser evil was choosing an evil in any case
which would serve to blur the people's perception of good and
evil. The PIF was to provide an alternative third force to the people
should their conscience choose to react against the "evil" of the
situation. The PIF was the vehicle to make the Jamāᶜat's message
clear to the people. "Seats are important, but zero seats with this
much achieved would be a far better result than eight or so seats
for ever and ever, as the price for defeating PPP and helping a
PPP-like party into power."[45]

The fact nevertheless remains that the contest in the elections
was between the two evils. The PIF/Jamāᶜat received only 2.4
percent of the popular votes compared with 38.2 percent for the
PPP and 39.7 percent for the Muslim League. Thus the Jamāᶜat's
vote bank was reduced to a little more than half when compared
to 1977. Qazi Hussain appears not to have learned the skills of
effective election campaign management. His anti-American
slogan was interpreted by the public as being anti-PPP and hence
benefited Nawaz Sharif's PML. Jamāᶜat's anti-feudal slogans turned
the landlords to assume a confrontational posture and hence support
the PML.[46]   Finally, the Jamāᶜat performed relatively better when
it sponsored a smaller number of candidates. An increase in the
number of candidates resulted in winning lesser number of seats.
The data in table 4.6 give a negative Spearman's rank-order
correlation ($r_s = -.37$) between seats contested and won by the
Jamāᶜat which is attributable to many factors. According to Mian
Tufail, however, the Front's election campaign managers had
committed excesses by adopting such un-Islamic practices as

Table 4.6
National Assembly seats contested and won by the
Jamā°at, 1970-1993

Year	Seats Contested	Seats won
1970	151	4
1977	31	9
1985	68	10
1988	26	8
1990	18	6
1993	103	3

dancing to the tune of film songs, creating the personality cult of the leader, and emotional slogan mongering. The public revolted against such practices adopted especially by the Jamā°at-e-Islāmī. Interestingly, the Pakistan Gallup Poll survey carried out in 1997 found that of the 5000 randomly selected respondents, 73 percent "preferred a relatively quiet election campaign without posters, banners, flags and rallies."[47]

The fear expressed by Maulana Amin Ahsan Islahi in the 1954 Machi Goth conference has come to be true. Continued participation in the political process has forced the Jamā°at to make costly compromises and to reassess its ideological stance on various issues. It has been forced to incorporate new strategies and policies into its ideology and to use secular symbols and tools in order to expand its support base. These changes, largely tactical and apparently subtle variations of the doctrine, have created tensions within the organization.

These changes might have damaged the popular appeal not only of the Jamā°at but of various Islamic institutions in Pakistan. The findings of a 1996 Pakistan Gallup Poll survey are revealing. Of the 821 randomly selected urban respondents, 78 percent expressed their trust in the military, 44 percent in religious scholars, and 34 percent in the courts.[48] Another survey conducted in Pakistan in 1997 found that the Pakistanis in general have low trust in major state institutions. About 82 percent of the 1162 respondents expressed their trust in the armed forces. Likewise, they expressed high trust in schools (72.5 percent), intellectuals (65.15 percent), and universities (58.55 percent). In contrast, only 46.1 percent expressed trust in the ʿulamā' and 40.65 percent in the mosque *imāms* (prayer leaders).[49]

QAZI HUSSAIN: RE-ELECTION AND RE-EVALUATION OF PARTY STRATEGY

For Qazi Hussain, participation in the 1993 election brought double trouble. Firstly, to capture political power, he rushed to form the Islamic Front and allowed the party's membership to swell, yet he lost the election. The general public perhaps did not find much difference between the Jamāʿat and other secular parties. The reconstituted Jamāʿat failed to translate popular support into electoral victory. Qazi Hussain was subjected to much criticism for the transformation of the Jamāʿat into a mass party. Secondly, again for the sake of capturing power, he adopted secular electoral symbols and tactics, yet he could win no more than three seats. This time he was subjected to scathing criticism for unethical campaign tactics as well as for losing the election. One thing became clear in the prevalent feudal based socio-cultural realities with its concomitant clientelist politics, ideology based parties stand no chance of winning elections in Pakistan. This realization, although it was clearly spelled out in the 1954 Machi Goth conference by those who opposed politicization of the Jamāʿat-e-Islāmī movement in Pakistan, has added to the despondency in some quarters of the party rank and file. There were allegations that Qazi Hussain had continuously been flouting the decisions of the party assembly and that he had lost the confidence of a majority of members of the party. The dissension in the organization reached such a point that Qazi Hussain felt obliged to tender his resignation from the party presidency.

The Jamāʿat assembly promptly appointed Chaudhury Rahmat Ilahi as acting president and decided to hold fresh elections for the post of the president. In the party elections that followed, the *majlis-e-shūrā* nominated three candidates for party presidency among whom Qazi Hussain Ahmad received the majority votes and was re-elected as the *amīr* of the Jamāʿat. Qazi Hussain polled 6093 or 76 percent of 7994 votes cast. This was just one percentage point less than the majority votes he garnered in the 1992 elections (5729 or 77 percent of the 7416 votes cast).[50] It must be noted that during the tenure of Qazi Hussain, the membership figure had been increasing by 8 percent per annum as compared to 7 percent during the tenure of his predecessor Mian Tufail.

The Jamāʿat did carry out a post-mortem of its electoral experience and declared that the 1993 electoral debacle was not due to any problem within the organization but to the unjust electoral system prevalent in Pakistan. It, therefore, reaffirmed that the Jamāʿat must remain in politics and that it must be mass based. However, it refused to form electoral alliances with those whose objectives and characters did not meet even the minimum requirements of the Jamāʿat as it would create confusion among the public and the objectives of the Jamāʿat would remain unrealized.[51] These decisions were not to the liking of many senior ranking members of the Jamāʿat. In 1995, fifteen of these senior leaders resigned from the party, as they could no longer tolerate the attention being paid to political activities to the detriment of the party's religious idealism. Their resignations, according to one report, was triggered by the sound of music, being prepared for the Jamāʿat's political rallies, which interrupted the sermon of a senior leader of the Jamāʿat, Mawlana Gawhar Rahman.[52] In any case, this did not deter the Jamāʿat leadership from implementing its political agenda. The Jamāʿat went ahead to diagnoze the problem, itemize its demands, and chalk out a new strategy to achieve its political objectives.

The Diagnosis
In its post-election evaluation, the Jamāʿat found that, first, the current electoral system requires great personal wealth and vote banks and it has repeatedly resulted in the election of wealthy, feudal, and industry/business representatives.[53] In other words, the electoral system helps perpetuate the feudal monopoly over politics in the country. Qazi Hussain pointed out that the majority

of those who sit in the parliament are not the "dear representatives of the people" but a group of people who patronise all illicit dealings and are the pillars of the cruel and unjust system. They lack honesty, competence, vision, and genuine commitment to the welfare of citizens. This pernicious influence of feudal aristocracy and wealth-culture has rendered the elections a sham and virtually disenfranchised the people. "The masses hate them but they find it difficult to free themselves from the clutches of these feudal politicians."[54]

Second, the electoral process is equally unjust. The people are subjected to political harangues, bribes, and threats, all intended to secure their support in elections. Sentimental slogans, coercion, and corruption were the sinews of electoral warfare in which all means were considered fair, including impersonation, bogus voting, tampering with ballot boxes, use of government transport and money, lavish expenditure on entertainment and enticement of the voters. Once elected to parliament and high posts, these oppressively status quo oriented feudal class treat the people and the country the way they treat their tenants, *kammis* (low caste professionals and artisans), and other dependants.[55] According to Qazi Hussain, "our elections have never been fair and just and hence real representatives of the people could never be elected to the parliament. Unless this entire system is reformed, it would be suicidal to take part in any future elections."[56]

Finally, the government has never been impartial and, worse still, in conducting elections, it has resorted to selective enforcement of the constitution. Thus, in none of the elections, has the government ever applied articles 62 and 63 of the constitution. Article 62 lays down some qualities like education, age, sagacity, righteousness, trustworthiness, adequate knowledge of Islamic teachings, piety, and clean past record as qualifications for eligibility of the candidates to the national and provincial assemblies. Article 63 lists such qualities as insanity, insolvency, moral turpitude, corruption, and holding of any opinion or acting in any manner, prejudicial to the ideology of Pakistan, or morality or the maintenance of public order as grounds for disqualification from being elected or chosen as, and from being, a member of the *majlis-e-shūrā* (see Appendix B). The two articles were intended to sift the good from the bad among candidates. Implementation of these two articles would have ensured the election of honest and less tainted politicians to the assemblies. Unfortunately, the government turned a blind eye to these constitutional requirements and has thus made it difficult for honest, trustworthy people to be elected to serve the ummah.

The above diagnosis shows the political maturity of the Jamāʿat in several ways. Firstly, it realized that elections are an important means for spreading the message of Islam. Campaigning during the elections is a means to mobilize the population behind the party's drive towards an Islamic socio-economic and political order. More importantly, however, elections are the means to capture political power which would provide the needed opportunity to implement sharīʿah which, in turn, would help restructure the society along Islamic lines. Under Qazi Hussain, the emphasis was on winning the election. The *daʿwah* or mobilization function inherent in the campaign process was used to rationalize the Jamāʿat's poor performance in the election. Secondly, winning the election requires broadening the mass base and effective campaign management. The Jamāʿat could embark upon the first but could not do the second effectively as it was characrterised by malpractices, corruption, vote-buying and other evils. A party promoting the cause of Islam cannot openly flout the Islamic norms of honesty, austerity, and decency.

Thirdly, and most importantly, the Jamāʿat realized that majority of the Pakistanis are at the beck and call of the feudal landlords. The feudal families have monopolised politics at both the grassroots and national levels and have manipulated the vital electoral institutions to perpetuate their coercive domination.[57] This feudal system must be tamed or if possible destroyed if any social engineering is to succeed. Consequently, the extraordinary meeting of the central shūrā of the Jamāʿat deliberated extensively on matters related to election and demanded, among other things, the following:[58]

1. The election commission should be reconstituted. It should be composed of the sitting or retired judges of the Supreme Court. It should be a permanent, competent and fully independent body with full-time staff and it should be adequately funded. Among other things, the commission should scrutinize all those who offer themselves for any public office. It should publicly announce their candidature and invite comments from the public by widely publicizing Articles 62 and 63 of the constitution. Only those who fulfill the requirements of the constitutional provisions should be allowed to stand for election. The resolution demanded that even if an elected member is found violating the said articles, his or her membership should be terminated immediately.

2. The commission must fix the limit for financial expenses during the election campaign and ensure that the limit is strictly adhered to. Any violation of this limit should result in the disqualification of the candidate.

3. Elections should be based upon proportional representation system. Under this system, parties acquire seats in explicit relation to the votes they receive. The most common form of proportional representation is the List system. According to this plan all candidates are grouped in lists according to their party labels and every party offers a list of its candidates up to the number of seats to be filled for each constituency. The total number of votes won by a party determines how many candidates are elected from that list. The number of votes gained by the individual candidates on the list determines which people are elected to represent that party. This list system, Jamāʿat believes, would free the electorate from the servitude of the landlords.[59] Election of a particular candidate would not depend on local feudal lords and therefore the party would be able to offer candidates on the basis of merit.

4. A high powered judicial commission, composed of sitting and retired judges of the supreme court and high courts, must be constituted to scrutinise and prosecute those who have abused power, embezzled funds and plundered the economy of the country. The commission should scrutinize not merely the politicians but also government officials and employees of the public sector agencies and organizations. Properties of those found guilty of misappropriation should be confiscated; they should be given exemplary punishment and, in case of politicians, be barred from taking part in any future elections. By this demand, if implemented by the government, the Jamāʿat would be able to banish many seasoned politicians from the scene and thus pave the way for its candidates to win the election without much competition.

5. All political parties should have equal access to the media and should have equal opportunity to present their message through nationally owned media. The media should not be allowed to preach indecency and immodesty, particularly on television.

THE JAMĀ^CAT AS A REVOLUTIONARY MASS MOVEMENT

The Jamāʿat was perhaps aware that its demands for a meaningful election implied total dismantling of the existing social structure of Pakistan. No Pakistani ruling elite would entertain these demands and certainly it would not be accepted by the president of Pakistan, Farooq Khan Leghari, a landlord from Dera Ghazi Khan. The Jamāʿat, however, believed that it could force the government to accept these demands. As such, the same *majlis-e-shūrā* decided to embark upon a mass contact movement to realize its demands. The objective of this movement was to compel the ruling authorities to accept proportional representation system, to undertake the process of accountability; to punish those guilty of embezzlement and fraudulent practices; to bar them from taking part in future elections; and to ensure that future elections are just and the

candidates are trustworthy and men of character.[60] The chief
characteristic of this resolute mass-contact movement is its peaceful
nature. To Qazi Hussain, Jamāᶜat is an exemplary, organized and
peaceful movement.

The interim government led by Malik Meraj Khalid in 1996
did respond to some of the demands of the Jamāᶜat. It published
lists of defaulters on loans and taxes and promulgated an
Accountability Ordinance but, other than recovering electricity,
and telephone bills, and the rent of the official residences, not
much came out of it.[61] By early 1997, the Jamāᶜat reached the
conclusion that the caretaker government had failed miserably to
stamp out corruption. It had ignored the timely and pertinent
demands and hence the ensuing elections would not be fair or
help promote democratic values in the country. Consequently, the
Jamāᶜat-e-Islāmī decided:

1. To boycott the elections of 3 February 1997.

2. To ask the party candidates, who had submitted their
    nomination papers in the hope of having effective
    accountability and the holding of transparent elections, to
    withdraw their nomination papers.

3. To appeal to the people of Pakistan not to take part in the
    electoral process because their just demand for accountability
    had not been fulfilled and Articles 62 and 63 of the constitution
    of Pakistan had also not been acted upon.[62]

Instead of taking part in what it called the "farcical elections,"
the party decided to organize public opinion to usher in "a true
democratic and welfare Islamic state." As usual, the *shūrā*
announced that the Jamāᶜat would not resort to violence of any
kind to obstruct the electoral process and that its protest would
remain peaceful.

In the February 3, 1997 general elections, the Pakistan Muslim
League led by Nawaz Sharif scored a major victory by capturing
137 national assembly seats as against 18 seats won by its nearest

rival, the Pakistan People's Party.[63] Most of the traditional seats belonging to the Jamāᶜat were captured by the PML. The PML, which formed the government, polled 45.95 percent of the total votes cast which amounted to about 16.32 percent of the total registered voters.

For the Jamāᶜat, the 1997 elections simply perpetuated the rule of the corrupt in society.

> The same feudal lords and capitalists were once again elected in the February '97 elections; the majority of whom, is devoid of honesty and trustworthiness. They have thoroughly plundered the nation's resources in the past, and continue to do so today. In our calculated opinion, these are the same people, who are responsible for all the miseries of Pakistan, since the past half-century.[64]

The redeeming feature of the elections, however, was that they registered the lowest voter turnout in the electoral history of Pakistan (see Table 4.7). To Jamāᶜat, this was an indication of its success in persuading the people to refrain from taking part in the elections. Furthermore, the Nawaz government's claim to have won a "big mandate" was a hoax, in that the PML actually polled

Table 4.7
Percent Voter Turnout in the National and Provincial Assemblies
Elections, 1985-1997

Year	National Assembly	Provincial Assemblies
1985	53.69	57.37
1988	43.07	43.20
1990	45.46	46.10
1993	40.32	42.76
1997	35.99	35.69

Source: Election Commission of Pakistan, *1997 General Elections Report,* Volume I (Islamabad: Printing Corporation of Pakistan Press, 1997), 195.

no more than 16.32 percent of the total registered voters.[65] This is yet another indication of the people's apathy with the prevailing political processes in the country. These indications were widely regarded by the Jamāᶜat as a vindication of its newfound strategy of ushering in a just moral order through "Islamic revolution."

THE EPOCHAL SHIFT
The revolutionary movement, announced in 1997 through the polls boycott decision, was already in the making since 1994. The *reasons*, the *nature* and the *strategy* of the revolutionary mass movement have, from time to time, been explained to the workers through various media. These explanations need to be threaded together to capture a comprehensive picture of the strategy of the revolutionary mass movement chalked out by the Jamāᶜat under the leadership of Qazi Hussain Ahmad. These changes constitute what Martin Marty calls "epochal shifts" characterized by "a complex set of radical religious changes, in which people sit and think religiously in ways that differ from those of the past."[66]

The Justification: The Jamāᶜat justifies its revolutionary movement through several interrelated arguments. These arguments are based upon its close readings of the Pakistani society, the Pakistani public, and the political experience of the Jamāᶜat over the last 50 years. First, the Jamāᶜat began with the observation that there exist sharp differences in language and culture, food and costumes, race and customs, and in the historical traditions of various regions which constitute Pakistan. Yet, a belief in the role of Islam constitutes a basic part of the social ideology of Pakistanis. Islam provides guidance for and regulates every aspect of life in Pakistan and occupies the center stage in the social, economic, and political life of all Pakistanis. However, Islam is not allowed to play its role by the feudal lords and capitalists who are at the top of the social pyramid with the peasantry forming the base. The tenants are held at the beck and call of the feudal lords who control the social, economic and political life of the tenants. They are averse to electoral reforms, politicization of the masses or any such radical transformation in the social sector. The electoral system in Pakistan helps to perpetuate the feudal monopoly over politics in the country. The landed aristocracy and the capitalist class contest elections for prestige as well as for reaping the attendant benefits that feudalist politicians have come to assume as their birthright. They spend most of their time, energies and resources on buying or trading shifting loyalties. Their emphasis has been on acquiring grants, foreign assistance, rural and urban property, tax evasions, and plundering of national resources. The Jamāᶜat, as declared by its *nā'ib amīr*, Liaquat Baloch, under the leadership of Qazi Hussain Ahmed, will bring about an Islamic revolution to solve the longstanding and chronic problems of the downtrodden masses.

Second, the Jamāᶜat had tried to bring about the desired transformation of the society by adopting the politics of alliance but it failed. It made an alliance with the Muslim League, and went from door to door asking for votes on their behalf. The Jamāᶜat leaders were promised that an Islamic System would be promulgated in the country, that Kashmir would be freed, and that justice provided to the people. The Muslim League betrayed the trust and honoured none of these promises.[67] The alliance politics, instead of helping the Jamāᶜat realise its goals, created confusion in the minds of the people about the message and the struggle of the organization. The Jamāᶜat, therefore, decided to shun the politics of alliance, distanced itself from the Muslim league "and purified our organisation from it."[68]

Third, the Jamāᶜat had actively participated in all of the elections hoping to bring about social transformations through constitutional, democratic means. Unfortunately, the elections in Pakistan have been neither fair nor free. The system is staked in favour of the loan defaulters, drug barons and tax-evaders. Under the prevailing electoral system, there is no opportunity for a new, representative and reforming leadership to emerge at local and national levels. The party organized rallies and meetings denouncing the corrupt system. It finally demanded from the government transparency in the system, accountability of the governors and the candidates, barring of all the unwanted persons

from public offices and the enforcement of Articles 62 and 63 of
the constitution of Pakistan. The government did not concede to
these legitimate demands. The people of Pakistan have become
increasingly apathetic about the entire process. They are fed up
with the Peoples Party and are frustrated with the Muslim League
and others.[69] They could not get anything from the elections and,
therefore, despair of voting, of democracy itself. The Jamā'at
leadership feels that this despair can only be removed by mobilizing
the public for an Islamic revolution.

Finally, the Jamā'at has realized that the movement has
significantly influenced the educated classes but its influence on
the common mass of people is much to be desired. It has developed
a new language of Islamic politics but it has still to work very hard
in overcoming the traditional sources of power in the country,
with the result that its moral and ideological weight is not being
fully and properly translated into political weight. It has been more
effective as an ideological force, or even as a pressure group with
immense street power, but not yet as a political power. The Jamā'at,
as such, feels the need to reorient its politics and make it people
oriented. Qazi Hussain assured the public that "We would not want
and let Martial Law to be imposed again [on Pakistan]; or to have
capitalists and feudal lords, debase it again, in the name of
democracy."

THE STRATEGY
To bring about an Islamic revolution the Jamā'at adopted a basic
strategy in 1994, under its five year plan. This strategy can be
summed up under three headings: education, social reform, and,
an all-out struggle.[70]

Education: The first strategy consists of an all-out campaign for
the regeneration and reconstruction of the collective life of the
community along Islamic concepts of life. The idea is to expose
people to pure Islamic teachings shorn of all false ideas and purged
of all unhealthy accretions. Islam would be presented as a complete
way of life and as an alternative civilization. It would explain not

merely the tenets and principles of Islam but also to show the relevance of Islam to the present-day world for developing a sound and healthy social, economic and political order. This would necessitate: One, a searching criticism of Western ideologies and philosophies. Two, a critical appreciation of the Muslim heritage. Finally, a judicious appropriation of healthy elements from both the Islamic and Western heritage through the revitalization of the spirit of *ijtihād*, i.e., exerting one's utmost to show how Islamic principles can be applied to new circumstances. The Jamāʿat, however, would not permit the slightest deviation as far as the teachings of the Qur'an and the Sunnah are concerned. "They are eternally binding and should be followed by Muslims in all periods of history."[71] Emphasis is placed on the establishment of educational institutions, arrangements for adult education, communication of basic teachings of Islam to the common people and trend setting reading rooms to create enlightenment.

Additionally, the meeting of the Central *majlis-e-shūrā*, Jamāʿat-e-Islāmī, Pakistan, on 22 December 1997, expressed anxiety over the Pakistani rulers' detached attitude towards education during the last 50 years resulting in what it called "anarchy on the ideological front."[72] It demanded, among others, a uniform syllabus with Urdu as the medium of instruction, improvement of the deplorable conditions of the state owned educational institutions; restoration of the traditional Islamic concept of *waqf* institutions, increase in educational budget to 5 per cent of the GNP, establishment of a women's university in every province, and revival of union activities in government and private educational institutions in the interest of healthy and purposeful activities.[73]

On its own, the Jamāʿat has decided to do two things: first, it would assist existing schools run by Jamāʿat sympathisers by improving their curriculum and by providing training to teachers. Second, it would set up a "city of knowledge" with a complex of institutes to carry out the task of rebuilding education and regenerating research. The Jamāʿat has acquired a big chunk of land in the suburb of Islamabad for an educational complex, a housing estate of 10,000 residential units, an industrial zone and a green belt, comprising lawns, parks and farm land.

Social Reform: The second component of the strategy is to start
an all-out campaign for the regeneration and reconstruction of the
collective life of the community along Islamic concepts of life.
This comprehensive program seeks to make the mosque the hub
of all Islamic activity. "An essential element of this program,"
according to the Jamāᶜat, "is moral uplift of the people and
cultivating in them the spirit to defend their rights."[74] People are
expected to extend help to weaker elements of society in protecting
their rights appropriately:

> At a highly personal level, the social program of the Jamāᶜat
> aims at inculcating in every human being the basic personal
> ethics of Islam. Ominously it starts with the creation of
> sense of personal hygiene and cleanliness and includes:
> fostering co-operation among people to ensure healthy
> conditions of living; listing orphans, widows, the crippled,
> the incapacitated, the poor students to arrange for their
> financial assistance, and catering for the health requirements
> of poor people. In fact, the objective is to foster the religious,
> moral, social and material welfare of the people and to create
> social conditions conducive for a healthy change in life.[75]

Social reform would develop a group of noble men in every
locality who would be in a position to suppress the bad elements
of the society and would strive to make the people of their own
area religious and honest. In this way a popular opinion will emerge
in the country which will suppress all kinds of evil or at least keep
people away from taking part in activities which have evil
consequences. Qazi Hussain believes that public opinion in
Pakistan has taken a positive turn, which is evident from low voter-
turn out in the 1997 elections. According to the Jamāᶜat's estimate,
no more than 20 percent of the people took part in the elections.
Even the official 35 percent turnout figure is the lowest in the
electoral history of Pakistan and is an indication of people's
disappointment with the corrupt political processes prevalent in

the country.[76]

Jihād **or All Out Struggle**: The final element of the party's strategy involves identifying and organizing all those who "are disposed to righteousness and who yearn to establish a noble and upright human society" under the banner of the Jamāᶜat. These people need to be exposed to such a programme for moral, intellectual and social upliftment that they become permeated with the true spirit of Islam. The movement needs people of this type. Without them, the movement can neither gain in strength nor grow in proportions.

To identify and organize such people, the Jamāᶜat embarked upon its membership drive in 1997. Instead of asking for votes, it now asked for membership of the Jamāᶜat. "Any one who consciously avoids sins, remains dutiful in obligatory deeds and his or her income and assets are never found dubious, is fully qualified to become our member."[77] This membership drive, according to Qazi Hussain, has been doubly beneficial. It has gradually transformed people's despair and frustration into hope and aspiration. They are showing signs of accepting Jamāᶜat's leadership role. It has also made the Jamāᶜat workers overcome their lethargy and become active. The Jamāᶜat has fixed the target of 5 million members. Once this figure is achieved, the situation will change. The Jamāᶜat is fully equipped to carry out its populist policy. The Jamāᶜat headquarters outside Lahore are an extensive complex of computerized offices, a school, a hospital and a mosque along with residential quarters. From here, the Jamāᶜat runs "
a nation-wide network of schools, reading rooms, clinics and other associated institutions."[78] A Jamāᶜat publicity section produces magazines, pamphlets and books in several languages. It has established its own website providing an overview of the Jamāᶜat objectives and goals, its views on national and global affairs, the directory of all Jamāᶜat run institutions and profile of the Jamaᶜat leadership "the most trust-worthy leaders of Pakistani people."[79]

Those joining the Jamāᶜat will be organized and the prominent and capable ones will join the "consultative committees" to be established at the local, city, district, province and central levels. Members of the respective committees will work as a team and will take initiative in solving people's problems in all walks of life. They will organize people against all kinds of exploitation and injustices. Depending upon the resources, they will open educational and welfare institutions and will help the needy, the orphans, the incapacitated and the like. Through these committees, the Jamāᶜat will be able to propagate its message which should also help dispel the image of the Jamāᶜat being a party of the select few. It is these people who will undertake *jihād* on all fronts and establish Allah's rule on earth. "We are at the threshold of working out a true revolution based upon Islam's just and balanced social system."[80]

The Jamāᶜat adopted another method of popularizing its movement for social justice. In 1998, it organized a national campaign urging ordinary citizens to sign on to a Jamāᶜat programme of Islamic social justice without necessarily becoming party members. According to reports available, the Jamāᶜat has succeeded in gathering some four million signatures.

NATURE OF THE ISLAMIC REVOLUTION

Qazi Hussain, it can be seen, has initiated what is the biggest project for social justice ever attempted by the Jamāᶜat-e-Islāmī or any other political party in Pakistan. He has been touring the country ceaselessly castigating the governments of both Benazir Bhutto and Nawaz Shariff, calling for the imposition of sharīᶜah law and emerging as one of the high-profile politicians. His vocabulary is littered with references to "feudals," "class," "masses" and "liberation" – words that might have been borrowed from Marx and Lenin. His desired restructuring of the society in favour of the oppressed is bound to be opposed by vested interests, which would make violence unavoidable. In 1997, the government banned Qazi Hussain Ahmad from entering the tribal areas. Though the ban was lifted, the local authorities came up with one excuse or the other to prevent the Jamāᶜat from addressing the crowd. Yet, the Jamāᶜat insisted that the revolution has to be peaceful. "We have to convince the people that a 'Bloody Revolution' is a path leading to destruction and the 'Islamic Revolution' is the path ensuring true change and deliverance."[81] In this respect, Qazi Hussain was following Syed Mawdudi whose advice, to the Arab Youth in Makkah in 1962, was

> ...not to resort to underground movements and use of arms for bringing a revolution. In fact, in your cherished path of revolution, impatience and haste have no place. A true revolution always evolves through popular movements. Give an open call to the people, change their thinking and win their hearts by exhibiting grand Islamic norms. Thus a revolution brought in a gradual way shall be so stable and firm that it would not be possible for opposite forces to obliterate it. If any revolution surfaces through artificial means in haste, it can be removed in the same way as it came.[82]

To the Jamāᶜat, violence is unacceptable. Islamic revolution is evolutionary and peaceful. It demands a movement that has a predetermined objective, and a predetermined leadership. In this movement, people rise in accord with an Islamic ideology and leadership. Changes are brought about by sacrifices, not through bloodshed. Jamāᶜat believes that once it attains the targeted membership of 5 million, it can easily guide the people in the direction of peaceful change. Being peaceful does not mean shying away from organizing and leading street demonstrations. In October 1996, in a bid to stage a sit-in outside parliament, Qazi Hussain personally led thousands of Jamāᶜat demonstrators into running battles with the police. This was a successful agitation that led to the dismissal of the Benazir Government in November 1996. Yet, Qazi Hussain reminded people that despite the gatherings of millions and despite police provocation during anti-Benazir agitation, no government or private property was destroyed and that not even a single glass pane was broken. The movement should face the challenges of injustice and oppressive government through mass mobilization with firm faith in Allah.[83] Agitation and demonstrations are also considered as tools for mobilization.

The transformation of the Jamāᶜat into a mass movement seems to have the support of the Jamāᶜat rank and file. This is evident from the re-election of Qazi Hussain Ahmad for the fourth consecutive time as the *amīr* of the Jamāᶜat. In the 1999 elections, Qazi Hussain Ahmad secured 79.38 percent votes. His popularity during the last 12 years, has increased by 17.38% (62% in 1987 to 79.38% in 1999).[84] Likewise, the membership drive has been very successful. Qazi Hussain claims that due to the membership drive, even the so-called 'dead' party-workers have become active.

THE JAMĀᶜAT AND THE MUSHARRAF COUP OF 1999

With this revived energy, Qazi Hussain launched the anti-government campaign with the avowed aim of sending the corrupt rulers packing and implementing sharīᶜah in the land of Allah. Fortunately for the Jamāᶜat and the opposition parties in general, the elected government led by Nawaz Sharif was devoid of a democratic spirit. Nawaz Sharif had established a firm control over state institutions through constitutional changes and political manipulation during 1997-99.[85] His personalized and whimsical political management, however, alienated the major political forces in the country. In August 1998, sections of the international media painted a bleak picture for Pakistan's future.[86]

These reports underlined the existence of high level of corruption, sectarian violence involving the Sunnis and the Shiites and political crises in Sindh. The economy as a whole was threatened by a low growth rate, a high balance of payment deficit, abysmal investor confidence, growing unemployment and poverty. Economic sanctions imposed in 1998, following Pakistan's explosion of nuclear devices, worsened Pakistan's economy. The *Asiaweek* talked "about a mess" and Nawaz Sharif being "under siege."[87] Ayeshal Jalal prophesied that "unless some miracle can help the Sharif government to bring the economy back from the brink of disaster, and restore its tarnished image, an unconstitutional coup is entirely on the cards."[88]

The opposition parties made several unsuccessful attempts to launch a movement to oust the Sharif government. To this end, they formed an alliance known as the Pakistan Awami Ittehad in 1998 that was rather short lived. In 1999 another broad-based alliance, the Grand Democratic Alliance, comprising 19 political parties, was formed which proved no better than its predecessor. Out of desperation, several opposition parties made direct and indirect appeals to the military to remove the Sharif government. The opposition anti-government agitation received momentum when prime minister Nawaz Sharif signed the Washington accord on July 4, 1999 and agreed to withdraw troops from Kargil heights in Indian occupied Kashmir and to enter into dialogue with India. The following day, the Jamā°at called for *jihād* against Sharif's government.[89] According to Qazi Hussain, "It is imperative for the resolution of the Kashmir issue and for the safety and solidarity of the country that Nawaz Sharif should be removed from the office of the Prime Minister."[90] Interestingly, Qazi Hussain Ahmad expressed the Jamā°at's willingness to lead opposition parties towards the formation of an interim administration and asked the Pakistan army to express unhappiness over the government's alleged conspiracies against the country. This coupled with Nawaz Sharif's attempt to replace General Musharraf with Lt. General Khwaja Ziauddin forced the Pakistan army to move in. Finally, when the army staged a bloodless military coup on Tuesday October 12, 1999, the Jamā°at claimed it "as the outcome of the popular movement."

Larry Diamond describes the October coup as "the single most serious reversal of democracy" as it ended 11 years of competitive party politics in Pakistan.[91] General Pervez Musharraf assumed the newly created position of Chief Exectuive. He declared a state of emergency, and suspended the constitution, national assembly, senate, and the provincial legislatures. The president and the Judiciary and the press were, however, left in place. General Musharraf apparently was not inclined to wield power and hence he declared that the armed forces would return to the barracks the moment they succeed in paving the way for true democracy to flourish in Pakistan.

The Jamāᶜat, however, asked the army and its leadership to act with "diligence and prudence" to implement the constitution which is based upon Islam, democracy and the principle of federation. It asked the army leadership not to allow the "Bhuttos and Sharifs who had set new records of corruption and fascism" to stage a comeback to power. Instead, the Jamāᶜat suggested for

> an interim setup, comprising of people who are not only faithful to Islam and Pakistan but who bear impeccable character and capability.... Through constitutional provisions, this setup should be given mandate and time enough to wipe out corruption of all past rulers, politicians and senior functionaries by conducting ruthless and above-board accountability; to reform the electoral system and its machinery so that free and fair elections could be held truly reflecting public opinion; and to rid the country of the feudals, capitalists and special interest mafias who have been devouring national resources like parasites. Moreover, the articles 62 and 63 of the constitution should be implemented. The *emergence of a capable, credible and sincere leadership from among the masses which is also accountable to them, presents the only solution to the country's problems (emphasis added).*[92]

5

SUMMARY AND CONCLUSION

The Jamā'at-e-Islāmī, in its British Indian phase, was not concerned with politics as the avenue for politicization was very much restricted. The post-Independence phase, however, was totally different. The vital principle of Pakistan to Quaid-e-Azam Muhammad Ali Jinnah was Islam, which he considered as "a realistic and practical code of conduct" for life. Pakistan was created for the Muslims who constituted a nation by any definition. However, the expectations of the Jamā'at for a sharī'ah-based Pakistan were rudely frustrated. The elite groups that successively ruled Pakistan had different perceptions about the role of Islam in the political process of Pakistan. Nevertheless, in the entire troubled history of Pakistan, rulers and politicians have declared the necessity of Islam in Pakistan.

The issue of Islam was vigorously debated during the period of "parliamentary democracy" (1947-1958) leading to the constitution of 1956 that made only a few symbolic concessions to Islam. The ruling elite, however, did not want the 'ulamā' to encroach on their monopoly of power and privilege. Consequently, the constitution was nullified by the military coup of 1958. The name Islamic Republic was dropped by General Ayub from the state nomenclature but was restored in 1963 under lengthy public debate over the issue. Almost all politicians and the military rulers, with a greater or lesser sincerity, vied with each other in proclaiming their devotion to Islam, often in a desire to legitimize their rule. Z.A. Bhutto, the authoritarian populist, did concede significant Islamic values during the last days of his rule. The devout Zia-ul-Huq continued the process of Islamization begun by his predecessor. He adopted a staunchly Islamic profile and instituted a number of reforms aimed at introducing Islam into the economics and politics of Pakistan. In May 1988, Zia was killed in a plane crash for which no official explanation has been provided. Since 1988, Pakistan has been operating an unstable political system run by civilians (alternating between Benazir Bhutto and Nawaz Sharif) whose Islamicity varied between secularism and a profession of moderate Islam. Thus Pakistan witnessed periods of uneasy democracy (1948-1958 and 1988 - October 1999) and long spells of military rule (from October 1958 to April 1971; from July 1977 to March 1988, and from October 1999 to the present). During the entire period of over half a century, successive regimes have tried in different ways to maintain a distance with the Islamic forces and to marginalise them by co-option if possible or by coercion if necessary.

During the entire troubled history of Pakistan, the Jamāʿat-e-Islāmī relentlessly pursued the cause of Islamization in Pakistan. All along it argued that since Islam is the main driving force for establishing Pakistan, it alone must rationalize the form of Pakistan's existence, permeate all its institutional arrangements, and define its code of social behaviour. It has succeeded in keeping the agenda of Islam in the forefront of the policy debates but in the process, the Jamāʿat has had to modify its policies several times and the organization itself has changed almost beyond recognition. Looking at the manner of transformation, it would be more accurate to say that the Jamāʿat evolved incrementally from a revolutionary ideological movement to an Islamic revolutionary movement.

THE TRANSFORMATION OF THE JAMĀʿAT

In the beginning, the Jamāʿat was an ideological revolutionary movement established to revive and preach Islam. Its aim was to implement Islam as a practical code of life for the Muslims. The activities of the Jamāʿat were not to be confined to one nation or country; it aimed at changing the moral, political, economic and social system of the whole world. It set a very high standard for its adherents to qualify as members. The Jamāʿat's emphasis was upon the purification of thought and social reforms. Politics received the lowest priority.

With the establishment of Pakistan, the Jamāᶜat subtly revised its mission and shifted its activities to Pakistan. Mawdudi argued that Pakistan was meant to be an Islamic state and hence it was incumbent upon all Muslims and in particular upon the Jamāᶜat to realize Islam in Pakistan. Organizationally, the Jamāᶜat functioned as a **pressure group**. Its energies were concentrated on social and educational work. It established small libraries, travelling dispensaries and educational institutions, and distributed Islamic literature for the religious training of the people. It organized public meetings, contacted members of the Constituent Assembly and mobilized strong public pressure to Islamize the government of Pakistan. At this stage, the aim was to reform the governing structures through lobbying and public pressure but certainly not through capture of power positions. Interestingly, the Jamāᶜat decided not to sponsor candidates but to support the righteous candidates contesting the elections from various platforms.

As a pressure group, the Jamāᶜat did achieve some of its objectives. It was nevertheless clear that the leaders of the newly created Pakistan were paying lip service to the idea of Islam in Pakistan. Consequently, the Jamā'at decided in 1954 at Machi Goth, to transform itself into a political party or **an Islamic political party**. Its aim was to work for the establishment of an Islamic government in Pakistan; hence it zeroed in on bringing about political change along Islamic lines. From then on, politics received preference over social and intellectual reforms. The most important goal of the Jamāᶜat became the replacement of the leadership of the wayward with those of the men of sterling character and piety. Sayyid Mawdudi, though he accorded primacy to politics, was not prepared to open the Jamāᶜat's membership to the general public. It was a party with carefully selected cadre members. It remained as a **cadre party** until Qazi Hussain Ahmad took over its leadership in 1983.

Between 1954 and 1992 the Jamāᶜat took part in all elections and participated in the **politics of alliance**. It joined the Combined Opposition Party in 1964, and the Pakistan National Alliance in 1977. For a time it joined the Zia regime as a junior partner but it clashed with him over the 1984 decision to ban student unions which included the student wing of the Jamaᶜat. The Jamāᶜat also formed part of the nine party alliance, Islami Jamhoori Ittehad (IJI), but soon distanced itself from it over differences in domestic and foreign policies. In 1993, the Jamāᶜat decided to contest the elections on its own and established the Pakistan Islamic Front to broaden its mass base. The election results were disappointing, since, according to the Jamāᶜat, the elections were neither free nor fair. This prompted the Jamāᶜat to boycott future elections, embark upon mass mobilization and membership drive, and carry out *jihād* to rid society of the feudal menace and restructure it along Islamic lines. In other words, the Jamāᶜat transformed itself into a **mass revolutionary movement.** Soon it mounted an anti-Nawaz Sharif government agitation which stopped only when the military staged a successful coup and ousted Nawaz Sharif from the post of Prime Minister. The transformation of the Jamāᶜat from an ideological movement through a pressure group to a political party and finally to a mass revolutionary movement is captured in Table 5.1.

It must be noted, however, that the transformation of the Jamāᶜat has been piecemeal and evolutionary. It is possible to identify several landmarks in the history of the Jamāᶜat. In 1941, it was formed as a **revivalist movement.** It became a **pressure group** in 1948. In 1954, in the aftermath of the famous Machi Goth Conference, it emerged as a **cadre party.** In 1993, the Jamāᶜat transformed itself into a **political party** via the formation of the Pakistan Islamic Front. In 1997, the Jamāᶜat boycotted the polls and vowed not to participate in elections till people are fully mobilized and the government is cleansed of all corrupt elements. Convinced of its successful membership drive, the Jamāᶜat mounted anti-government agitation which stopped with the military coup of October 12, 1999.

THE ELITE STRUCTURE AND THE TRANSFORMATION OF THE JAMĀᶜAT

It is also interesting that the transformation of the Jamāᶜat took place during the civilian era. Indeed, the impetus for these

Table 5.1
Transformation of the Jamāʿat-e-Islāmī

Period	Leader	Elite Composition	Regime Type	Nature of Organization
1941-47	Mawdudi	Ulama' dominant	Colonialism	Ideological Movement
1947-54	Mawdudi	Ulama dominant	Parliamentary Democracy	Pressure Group
1954-1958	Mawdudi	Ulama/Western educated	Parliamentary Democracy	Cadre Party
1958-1972	Mawdudi	Balanced	Military rule	Cadre Party
1972-1977	Mian Tufail	West dominant	Parliamentary rule	Cadre Party/Alliance
1977-1987	Mian Tufail	West dominant	Military rule	Cadre Party/Alliance
1987-1992	Qazi Hussain	Westernized	Parliamentary Democracy	Cadre Party/Alliance
1992-1997	Qazi Hussain	Westernized	Parliamentary Democracy	Mass-based Political Party
1997- Present	Qazi Hussain	Westernized	Parliamentary Democracy	Revolutionary Movement

organizational changes was provided by the long spell of military rule during which the Jamāʿat acted as a successful opposition movement. Additional reason for the transformation is to be found in its inability to muster enough votes or seats to capture power. In the 1970 elections, the Jamāʿat won not a single seat in the national legislature. In 1993, it won only three seats. The Jamāʿat's electoral performance was better when it took part in alliance politics but then it was obliged to act as a junior partner - a role which the Jamāʿat did not enjoy playing.

The transformation of the Jamāʿat is associated with both leadership and elite structure of the Jamāʿat itself. During the revivalist phase, the Jamāʿat was dominated by the ʿulamā'. The cadre party phase of the Jamāʿat was made possible only after the expulsion of a number of leading ʿulamā' from the decision making structure. The Jamāʿat embarked upon its mass politics phase only when the central consultative council of the Jamāʿat was under the control of the Western educated elite. Likewise, during the leadership of both Sayyid Mawdudi and Mian Tufail, the party remained more or less elite based. Sayyid Mawdudi, despite his insistence on political participation, refused to open the party membership to the masses and rigorously pursued the character development programme of the Jamāʿat members. Qazi Hussain Ahmad, with his Western education and business mentality and aided by Khurram Murad and others, is solely responsible for broadening the base of the Jamāʿat first through the Pakistan Islamic Front and later through the membership drive.

In its attempt to Islamize Pakistan, the Jamāʿat was forced to choose between two seeming incompatibles – principles and power. The Jamāʿat refused to recognize this incompatibility and struggled to capture power without sacrificing its principles. It embraced public discussion, press conferences, vote-getting, and parliamentary numbers, rather than terrorism, street violence, and dreams of a revolutionary putsch. Indeed, the Jamāʿat, by remaining faithful to its own principles and to these democratic procedures, failed to achieve governmental power. Its participation in electoral practice did leave an adverse effect on the moral behaviour of Jamā^cat members. The irony is that despite its toleration of unethical behaviour, or perhaps because of it on the part of some of its members during the election campaigns, the Jamā^cat failed to capture political power. This failure is also due to the fact that its opponents did not abide by the rules of democracy. They indulged in all kinds of corrupt practices. Time and again the Jamā^cat found itself outwitted, censored, beaten up, and jailed. The Jamā^cat nevertheless remained steadfast and continued its pursuit of power.

It is to the credit of the Jamā^cat that it did not abandon the democratic method temporarily to attain power by violence. It argues that a movement for democratic Islamic framework that resorts to despotic methods to achieve its goals would not remain an Islamic or a democratic movement for long. Its chosen means will devour its chosen ends. Consequently, the Jamā^cat embarked upon what it called an Islamic revolution through education and moral upliftment of the Pakistani society. It launched a mass mobilization programme, through peaceful means, to put pressure upon the government to purge itself of all corrupt elements and to conduct ethical elections as stipulated in the constitution of Pakistan.

THE FUTURE

The tangible result of the Jamā^cat's mass movement phase is yet to be seen. In the mean time, the Jamā^cat can make its demand much more compelling by enlisting rural support. This can be done through the articulation of a social mission for Islam. The Jamā^cat should take the traditional concept of *da^cwah* (call to Islam) seriously. Instead of confining *da^cwah* to unbelievers, it must make its central purpose the return of nominal Muslims to the true Islamic path. In addition to the obvious emphasis on education, a social welfare network of impressive proportions must be evolved as integral to this new sense of mission. Islamic hospitals and health clinics, housing cooperatives, and benevolent societies for widows and orphans should be established. Heavy emphasis upon *da^cwah* and welfare activities through various Jamā^cat-managed institutions like mosques, clinics and schools, would help alleviate the material and spiritual poverty of the masses, cultivate grassroots networks; attract followers to the cause, and challenge the inefficient, competing institutions of the state.

APPENDIX A

Our Programme: An Islamic Revolution[*]
Qazi Hussain Ahmed

Election 1997 and Jamāᶜat-e-Islāmī

Why did we not take part in the last elections? Why did we not make an alliance with another political party? And what did we gain from this boycott?

The answer to this question is that this was not an emotional decision, but a well contemplated one. We knew that the Islamic movement could face a situation when, compared to taking part in an election, a boycott would benefit them more. However, not to have taken part in the elections, certainly does not mean that we shall not contest elections in the future.

Taking part in the 1997 elections would, in our opinion have been, a total loss. Before that, we had tried our utmost to change the present electoral system, so that one group of looters may not replace another through elections. But the electoral system could not be changed, because the real power lay in the hands of the protectors of this system. In spite of our demand, Articles 62 & 63 of the constitution were not implemented. In other words, the way was paved for the nomination and election of the same corrupt people, who were directly responsible for the devastation of the country in the past. It was useless to participate in elections under these circumstances, and our doubts were proven correct. The same feudal lords and capitalists were once again elected in the February

---
[*] Source: *The Jang* (daily, Rawalpindi) August 27, 1997. Translated from Urdu by Abdul Rashid Moten.

1997 elections. Majority of those elected are devoid of honesty and trustworthiness. They have thoroughly plundered the nation's resources in the past, and continue to do so today. In our calculated opinion, these are the same people who have been responsible for all the miseries of Pakistan, since the past half-century. The nation can neither get out of this vortex of lawlessness, poverty and injustice, nor change the present, unjust and oppressive system, unless it gets rid of them.

The overwhelming majority of these people, who have formed the present government, belong to the same, selfish lot. We are absolutely sure that they cannot remove the imperfections of the present system. They cannot bring Pakistan out of the present crisis because honesty and integrity are not constituent elements of their brew. Nor can they establish an Islamic system. Pakistan, it must be noted, cannot get out of its present predicament without the establishment of an Islamic order. Let alone an Islamic system, these people are not even capable of establishing and running a western system which they represent.

Take *iḥtisāb* for example, which the present government used as a slogan to come to power. Can there be real accountability with Nawaz Sharif's present policy of accountability? He has altogether eliminated a complete era, 1985 to 1990, from the *iḥtisāb* Bill; whereas, most of the discrepancies had occurred during this period. The extent to which corruption was committed during that period had never been committed before. Who does not know who took how many loans, and how many of these were written-off?. There are complete records of this corruption with the State Bank and other banks. But this black era was whitened by Nawaz Sharif. In reality, there is darkness all around the present government, and its own dignitaries and patrons are involved in this wickedness. The Muslim League, which is equally involved in corruption, wants to escape accountability of the corruption.

A claim is being made, that the appeal against the [FSC's decision about the] abolishment of 'interest' from the economy, pending hearing at [Sharīʿah Appellate Bench of] the Supreme Court, was withdrawn. In reality, a fresh appeal has been made to the Sharīʿah Court to review its decision. This is also an act of fraudulence. What was actually required of them was to reverse their decision, instead of taking back the appeal. But they instead asked for a grace period to keep imposed a curse like interest, on the nation, for another two years. They believe they will get a period of another two years, but, with such acts as theirs, who knows whether they will get that chance at all.

During Zia-ul-Haq's era, there was deceit and deception for eleven years, under the guise of 'Interest-free Banking.' Then, another nine years passed with 'interest,' through lies and deception. Now, they want to pass another two years, through treachery, by lodging an appeal with the court to change its decision, but which is falsely being posed as taking back the appeal from the Appellate Bench. Does not Allah, clearly command, regarding 'interest,' that it amounts to declaration of war against Allah and His Prophet (s.a.w)? How can we make peace with those who are asking for a respite of two years to continue the war with Allah and the Prophet (s.a.w)?

Jamāʿat-e-Islāmī's Membership Drive (1997)
We had, in the past, made an alliance with the Muslim League, and went from door to door, asking for votes on their behalf, because we were promised that the Islamic system would be promulgated in the country; that there would be no subordination to the West; that there would be no 'interest in economy'; that there would be no friendship with India without first settling, the basic issues; that Kashmir shall be freed; that peace will be established in Afghanistan; that peace would be established within the country; and that justice would be provided to the people. But none of these promises were honoured. The Muslim League was not able to do anything. Therefore, we withdrew from the alliance

and purified our organisation. We have now organised our political
movement by ourselves. We now ask the people, from whom we
used to seek votes, to become members of the party which will
promulgate the Islamic system. In that decision alone, lies
salvation, yours, ours, and of the whole country. Our experience
shows that persons who have become members display a rapid
change. If they have changed, and if they realise that they have
joined a good organisation, then, *inshā Allāh*, no one will ever be
able to use them for propagation of evil. There are many good
people in our society, who were not with us in the past; we have
now gained access to them. We want them to join us because of
their inherent goodness and love for, and attachment to, Islam.
We are sure that if a majority of good people gather under the
banner of '*Lā ilāha illā Allāh Muḥammad al Rasūl Allāh,*' then,
the country will see true revolution, whose groundwork we have
already laid. Then, *inshā Allāh,* there will be sunshine all around,
and the clouds of darkness will remove themselves.

We had many pleasant experiences during this membership drive.
The people are open hearted. If they meet a true Muslim and a
patriot, they readily embrace him. Until today, they have been
deceived by the same claim. But now, they are beginning to
differentiate between the true and the fake claim. Indeed, our own
workers and activists are becoming motivated. According to reports
that we have collected regarding effects of the membership drive,
even the so-called 'dead' party-workers have risen and are
becoming active. Slowly and steadily, those who had given up all
hope are showing inclination for work. We have broken the
impasse; just as running water gets cleansed of its germs, so too,
with the movement of a caravan, its members overcome their
physical and spiritual problems.

Remedy for Despair
Admittedly, the people of Pakistan are, in general, victims of
despair. Those, who were fed up with the Peoples Party, are now

frustrated with the present government and the Muslim League. They could not get anything from the elections and are therefore, despairing about democracy and voting itself. They hold little hope of anything good arising from martial law or the military. We feel that this despair can only be removed by making contact with the public. Our workers will, *inshā Allāh*, establish offices of Jamā°at-e-Islāmī in every street. The public will be convinced that there is now only one way left to follow: 'the way of Islam', the way of Jamā°at-e-Islāmī. Critics say that the "Jamā°at-e-Islāmī is a small party, it cannot come to power." This notion should now be dispelled. When it has 5 million members, and an office in every street and neighbourhood, this false notion will disappear by itself. The light of hope will illuminate in the hearts of people. I am sure that within three or four months, this whole scene of frustration will change into one of hope and aspiration. I am sure that when Allah's blessings are with us, people will witness the change with their own eyes.

Those who want to rectify the situation through martial law, are mistaken. Martial Law will no longer be imposed once Jamā°at-e-Islāmī comes into power. And this concept of democracy, in which only feudal lords, capitalists and a special breed of cunning people succeed, will also vanish. When Jamā°at-e-Islāmī enters the halls of government, all doubts and fears will be dissipated. We will not cure disease with disease, nor terminate evil with evil. Our faith is: "No doubt, only good deeds can end evil." (al-Qur'ān). We would not want and will not let martial law to be imposed again or to have capitalists and feudal lords debase it again, in the name of democracy. We will, *inshā Allāh*, try to avoid that.

Bloody Revolution or An Islamic Revolution?
When people become frustrated, without thinking, they say that the only remedy for the country is 'a bloody revolution.' This is a dangerous mood. We must make the people realise that resorting to bloody revolution would be inviting a new catastrophe. Blood

is already cheap in Pakistan; there is bloodshed every day. Has this bloodshed brought about a revolution? If there were blood flowing all around, what kind of revolution would come about? The concept of a bloody revolution is inhuman and not Islamic. There is only one way to cause an Islamic revolution, and that is, to start a movement which has a predetermined objective, and a predetermined leadership. When the people rise in accord with an Islamic ideology and leadership, definitely no one can stop such a movement. If someone does try to oppose it, he will not be able to confront it. If an attempt is still made to create unrest, then people will not hesitate, even if it means sacrifing their lives. Changes are brought about by sacrifices, not through bloodshed. When four of our men were martyred last year (June 1996), all of Pakistan witnessed how big a change that brought about. It resulted in a movement against the government of the Peoples' Party, a clash we had tried to avoid. In spite of the government's provocation, our men avoided resorting to violence. Although the government had unwittingly created an opportunity for violence, we chose peace.

Nowadays, there is a need to create awareness among the people as to how to elect an honest leadership. After accepting such a leadership, and under its guidance, a journey on the path of change, through peaceful means, will become easy. Jamāᶜat-e-Islāmī, after completing its target membership of 5 million, can easily guide the people in this direction. When people rise from every street, neighbourhood, city and town, this dilapidated system will automatically crumble and give way. We have to tell the people which leadership can take care of the country and which cannot. Even the greatest of evil forces surrenders, when confronted with mass awareness. The present system will also give way. If it does not, it will be compelled to do so under subjugation.

The 'Objectives Resolution' is part of the constitution of Pakistan. This Resolution which lays a good foundation, holds the potential of an enormous change within itself. During the half-century history of Pakistan, because of the struggles and demands of the Islamic movement, a lot of positive changes have already taken place. Islam has become a compulsory subject in the schools. No one now has enough courage to steer the country towards a secular path. 'Motivation cells' have been established in sensitive institutions and a fairly large amount of work, on Islamic teachings, has been carried out. However, lot more needs to be done in this respect.

The system of the armed forces also needs to be changed just like the other organs of the government. It is a remnant of the era of subjugation, and needs to be changed in a manner befitting Pakistan's Armed Force's motto of faith, piety and *Jihād fī sabīl Allāh*. Laws and the constitution need to be amended. The recommendations prepared by the Council of Islamic Ideology provide sufficient Islamic basis, to bring about the changes in the judicial system. In the presence of the constitution, moulding the entire legal framework into an Islamic structure is not difficult any more.

Such institutions as the Judiciary and the Council of Islamic Ideology are there to remove any confusion. The Council of Islamic Ideology can be reorganised, so that 'ulamā', jurists and scholars rise above compromises, ... have a true concept of *dīn*, ... are pious, content and able to pass judgement. The Council of Islamic Ideology thus has a very important and basic role to play. Once it has been restructured, people will have faith in it and realise that they are being guided in the right direction. We have to convince the people that a 'bloody revolution' is a path leading to destruction and the 'Islamic Revolution' is the path ensuring true change and deliverance.

Our Defence In Our Hands
The country is richly endowed with resources, but these are being wasted either through corruption or being transferred abroad.

Economic devastation has crossed the limits. But it will be very wrong if, instead of ending corruption, an attempt is made to reduce defence spending. We do not want our defence to be weakened. We want to make the state strong. Strengthening of the defence and the capabilities of the armed forces is a requirement of our faith and belief. Especially now when disguised capitalist NGOs and multinationals are active all around, its importance has increased even more. If we reduce our defence budget or weaken the defence of our country because others have demanded so, we would not be able to maintain our independence. Even allowing such a thought is extremely foolish. This is akin to handing over the government to the Jews and other anti-Islamic powers. We should not let international financial agencies to gain free control of our internal, external and defence projects. We believe that these so-called NGOs and the multinationals should not be allowed to wander about unchecked. We want the state to have assured superiority over all its affairs and organs. If it is being alleged that western powers want to control the freedom of Pakistan, it is because of the direct and indirect interference by the international colonialist powers, under the guise of private investment. We believe in proper rules and regulations for international investment that would protect national security and dignity. Just as we are against securing foreign loans, we are against allowing any foreign investor to have the right of making important decisions in our country.

Improvement of the Economy
When Jamā'at-e-Islāmī comes to power, improvement of the economy will be one of its first priorities. To begin with, we will bring back the plundered wealth. We shall then organise a moral education of the administration and the bureaucracy so that they will consider themselves caretakers and guardians of the national and state wealth and not the owners and inheritors. We will make education common so that every person in society understands consciously the meaning of trusteeship and trustworthiness. The difference between us and communists is that they take financial

and material matters as the prime root of the problem whereas we take educational and moral aspects as the most important factors. In our view only better education and training in good moral behaviour can correct the system at large permanently. We will, *inshā Allāh*, try to reform the mass media and educational institutions. In this modern era, the importance of the mass media has substantially increased for the propagation and improvement of education. A complete reform of the educational structure is a permanent component of our program. Teaching staff will be organised in such a manner that they could educate the students in the best possible way. For this purpose, both long and short term programs will be planned.

National training and moral development, in our opinion, is a continuous process. By augmenting an atmosphere of morality, benevolence and honesty will flourish. For this to happen, it is essential that the rulers present themselves as models of austerity and honesty, and bring their standard of living down to that of the average citizen. By doing so, the rat-race of trying to become rich overnight will end by itself, and a culture based on brotherhood and co-operation will be established. Instead of competing in the construction of palaces, people will try to excel each other in morality and character. The simple living standards of the rulers will be presented to the public through the media, and that would be a model which everyone will be required to follow. Through articles, magazines, newspapers and other means of communications, the thinking mode of the citizens will be moulded so that they prefer to live simple lives.

We will give incentives to the people for the improvement of the economy, and in this context, the basic, underlying theme will be good conduct and honesty. The fire of sectarianism in which the nation is burning nowadays can only be extinguished by the enforcement of the law of brotherhood. The holy Qur'ān has declared the 'wealth' of fraternity a 'gift from Allah.' We will make this gift available to everyone.

Boosting industrial and agricultural production is one of our main
targets for strengthening the security of the country and the ummah.
This task is possible only through the spirit of continuous struggle.
Trade with Islamic countries will be expanded; this will give stability
and strength to the ummah. We will increase productivity in a
manner that would fulfil the needs of the Muslim nations, and also
help our own national requirements.

A Model Pakistan
Progress and development is an integral part of the model for
Pakistan, which we hold in our imagination. Nations prosper with
the prosperity of their people. We want to give the 130 million
Pakistanis equal access to national resources. The elitist groups
will not be able to exploit the weak and poor people. Everyone
will have equal opportunities for progress. Love and co-operation
will be used, instead of hate and revenge, in the distribution of
rights. Imagine a Pakistan in which, instead of the dominance of a
few hundred big industrialists, businessmen and capitalists, tens
of millions of people will be owners of industries and partners in
the development of trade, agriculture and other sectors.

Imagine that ideal Pakistan, where the child of every poor person
would be educated at the best possible educational institutions,
where a poor labourer will have access to modern medical facilities,
and where there will be no discrimination between a top boss and
a junior functionary. The President and the Prime Minister of the
country will also live in ordinary houses, where there will not be
an army of servants. The members of these households will do
their work themselves. *Alḥamdulillāh,* workers of the Jamāʿat-e-
Islāmī are already living such lives. For them, keeping this standard
of living, even after reaching high offices, will not be difficult.

The assumption that we will deprive people of healthy
entertainment and enjoyment is also not correct. In fact, we would

want the whole society to become a house of happiness and delight. Our style of sports will also be unique. Separate playgrounds for children and women will be constructed. Men will have their own sports complexes. Our model is such that even in play the spirit of gentleness, co-operation and brotherhood should prevail.

We intend to construct model villages. People will be encouraged to establish these exemplary towns in such a way that they would be envied by the big cities. *Inshā Allāh*, we will plan these model towns even better than Europe and America. Our exemplary towns will later become models, which the whole world would want to replicate. We will seek to prevent in our towns those problems, which are very common all over the world. They will also have all those amenities which can be found in any of the most advanced, modern, welfare societies.

The foundation of our society will be laid, not on enmity or revenge, but on love and sincerity. If someone believes that heads will be raised on lances, and hands and feet will be amputated, then he had better change his convictions. We have the courage and ability to forgive our worst enemies. We have the example of our beloved Prophet (s.a.w) before us. He ordered general amnesty, when he conquered Makkah, and even pardoned all the past crimes of his worst enemies, and adopted an attitude of mercy towards them. When we enter this new era, we will try to avoid all sorts of retaliatory actions, though all looted wealth will definitely be taken back from the embezzlers. For this purpose, the system of reward and punishment, which Islam has given us, will guide us to make the right decisions.

APPENDIX B

Articles 62 and 63 of the Constitution of Pakistan·

62.   A person shall not be qualified to be elected or chosen as a member of Majlis-e-Shoora (Parliament) unless:

    a.   he is a citizen of Pakistan;

    b.   he is, in the case of National Assembly, not less than twenty-five years of age and is enrolled as a voter in any electoral roll for election to a Muslim seat or a non-Muslim seat as the case may be in that Assembly;

    c.   he is, in the case of Senate, not less than thirty years of age and is enrolled as a voter in any area in the Province or, as the case may be, the Federal Capital or the Federally Administered Tribal Areas, from where he seeks membership;

    d.   he is of good character and is not commonly known as one who violates Islamic injunction;

    e.   he has adequate knowledge of Islamic teachings and practises obligatory duties prescribed by Islam as well as abstains from major sins;

    f.   he is sagacious, righteous and non-profligate, honest and ameen;

    g.   he has not been convicted for a crime involving moral turpitude or for giving false evidence;

    h.   he has not, after the establishment of Pakistan, worked against the integrity of the country or opposed the Ideology of Pakistan.

---

*Source: *The Constitution of the Islamic Republic of Pakistan* (Islamabad: Ministry of Law, Justice and Parliamentary Affairs, 1990), 43-48.

Provided that the disqualifications specified in paragraphs
(d) and (e) shall not apply to a person who is a non-Muslim,
but such a person shall have good moral reputation; and

i.   he possesses such other qualifications as may be
      prescribed by Act of Majlis-e-Shoora (Parliament).

63. (1). A person shall be disqualified from being elected or
     chosen as, and from being, a member of the Majlis-e-Shoora
     (Parliament), if:

a.   he is of unsound mind and has been so declared by a
      competent court; or
b.   he is an undischarged insolvent; or
c.   he ceases to be a citizen of Pakistan, or has acquired
      the citizenship of a foreign State; or
d.   he holds an office of profit in the service of Pakistan
      other than an office declared by law not to disqualify
      its holder; or
e.   he is in the service of any statutory body or any body
      which is owned or controlled by the Government or in
      which the Government has a controlling share or
      interest; or
f.   being a citizen of Pakistan by virtue of section 14B of
      the Pakistan Citizenship Act, 1951 (II of 1951), he is
      for the time being disqualified under any law in force
      in Azad Jammu and Kashmir from being elected as a
      member of the Legislative Assembly of Azad Jammu
      and Kashmir; or
g.   he is propagating any opinion, or acting in any manner,
      prejudicial to the Ideology of Pakistan, or the
      sovereignty, integrity or security of Pakistan, or
      morality, or the maintenance of public order, or the
      integrity or independence of the judiciary of Pakistan,
      or which defames or brings into ridicule the judiciary
      or the Armed Forces of Pakistan; or
h.   he has been, on conviction for any offence which in
      the opinion of the Chief Election Commissioner

involves moral turpitude, sentenced to imprisonment for a term of not less than two years, unless a period of five years has elapsed since his release; or

i.   he has been dismissed from the service of Pakistan on the ground of misconduct, unless a period of five years has elapsed since his dismissal; or

j.   he has been removed or compulsorily retired from the service of Pakistan on the ground of misconduct unless a period of three years has elapsed since his removal or compulsory retirement; or

k.   he has been in the service of Pakistan or of any statutory body or any body which is owned or controlled by the Government or in which the Government has a controlling share or interest, unless a period of two years has elapsed since he ceased to be in such service; or

l.   he is found guilty of a corrupt or illegal practice under any law in force, at that time unless a period of five years has elapsed from the date on which that order takes effect; or

m.   he has been convicted under section 7 of the Political Parties Act, 1962 (III of 1962), unless a period of five years has elapsed from the date of such conviction; or

n.   he, whether by himself or through any person or body of persons in trust for him or for his benefit or on his account or as a member of a Hindu undivided family, has any share or interest in a contract, not being a contract between a cooperative society and Government, for the supply of goods to, or for the execution of any contract or for the performance of any service undertaken by the Government:

Provided that the disqualification under this paragraph shall not apply to a person:

i.   where the share or interest in the contract devolves on him by inheritance or succession or as a legatee,

executor or administrator, until the expiration of
six months after it has so devolved on him; or

ii. where the contract has been entered into by or on
behalf of a public company as defined in the
Companies Ordinance, 1984 (XLVII of 1984), of
which he is a share – holder but is not a director
holding an office of profit under the company; or

iii. where he is a member of a Hindu undivided family
and the contract has been entered into by any other
member of that family in the course of carrying on
a separate business in which he has no share or
interest; or

Explanation - In this Article "goods" does not include
agricultural produce or commodity grown or produced
by him or such goods as he is, under any directive of
Government or any law for the time being in force,
under a duty or obligation to supply.

o. he holds any office of profit in the service of Pakistan
other than the following offices, namely:

i. an office which is not full time, remunerated either
by salary or by fee;

ii. the office of Lumbardar, whether called by this or
any other title;

iii. the Qaumi Razakars;

iv. any office the holder whereof, by virtue of such
office, is liable to be called up for military training
or military service under any law providing for the
constitution or raising of a Force; or

p. he has for the time being been disqualified from being
elected or chosen as a member of the Majlis-e-Shoora
(Parliament) or of a Provincial Assembly under any law
in force at that time.

(2) If any question arises whether a member of the Majlis-e-
     Shoora (Parliament) has become disqualified from being a
     member, the Speaker or, as the case may be, the Chairman
     shall refer the question to the Chief Election Commissioner
     and if the Chief Election Commissioner is of the opinion
     that the member has become disqualified, he shall cease to
     be a member and his seat shall become vacant.

NOTES

I Introduction: A Framework to Analysis

1. According to Sharabi, Islam had survived in three main forms: in the instinctive belief of the common man, in the self-image of the urban Muslim, and in "the shape of the moulds in which thought and evaluations are cast." Hisham Sharabi, "Islam and modernization in the Arab World" in J.H. Thompson and R. D. Reischauer (eds.), *Modernization of the Arab World* (New York: D. Van Nostrand Company, Inc., 1966), 26-27.

2. Yusuf ibn Abd al-Barr al-Qurtubi, *Jāmiʿ Bayān al-ʿIlm wa Faḍluh* (Madinah: al-Maktabah al-ʿIlmiyah, n.d.), Vol. I, 62.

3. Ibn Qutaybah, *ʿUyūn al-Akhbār,* Vol. I in Bernard Lewis (ed.), *Islam: From the Prophet Muhammad to the Capture of Constantinople* (London: The Macmillan Press, Ltd., 1976), Vol. I, 184.

4. G.H. Jansen, *Militant Islam* (London: Pan Books, 1979), 17.

5. Sir Muhammad Iqbal, *The Reconstruction of Religious Thought in Islam* (Lahore: Sh. Muhammad Ashraf, 1971), 154.

6. For a discussion of the transformation of the ideal caliphate into the dynastic rule, see Abul Aʿla Mawdudi, *Khilāfat wa Mulūkiyat* (Caliphate and the Dynastic Rule) (Lahore: Idarah Tarjuman al-Qurʾān, 1975).

7. However, under the Delhi Sultan Firuz Tughlaq (1351-1388) and the Mughal emperor Awrangzeb (1658-1707), the administration was run on the basis of sharīʿah. Tughlaq was a religious person. "Until Aurangzeb, in fact, no other ruler made such a serious endeavour to champion orthodoxy as a guide for the state." S.M. Ikram, *Muslim Civilization in India* (New York: Oxford University Press, 1964), 74.

8. Khurshid Ahmad, "The Nature of Islamic Resurgence" in John L. Esposito ed., *Voices of Resurgent Islam* (New York: Oxford University Press, 1983), 219-20.

9. *Tajdīd* means renewal, an effort to regenerate the authentic Islamic spirit, to return to the fundamental principles of Islam as found in the Qurʾān and the Sunnah.

10. *New York Times,* June 22, 1992.

11. *Washington Times,* January 17, 1995.

12. Bernard Lewis, "The Roots of Muslim Rage," *Atlantic Monthly,* September 1990, 47-60.

13. Ibid., 59.

14. Judith Miller, "The Challenge of Radical Islam," *Foreign Affairs,* Vol. 72, No. 2, 1993, 45.

15 Samuel P. Huntington, "The Clash of Civilizations?," *Foreign Affairs,* Vol. 72, No. 3, 1993, 22-49.

16 Ibid., 25.

17 See John L. Esposito, *The Islamic Threat: Myth or Reality?* (Oxford: Oxford University Press, 1992).

18 Peter Rodman, "Islam and Democracy," *National Review,* May 11, 1992, 28-29.

19 Judith Miller, "The Challenge of Radical Islam," 55.

20 Samuel Huntington, "The Clash of Civilizations?," 47.

21 Daniel Pipes, "An Islamic International," *Forward,* July 22, 1994, 7.

22 Thomas Lippman, *The Washington Post,* December 28, 1994.

23 Robin Wright, "Islam, Democracy and the West," *Foreign Affairs,* Vol. 71, No. 3, 1992, 131-145.

24 Leon Hadar, "What Green Peril?," *Foreign Affairs,* Vol. 72, No. 3, 1993, 27-42.

25 John Esposito, "Political Islam: Beyond the Green Menace," *Current History,* January 1994, 19-24.

26 Mawdudi wrote to a convert: "...Whatever I have done, I have always done it openly within the boundaries of law and existing constitution, so much that I have never violated even those laws which I have fought hard to oppose. I have tried to change them through lawful and constitutional means and never adopted the path of violation of the law." *Nawa-i-Waqt,* November 10, 1963 quoted in Maryam Jameelah, *Islam in Theory and Practice* (Lahore: Mohammad Yusuf Khan & Sons, 1978), 334.

27 Abul A°la Mawdudi, *Islamic Law and Constitution* tr. & ed., Khurshid Ahmad (Lahore: Islamic Publications, Ltd., 1967), 101.

28 Abul A°la Mawdudi, *Jamāʿat-e-Islāmī: Tārikh, Maqṣad, Awr Lāiheh-e-ʿAmal* (Jamāʿat-e-Islāmī: History, Aims, and Plan of Action) (Lahore: Islamic Publications, 1963), 205.

29 Abul A°la Mawdudi, *Come Let Us Change the World* tr. Kaukab Siddique (Washington: The Islamic Party of North America, 1972), 143.

30 Vilfred Pareto, *The Mind and Society* (London: Jonathan Cape,1935); *Vilfred Pareto: Sociological Writings*, selected and introduced by S.E. Finer, translated by Derich Mirfin (New York: Praeger, 1966); Gaetano Mosca, *The Ruling Class* ed., Arthur Livingston (New York: McGraw Hill, 1939); Robert Michels, Political Parties tr., Eden and Cedar Paul (New York: Collier Books, 1962); Harold D. Lasswell, Daniel Lerner and C.E. Rothwell, *The Comparative Study of Elites* (Stanford: Hoover Insatitute, 1951); C. Wright Mills, *The Power Elite* (New York: Oxford University Press, 1956); Robert Dahl, *Who Governs?* (New Haven: Yale University Press, 1961).

[31] Michels, *Political Parties*, 389-90.

[32] Lasswell et. al., *The Comparative Study of Elites*, 7.

[33] Mills, *The Power Elite*; also G. William Domhoff and H.B. Ballard eds., *C. Wright Mills and the Power Elite* (Boston: Beacon Press,1968).

[34] Quoted in Haroon Khan Sherwani, *Studies in Muslim Political Thought and Administration* (Lahore: Sh. Muhammad Ashraf, 1970), 72-73.

[35] See Muhammad Qamaruddin Khan, "Al-Mawardi" in M. M. Sharif ed., *A History of Muslim Philosophy* (Delhi: Low Price Publications, 1995), Vol. I, 717-731.

[36] See L. Binder, "Al-Ghazali's Theory of Islamic Government," *The Muslim World*, Vol. 95, No. 3 (1955); also Erwin I.J. Rosenthal, *Political Thought in Medieval Islam: An Introductory Outline* (Cambridge: The University Press, 1968), 38-43.

[37] Sayyid Abul A'la Mawdudi, *The Islamic Movement: Dynamics of Values, Power and Change*, ed., Khurram Murad (Leicester: The Islamic Foundation, 1984), 77.

[38] Hadith quoted in Ibid., 84.

[39] See, among others, J.O. Morris, Elites, *Intellectuals and Consensus: A Study of the Origins of the Industrial Relations Systems in Chile, 1900-1938* (Ithaca, New York: Cornell University Press, 1966); C. Wright Mills, *The Power Elite*; H.D. Lasswell and D. Lerner eds., *World Revolutionary Elites* (Cambridge, Mass.: Cambridge University Press, 1966); Abdul Rashid Moten, "Political Elites and Political Instability in Pakistan" (Unpublished Ph.D. Thesis, Department of Political Science, The University of Alberta, Canada, 1982).

[40] Edmund Leach and S.N. Mukherjee eds., *Elites in South Asia* (Cambridge, Mass: The University Press, 1970), x.

[41] Harold Lasswell, *Politics: Who Gets What, When, How?* (New York: Peter Smith, 1950), 3.

[42] Field and Higley, *Elites in Developed Societies: A Theoretical Reflection on an Initial Stage in Norway* (Beverly Hills: Sage Publications, 1972), 9-10.

[43] See Richard L. Merritt, *Systematic Approaches to Comparative Politics* (Chicago: Rand McNally & Co., 1970), 104-40.

2 Socio-Political Environmental and the Jamā'at

[1] See Mumtaz Ahmad, "Islamic Fundamentalism in South Asia: The Jamaat-i-Islami and the Tablighi Jamaat" in Martin E. Marty and R. Scott Appleby, eds., *Fundamentalisms Observed* (Chicago: University of Chicago Press, 1991), 457-530; Rafiuddin Ahmed, "Redefining Muslim Identity in South Asia: The Transformation of the Jamaat-i-Islami" in Martin E. Marty and

R. Scott Appleby, eds., *Accounting for Fundamentalisms: The Dynamic Character of Movements* (Chicago: University of Chicago Press, 1994), 699-705; Seyyed Vali Reza Nasr, *The Vanguard of the Islamic Revolution: The Jamāᶜat-i-Islāmī of Pakistan* (Berkeley: University of California Press, 1994).

2   *Wathā'iq-e-Mawdudi* (Mawdudi's Documents) (Lahore: Islamic Research Academy, 1984), 97.

3   Ibid.

4   Sayyid Mawdudi's elder brother Abul Kahir Mawdudi's statement in weekly *Ain* (Lahore), October 17, 1968.

5   For certificates see *Wathā'iq-e-Mawdudi*, 11-14.

6   Asim Nu'mani (compiled), *Makāteeb Sayyid Abul Aᶜla Mawdudi* (Writings of Mawdudi)(Lahore: Islamic Publications, 1981), 312.

7   Muhammad Yusuf Buhtah, *Mawlana Mawdudi Apnī aur Doosron kī Nazar Mein* (Mawlana Mawdudi as seen by himself and others) (Lahore: Idarah Ma'arif-e-Islami, 1980), 39.

8   *Wathā'iq-e-Mawdudi*, 18.

9   S. Zakir Aijaz tr., *Selected Speeches and Writings of Mawlana Mawdudi* (Karachi: International Islamic Publications, 1982), Vol. II, 1-2.

10 Khurshid Ahmad, "Mawdudi's model for Islamic Revival," *Al-Ittihad*, Vol. 15, No. 4, October 1978, 45-64.

11 S. Zakir Aijaz tr., *Selected Speeches and Writings of Mawlana Mawdudi*, 1-2.

12 See Abdul Rashid Moten, *Islam and Revolution: Contributions of Sayyid Mawdudi* (Kano: Bureau for Islamic Propagation, 1988).

13 Sayyid Abul Aᶜla Mawdudi, *Jamāᶜat-e-Islāmī ke 29 Sāl* (Twenty Years of Jamāᶜat-e-Islāmī) (Lahore: Jamāᶜat-e-Islāmī, 1976), 25.

14 Abul Aᶜla Mawdudi, *Musalmān aur Mawjūdah Siyāsī Kashmakash* (Muslims and the Current Political Crisis) (Lahore: Shuᶜbah-e-Nashr wa Ishaᶜat-e-Jamāᶜat-e-Islāmī, Pakistan, 1970).

15 Ishtiaq Husain Qureshi, *Ulema in Politics* (Karachi: Ma'arif Limited, 1972), 339, 351.

16 ᶜAllāmah Muhammad Iqbal, the son of a tailor, was from a respectable lower middle class family in the Punjab. His Kashmiri forefathers had recently converted from Hinduism. As a mature student he arrived in Cambridge in 1905 and went on to complete his Ph.D. at Heidelberg. He died in 1938.

17 Khalid Bin Sayeed, *Pakistan: The Formative Phase, 1857-1948* (London: Oxford University Press, 1972), 103-104.

[18] Interestingly, in the late 1930s, Sayyid Mawdudi was also critical of the Indian National Congress and argued that Muslims and Hindus formed two distinct and separate entities. He also proposed a federation of nations in which the federating nations would be represented in the central government of India according to their proportion in the total population. Mawdudi's alternative proposal was to allocate to each nation a specific territory with a provision made for a transfer of populations over a 25-year period. See Mawdudi, *Musalmān awr Mawjūdah Siyāsī Kashmakash*, Vol II, 206-19.

[19] Muhammad Ali Jinnah, referred to as the "Quaid-e-Azam" (the Great Leader), was born in Karachi to a Khoja family. He went to London for his studies and was called to the bar in 1896 at Lincoln's Inn. It is said that Jinnah chose Lincoln's Inn because he saw the name of Prophet Muhammad (s.a.w) at the entrance. Already a member of the Indian National Congress, *Jinnah* also joined the Muslim League in 1913 to bring about co-operation between the two organizations. He broke away from the Congress in 1920 but continued to work for Hindu-Muslim unity in which he failed miserably. Accordingly, Jinnah came to espouse the Two Nation Theory and eventually sponsored the Lahore Resolution of 1940. He was the President of the All India Muslim League, in 1916, 1920, and 1934-1948. He was the Governor General and the President of the Constituent Assembly of Pakistan. He died on September 11, 1948. For a perceptive account of Jinnah's heroic achievement and his human face, see Akbar S. Ahmed, *Jinnah, Pakistan and Islamic Identity: The Search for Saladin* (London: Routledge, 1997).

[20] Jamil-ud-Din Ahmad ed., *Some Recent Speeches and Writings of Mr. Jinnah* (Lahore: Mohammad Ashraf, 1947), Vol. I, 178, 180.

[21] For details, see Khalid Bin Sayeed, *Pakistan: The Formative Phase.*

[22] Sayyid Abul A'la Mawdudi, "Ham ne Taḥrīk-e-Pakistan kā Sāth Nahin Diyā Thā" (We did not support the Pakistan Movement), *Nawa-e-Waqt*, August 15, 1973, 3.

[23] Leonard Binder, *Religion and Politics in Pakistan* (Berkeley: University of California Press, 1961), 94.

[24] Government of Pakistan, *Report of the Court of Enquiry Constituted Under Punjab Act II of 1954 to Enquire Into the Punjab Disturbances of 1953* (Lahore: Superintendent Government Printing, 1954), 255. This is popularly known as the Munir Report.

[25] °Allamah Shabbir Ahmad Uthmani, *Paighām* (Message) (Lahore: Hashimi Book Depot, 1945), 12-25.

[26] Mawdudi, *Jamā'at-e-Islāmī Ke 29 Sāl*, 22-23.

27 See Mawdudi, *Tanqiḥāt* (Inquiries) (Pathankot: Maktabah Jamaᶜat-e-Islami, 1939).

28 Mawdudi, *Jamāᶜat-e-Islāmī Ke 29 Sāl*, fn.1, 24.

29 Liaquat Ali Khan, referred to as the Quaid-e-Millat (leader of the nation), was born in Karnal, Punjab, in 1896. Son of a landlord, he was educated at Aligarh, Allahabad, and Exeter College, Oxford. He chose law as his profession and was called to the Bar in the Inner Temple in 1922. He was very close to Muhammad Ali Jinnah and was appointed as general secretary of the Muslim League in 1936. After a brilliant public career, he became the first prime minister of Pakistan in 1947. He was felled by an assassin's bullet in Rawalpindi on October 16, 1951.

30 W.C. Smith, *Islam in Modern History* (Princeton: Princeton University Press, 1959), 226.

31 For details on the "Views of the Board of Taᶜlimāt-I Islāmīyah," see Leonard Binder, *Religion and Politics in Pakistan*,155-182; 383-429. Mawlana Sayyid Suleiman Nadvi and Mawlana Zafar Ahmad Ansari were respectively the president and secretary of the Board. Among its members were Mawlana Shabbir Ahmad Usmani and Mufti Mohammad Shafi.

32 Abul Aᶜla Mawdudi, *Islamic Law and Constitution tr. & ed.* Khurshid Ahmad (Lahore: Islamic Publications Ltd., 1967), 20.

33 Government of Pakistan, *Report of the Court of Inquiry Constituted Under Punjab Act 11 of 1954 to Enquire Into the Punjab Disturbances of 1953*, 210.

34 Ibid., 231-32.

35 Constituent Assembly of Pakistan *Debates*, Jan. 31, 1956. Vol.I, 2231.

36 Sayyid Abul Aᶜla Mawdudi, *Process of Islamic Revolution* (Delhi: Markazi Maktabah Jamāᶜat-e-Islāmī, Hind, 1970), 9.

37 Mawdudi, *Islamic Law and Constitution*, 235.

38 Ibid., 239.

39 In terms of legislation, Mawdudi makes a distinction between that part of the sharīᶜah which has a permanent and unalterable character and that which is flexible. The former comprised (a) the laws derived from Qur'ān and Sunnah like the prohibition of alcoholic drinks, interest and gambling; (b) the directive principles such as prohibitions of use of intoxicants in general, of all transactions not entered freely by both parties, and the principle that men are protectors and in charge of women; and (c) the limitation in the number of wives, of divorces and in the amount of inheritance. The flexible part which is very wide is subject to modification according to the needs and requirements of the changing circumstances. This flexible part is the result of the application of *ta 'wīl* (interpretation),

qiyās (analogous deduction), *ijtihād* (disciplined judgement of jurists) and *istiḥsān* (juristic preference). But these four types of legislation can be exercised by persons well-qualified in Islamic law and within limits prescribed by Islam. See Ibid., 60-62.

40 Ibid., 148.

41 Pakistan, according to the Census of 1961, had a population of about 93.8 million compared to 72.99 million in 1951. The growth rate was estimated at 2.2 percent per annum. The greater part of the population, 54.3 percent, lived in East Pakistan and 45.7 percent in West Pakistan. In the latter, the Punjab contained the largest concentration of the population (about 60 percent of West Pakistan's population in 1961). Punjab exerted the greatest degree of social, economic and political influence in the country. See Abdul Rashid Moten, "Political Elites and Political Instability in Pakistan" (Unpublished Ph.D. thesis, Department of Political Science, The University of Alberta, Canada, 1982), ch. II.

42 Jamil-ud-Din Ahmad ed., *Some Recent Speeches and Writings of Mr. Jinnah*, Vol. II, 393.

43 The Constituent Assembly of Pakistan *Debates*, Feb. 24, 1948, Vol. II, No. 1, 7.

44 See Abdul Rashid Moten, "Political Elites and Political Instability in Pakistan," 97; also *The Azad* (Dacca) March 31, 1954.

45 K. B. Sayeed, "The Jamaᶜat-e-Islami Movement in Pakistan," *Pacific Affairs*, Vol. 30, No. 2, 1957, 64.

46 Abul Aᶜla Mawdudi, *Come Let Us Change the World, tr. Kaukab Siddique* (Washington: The Islamic Party of North America, 1972), 143.

47 *Quaid-i-Azam Mohammad Ali Jinnah: Speeches as Governor-General of Pakistan (1947-48)* (n.p., June 1963), 21.

48 Ibid., 154.

49 Ibid., 16, 19, 30, 61.

50 Ibid., 65.

51 Quoted in W.S. Metz, *Pakistan: Government and Politics* (New Haven, Conn.: Human Relations Area Files Inc., 1956), 10.

52 For his presidential address, see The Constituent Assembly of Pakistan *Debates* (Karachi: Government of Pakistan, August 1947), Vol. 1, No. 2, 20.

53 Ibid.

54 The Constituent Assembly of Pakistan *Debates* (Karachi: Government of Pakistan, 1949), Vol. 5, No. 1, 2.

55 Ibid., 4.

56 Ibid., Vol. 5, No. 3, 62.

[57] Ibid., Vol. 5, No. 1, 7.

[58] S. *Zakir Aijaz tr., Selected Speeches and Writings of Mawlana Mawdudi*, (Karachi: International Islamic Publications, 1982), Vol. I , 70.

[59] W.C. Smith, *Islam in Modern History* (Princeton: Princeton University Press, 1959), 226, 231.

[60] Asaf Hussain, *Elite Politics in an Ideological State: The Case of Pakistan* (England: William Dawson & Sons, 1979), 83.

[61] See Moten, "Political Elites and Political Instability in Pakistan," ch. III.

[62] One of the cardinal principles of Islam has been the finality of Prophet Muhammad (s.a.w) and the Qur'ān. The proclamation of Mirza Ghulam Ahmad as the Messiah puts him outside the fold of Islam. Allamah Iqbal considered Ahmadis not only non-Muslims but rather a great danger to Islam on account of their splitting the solidarity of the Muslim ummah. See Muhammad Iqbal, *Islam and Ahmadism* (Lahore: Anjuman-e-Khuddam al-Din, n.d.). Mawlana Mawdudi was also very vehement in his condemnation of Ahmadism and Ahmadis. See S. Abul A'la Maududi, *The Qadiani Problem* (Lahore: Islamic Publications Ltd., 1979).

[63] Government of Pakistan, *Report of the Court of Inquiry Constituted Under Punjab Act 11 of 1954 to Enquire Into the Punjab Disturbances of 1953*, 131.

[64] See John L. Esposito, "Pakistan: The Quest for Islamic Identity," in John L. Esposito ed., *Islam and Development: Religion and Sociopolitical Change* (Syracuse: Syracuse university Press, 1980), 139-162; and John L. Esposito, "Islam: Ideology and Politics in Pakistan," in Ali Banuazizi and Myron Weiner eds., *The State, Religion, and Ethnic Politics: Afghanistan, Iran, and Pakistan* (Syracuse: Syracuse University Press, 1986), 333-369.

[65] S. *Zakir Aijaz tr., Selected Speeches and Writings of Mawlana Mawdudi*, Vol. I, 99.

[66] National Assembly of Pakistan, Parliamentary *Debates*, Official Reports (Karachi; Government of Pakistan Press, 1956), Vol. II, No. 3, 167-168.

[67] *The Constitution of the Islamic Republic of Pakistan* (Karachi: Government of Pakistan Press, 1956).

[68] Aziz Ahmad, *Islamic Modernism in India and Pakistan, 1857-1964* (London: Oxford University Press, 1967), 243.

[69] All the quotations are from Freeland Abbot, *Islam and Pakistan* (Ithaca, N.Y.: Cornell University Press, 1968), 208.

[70] General Iskander Mirza's unpublished memoirs, 109-10 as cited in Seyyed Vali Reza Nasr, *The Vanguard of the Islamic Revolution*, 147.

[71] Muhammad Ayub Khan belonged to a Pathan tribe called Tareen. He was born on May 14, 1907 in the village of Rehana, fifty miles north of

Rawalpindi. His father was a subedar major (non-commissioned officer) in the British Indian Army. Ayub Khan was educated at Muslim University, Aligarh, India and Royal Military College, Sandhurst. He was commissioned in 1928 and in 1951 he succeeded Sir Douglas Gracy as the first Pakistani Commander-in-Chief of the Pakistan Army. He became the President of Pakistan following the military coup in 1958 and remained the head of state until he was forced to resign on March 25, 1969.

[72] Gunnar Myrdal, *Asian Drama: An Inquiry into the Poverty of Nations* (Great Britain: The Penguin Press, 1968), Vol. I, 326.

[73] Samuel P. Huntington, *Political Order in Changing Societies* (New Haven: Yale University Press, 1968), 250-51.

[74] In 1959, Ayub promulgated the Basic Democracies Order that provided for a five-tier pyramidal hierarchy of interlocking levels of legislative councils from the village to the provincial level. It began with union counicls or Town Committees and proceeded upward via tehsil (subdistrict) counicls, zilla (district) councils, divisional councils and the provincial development councils. The council members were partly elected and partly nominated. In 1960, the elected members of the union councils voted to endorse Ayub's presidency and under the 1962 constitution they formed an electoral college to elect the president and the national and provincial legislatures. The Basic Democracies were concerned with no more than local government and rural development.

[75] See Gustav F. Papanek, *Pakistan's Development: Social Goals and Private Incentives* (Cambridge, Mass.: Harvard University Press, 1967), 240-43; Rounaq Jahan, *Pakistan: Failure in National Integration* (New York: Columbia University Press, 1971).

[76] Mohammad Ayub Khan, *Friends Not Masters: A Political Autobiography* (London: Oxford University Press, 1967), 202-203.

[77] Ibid., 203-204.

[78] Mohammad Ayub Khan, *Speeches and Statements* (Karachi: Pakistan Publications, 1960-61), 5.

[79] See Fazlur Rahman, "The Controversy Over the Muslim Family Laws" in Donald E. Smith, *South Asian Religion and Politics* ed. (Princeton: Princeton University Press, 1966), 414-27.

[80] Fazlur Rahman admitted his failure to bridge the gap between "tradition" and "modernity." He wrote: "The case of this institute illustrates the real dilemma of the purposeful and creative Islamic scholarship. On the one hand are the traditional Madrasas, which are incapable of even conceiving what scientific scholarship is like and what its criteria are. On the other hand there has been a constant flow of those scholars who have earned their Ph.Ds from Western universities - but in the process have become

"orientalists." That is to say, they know enough of what sound scholarship is like, but their work is not Islamically purposeful or creative. They might write good enough works on Islamic history, or literature, philosophy, or art, but to think Islamically or to rethink Islam has not been one of their concerns." Fazlur Rahman, *Islam and Modernity* (Chicago, Illinois: University of Chicago Press, 1982), 124. Under pressure from the Islamist lobby, Fazlur Rahman resigned as the director of the Institute which then, effectively, collapsed.

[81] Nasr, *The Vanguard of the Islamic Revolution*, 150.

[82] Ibid., 153.

[83] *The Pakistan Times* (Lahore), 18 June 1964.

[84] To a journalist who enquired if he would like to be the next president of Pakistan if the legislators elected him, he said "I have never thought of it and I am not after position," *Morning News* (Dhaka), December 24, 1969.

[85] *Morning News*, August 14, 1969.

[86] Ibid., November 29, 1969.

[87] Ibid., April 11, 1969.

[88] Safdar Mahmood, *Pakistan: Political Roots and Development* (New Delhi: Sterling Publishers, 1990), 265.

[89] *Selected Speeches and Writings*, Vol. II, 90.

[90] Quoted in Maryam Jameelah, *Islam in Theory and Practice* (Lahore: Mohammed Yusuf Khan & Sons, 1978), 305.

[91] *Selected Speeches and Writings*, Vol. II, 323.

[92] Jamil-ud-Din Ahmad ed., *Some Recent Speeches and Writings of Mr. Jinnah*, Vol. II, 393.

[93] Zulfiqar Ali Bhutto was the son of Sir Shahnawaz Bhutto, a wealthy landlord from central Sindh. He attended Oxford University and the universities of Southern California and Berkeley. He first sprang to prominence in 1958 when he was made minister of fuel and natural resources in Ayub's first cabinet; later he became foreign minister. Following the 1965 war with India, Bhutto broke with Ayub and founded the Pakistan People's Party in 1967. After the emergence of Bangladesh, Bhutto was appointed as the president and chief martial law administrator. After the promulgation of the 1973 constitution, he redefined his position as prime minister, a position he retained until he was removed by the Army following the large scale civil unrest in 1977. He was convicted of murder and was hanged on April 4, 1979.

[94] *Foundation Document of the Pakistan People's Party* (Lahore: Mubashar Hassan, 1967).

[95] G.W. Choudhury, "New Pakistan's Constitution," *The Middle East Journal,* Vol. 28, No. 2, 1974, 11.

[96] See *Criterion*, Vol. 5, no. 4, 5:4, 1970, 62-63.

[97] William Border, "Bhutto in Crackdown on Critics: Orders Martial Law for Three Cities," *New York Times*, 22 April 1977, 1.

[98] Surendra Nath Kaushik, "Aftermath of the March 1977 General Elections in Pakistan," *South Asian Studies*, Vol. 13, no. 1, 1978, 75.

[99] *Chairman Bhutto's Reply to Gen. Zia's 2nd Statement in the Supreme Court, 31 October 1977* (Lahore: Pakistan People's Party publication, n.d), 88.

[100] Mohammad Zia-ul-Haq was born in Jullundur, East Punjab, India. He was a career military officer serving with British Indian forces during World War II. He received his commission in 1945 from the Indian Military Academy at Dehra Dun. He was promoted to Colonel in 1968, Brigadier in 1969, Major General in 1972, Lieutenant General in 1975 and Chief of Army Staff in 1976. Zia staged the coup in 1977 and retained power for over eleven years as Chief Martial Law Administrator (1977-1985) and as president of Pakistan (1979-1988). He died in a plane crash on August 17, 1988.

[101] See Government of Pakistan, Cabinet Division, *Ansari Commission's Report on Form of Government, 4th August 1983* (Islamabad: Manager, Printing Corporation of Pakistan Press, 1984).

[102] *Pakistan Times* (Lahore) July 6, 1977.

[103] Ibid., June 16, 1988.

[104] Nasr, *The Vanguard of the Islamic Revolution*, 188.

[105] Ibid., 191.

[106] Mumtaz Ahmad, "Islamization and Sectarian Violence in Pakistan," *Intellectual Discourse*, Vol. 6, no. 1, 1998, 17.

[107] Ibid.

[108] Richard Reeves, "Journey to Pakistan," *New Yorker*, LX: 33 (1 October 1984), 97-98.

[109] See *The Constitution of the Islamic Republic of Pakistan, as modified up to 30 December 1985* (Islamabad: Ministry of Justice and Parliamentary Affairs, n.d.), 5.

[110] *Political Plan Announced: Address of President Zia at the Seventh Session of the Federal Council on 12 August 1983* (Islamabad: Ministry of Information and Broadcasting, August 1983), 16.

[111] William L. Richter, "The Political Meaning of Islamisation in Pakistan," in Anita M. Weiss ed., *Islamic Reassertion in Pakistan: The Application of Islamic Laws in a Modern State* (New York: Syracuse University Press, 1986), 132; The Economist, 19 January 1985, 33.

[112] However, it was Miss Fatima Jinnah, sister of Quaid-e-Azam M.A. Jinnah, who first mounted a vigorous campaign to capture the presidency of the

country in 1964. She lost the election largely due to the unfair means adopted by the incumbent president, General Mohammad Ayub Khan.

113 Quoted in Rafiq Zakaria, *The Struggle Within Islam: The Conflict Between Religion and Politics* (New York: Viking Penguin, 1988), 238.

114 It is reported that on the suggestion of the army chief, General Aslam Beg, the Inter-Services Intelligence "created the IDA [the Islamic Democratic Alliance headed by Nawaz Sharif] to promote democracy after the August 1988 death of President Zia ul-Haq in an air crash ... Without the IDA, Gul [the head of the ISI] claimed that Pakistan could not have returned to electoral politics." See Salamat Ali, "Tarnished Brass: Scandal Over Soldiers Playing Politics," *Far Eastern Economic Review*, 15 October 1992.

115 "Enemies and More Enemies," *Newsweek*, 13 January, 1992.

116 See Ajay Singh and Ayaz Gul, "Talk About a Mess: Nawaz Sharif is Under Siege," *Asiaweek*, Vol. 24, no. 40, October 16, 1998, 37; Ayesha Jalal, "Pakistan's Tangle: The Politics of Conflicting Security and Economic Interests," *Government and Opposition*, Vol. 34, no. 1, 1999, 92.

117 Ahmed Rashid, "Feud Worsens as Bhutto Returns to the Fray," *The Sunday Times* (London), 22 November 1992.

118 *The Economist*, 9 November 1992.

119 Kathy Evans, "Sex Scandal Shocks Pakistani Elite," *The Guardian*, 4 November 1991.

3 Jamāʿat-i-Islāmī: Transformation of A Movement

1 E.I.J. Rosenthal, *Islam in the Modern National State* (Cambridge: Cambridge University Press, 1965), 247.

2 A.A. Mawdudi, *Tafhīm al-Qurʾān* (Towards Understanding the Qurʾān) (Lahore: Idarah Tarjumanul Qurʾān, 1973), Vol. I, 33.

3 Sayyid Abul Aʿla Mawdudi, *The Islamic Movement: Dynamics of Values, Power and Change,* ed., Khurram Murad (Leicester: The Islamic Foundation, 1984), 79.

4 Ibid.

5 Seyyed Vali Reza Nasr, *The Vanguard of the Islamic Revolution: The Jamāʿat-i-Islāmī of Pakistan* (London: I.B. Tauris Publishers, 1994), 10

6 S. Zakir Aijaz, tr., *Selected Speeches and Writings of Mawlana Mawdudi,* (Karachi: International Islamic Publications, 1982), Vol. I, p. 7.

7 Ibid., Vol. II, p. 94.

8 See Sayyid Asʿad Gilani, "Jamāʿat-e-Islāmī, 1941-47," (Ph.D. dissertation submitted to the Department of Political Science, University of Punjab, 1989-90), 360-65.

9 S. Zakir Aijaz, tr., *Selected Speeches and Writings of Mawlana Mawdudi,* Vol. I, 3.

10 Sayyid Abul Aᶜla Mawdudi, *Process of Islamic Revolution* (Delhi: Markazi Maktabah Jamāᶜat-e-Islāmī Hind, 1970), 2.

11 Ibid., 24-42.

12 Ibid., 41.

13 See A. Rashid Moten, *Islam and Revolution: Contributions of Sayyid Mawdudi* (Kano, Nigeria: Bureau for Islamic Propogation, 1988), 54-58.

14 Mawdudi, *Process of Islamic Revolution,* 28.

15 *Correspondence Between Maulana Maudoodi and Maryam Jameelah* (Lahore: Mohammed Yusuf Khan, 1973), 57-58.

16 Charles J. Adams, "The Ideology of Mawdudi," in D.E. Smith ed., *South Asian Politics and Religion,* (Pinceton: Princeton University Press, 1966), 375.

17 S.A.A. Mawdudi, *System of Government Under the Holy Prophet* (Lahore: Islamic Publications, 1978), 19.

18 Israr Ahmad, *Teḥrīk-e-Jamāᶜat-e-Islāmī: Ek Tahqīqī Muṭālaᶜah* (The Jamāᶜat-e-Islāmī Movement: A Critical Study) (Lahore: Markazi Anjuman Khuddam al-Qur'ān, 1990), 83-99.

19 Ibid., 100-106.

20 Nasr, *The Vanguard of the Islamic Revolution,* 83.

21 Mawdudi, *Process of Islamic Revolution,* 41.

22 S. Zakir Aijaz tr., *Selected Speeches and Writings of Mawlana Mawdudi,* Vol. I, 29-34.

23 Ibid., 9.

24 Ibid., 40.

25 *Rudād Jamāᶜat-e-Islāmī* (Proceedings of the Jamāᶜat-e-Islāmī) (Lahore: Shuᶜbah Nashr-o-Ishaᶜat, Jamāᶜat-e-Islāmī Pakistan, 1994), Vol. 6, 403-16. See also Moten, *Islam and Revolution: Contributions of Sayyid Mawdudi,* 24.

26 Sayyid Abul A'la Mawdudi, *Teḥrīk-I Islamī ki Akhlāqī Bunyādin* (Lahore: Islamic Publications, 1968), 3.

27 *Rudād Jamāᶜat-e-Islāmī* (Lahore: Shuᶜbah Nashr-o-Ishaᶜat Jamāᶜat-e-Islāmī, 1996), Vol. I, 50-1.

28 Ibid., vol. 7 (1955), 1138.

29 Israr Ahmad, *Teḥrīk-e-Jamāᶜat-e-Islāmī: Ek Tehqīqī Muṭālaᶜah.* 123-26.

30 Ibid., 118-21.

31 See Mawdudi, *Tafhīm al-Qur'ān,* Vol. I, 36.

32 Abul Aᶜla Mawdudi, *Islamic Law and Constitution,* tr. & ed. Khurshid Ahmad (Lahore: Islamic Publications, 1967), 107; also Dr. Israr Ahmad,

Teḥrīk-e-Jamāᶜat-e-Islāmī, 126.

33 Cited in Safdar Mahmood, *Pakistan: Political Roots and Development* (New Delhi: Sterling Publishers, 1990), 256-57.

34 *S. Zakir Aijaz tr., Selected Speeches and Writings of Mawlana Mawdudi*, Vol. I, 170.

35 *Rudād Jamāᶜat-e-Islāmī*, Vol. 6, 115.

36 Between 1947 and 1970, Pakistan had four provincial elections (Punjab, March 1951; NWFP, December 1951; Sindh, May 1953; and East Bengal, April 1954) on adult-franchise basis; two national and provincial elections (1962 and 1965) and the presidential election (1965) under president Ayub Khan's ingenious Basic Democracy (BD) system of indirect elections, and the December 1970 national and provincial assembly elections on adult-franchise and "one-man one-vote" basis. All these elections were conducted by an election machinery set up by the government; but the 1970 elections were the only ones in which the regime was not directly involved as an interested party. Hence the 1970 elections, often considered Pakistan's first general elections, were also the only free and fair elections to be held under a neutral regime.

37 Israr Ahmad, *Teḥrīk-e-Jamāᶜat-e-Islāmī,*154.

38 *Rudād Jamāᶜat-e-Islāmī*, Vol. 6, 115-117.

39 Ibid., 117. Also, Kalim Bahadur, *The Jamāᶜat-e-Islāmī of Pakistan: Political Thought and Political Action* (Lahore: Progressive Books, 1978), 63.

40 Ibid., 64.

41 *Rudād Jamāᶜat-e-Islāmī*, Vol. 6, 120.

42 Ibid., 119.

43 Ibid., 414.

44 Abul-Afaq, *Sayyid Abul Aᶜla Mawdudi, Sawānih, Afkār, Teḥrīk* (Sayyid Abul Ala Mawdudi: Biography, Thought, Movement) (Lahore: Islamic Publications, 1971), Vol. I, 454. Dr. Israr Ahmad, *Teḥrīk Jamāᶜat-e-Islāmī.*

45 The committee of four was comprised of all ᶜulamā': Abdul Rahim Ashraf, Abdul Gaffar Hasan, Abdul Jabbar Ghazi and Sultan Ahmad. See Dr. Israr Ahmad, *Tārīkh Jamāᶜat-e-Islāmī ka ek Gumshudah Bāb* (A Lost Chapter of the History of the Jamāᶜat-e-Islāmī) (Lahore: Tanzim-e-Islāmī Pakistan, 1990), 8.

46 Ibid., 24.

47 See Israr Ahmad, *Teḥrīk-e-Jamāᶜat-e-Islāmī: Ek Tehqīqī Muṭālaᶜah*, 182-239; also *Tārīkh Jamāᶜat-e-Islāmī kā ek Gumshudah Bāb.*

48 See Kalim Bahadur, *The Jamaᶜat-i-Islami of Pakistan*, 87-94.

49 Ibid., 92.

50 This speech clearly spells out Mawdudi's views on religion and politics and is published as *Teḥrīk-e-Islāmī ka Ā'indah Lā'iḥa-e-ᶜAmal* (The Islamic Movement's Future Course of Action) (Lahore: Islamic Publications, 1986).

51 *Tarjumān al-Qur'ān*, Vol. 87, No. 6 (June 1961), 380-81.

52 Nasr, *The Vanguard of the Islamic Revolution*, 38.

53 Ibid., 39.

54 See Muhammad Nejat Allah Siddiqui, *Teḥrīk-e-Islāmī Asr-e-ḥāḍir main* (Islamic Movements in the Contemporary Period) (Delhi: Markazi Maktaba-I-Islami Publishers, 1995), 156.

55 Mawdudi, *Islamic Law and Constitution*, 177.

56 Mawdudi, *Teḥrīk-e-Islāmī ka Ā'indah Lā'iḥa-e-ᶜAmal*, 205. According to a sincere convert, "Mawdudi was convinced beyond doubt that the Pakistanis could be properly educated to reform and purify elections to make them sober, clean, fair and just. He believed that, if virtuous candidaters of the Jamāᶜat-e-Islāmī actively campaigned in the national elections like ordinary politicians, ultimately the people would vote them into power and in this way a revival of a true Islamic state modeled after the khilafat Rashidun would take place." Maryam Jameelah, "An Appraisal of Some Aspects of Maulana Sayyid A'la Maudoodi's Life and Thought," *The Islamic Quarterly*, Vol. 31, No. 2, 1987, 125.

57 Nasr, *The Vanguard of the Islamic Revolution*, 41.

58 K.B. Sayeed, "The Jamāᶜat-e-Islāmī Movement in Pakistan," *Pacific Affairs*, Vol. 30, No. 2, 1957, 64.

59 Ibid., 145.

60 Leonard Binder, *Religion and Politics in Pakistan* (Berkeley: University of California Press, 1961), 374.

61 See *Election Manifesto of Jamāᶜat-e-Islāmī* (Karachi: Jamāᶜat-e-Islāmī, 1958).

62 See the statement by General Mohammad Ayub Khan, *Dawn* (Karachi), October 8, 1958.

63 See *Tarjumān al-Qur'ān*, Vol. 88, No. 6, 1962, 322.

64 "To his last days, he [Mawdudi] was convinced that the restoration of Western-style democracy in Pakistan would provide most fertile soil favourable to Islamic revival and a true Islamic state." Maryam Jameelah, "An Appraisal of Some Aspects of Maulana Sayyid Aᶜla Maudoodi's Life and Thought," 124.

[65] The Combined Opposition Party (COP) was formed to oppose Ayub Khan in the 1965 elections. It was composed of the Council Muslim League, the Jamāᶜat-e-Islāmī, the Awami League, National Awami Party, and Nizam-e-Islam Party.

[66] *Dawn* (Karachi) December 6, 1964.

[67] *Mashriq* (Lahore) December 7, 1964.

[68] *Pakistan Observer* (Dacca) October 3, 1964.

[69] Khurram Murad, *Lamḥāt* (Moments) (Lahore: Masnshurat, 2000), 341.

[70] Ibid., 84.

[71] Sarwat Saulat, *Maulana Maududi* (Karachi: International Islamic Publishers,1979), 70.

[72] See *Election Manifesto* (Lahore: Jamāᶜat-e-Islāmī, Pakistan, 1970).

[73] Sarwat Saulat, *Maulana Maududi*, 71.

[74] See *Report on the General Elections, Pakistan 1970-1971* (Islamabad: Election Commission of Pakistan, n.d.), Vol. 2.

[75] Sharif al Mujahid, "Pakistan's First General Elections," *Asian Survey*, Vol. 11, no. 2, 1971, 170.

[76] Ibid.

[77] Sarwat Saulat, *Maulana Maududi*, 72.

[78] The six-point programme outlined a situation of maximum political, economic and administrative autonomy for East Bengal within a confederal Pakistan. The six point programme outlined the following:

1. Pakistan should be a federation on the basis of the Lahore Resolution of 1940 (which implied the existence of two similar entities) and should have a parliamentary set-up with the legislature elected on the basis of universal adult franchise.

2. The federal government should deal solely with defence and foreign affairs.

3. There should be two separate but freely convertible currencies. East Pakistan would have a separate banking reserve as well as separate fiscal and monetary policies.

4. The federated units would have the sole power of taxation. The central government should be granted a share in the state taxes for meeting its required expenditures.

5. Separate accounts from foreign exchange earnings would be maintained. The federating units would be free to establish trade and commercial relations and set up trade missions in, and enter into agreements with, foreign countries.

6. There should be established "a militia or a para-military force for East Pakistan."

Sheikh Mujibur Rahman, "6-Point Formula - Our Right to Live" in *Bangladesh Documents* (New Delhi: Minitry of External Affairs, n.d.), 23-33.

79   Khurram Murad, *Lamḥāt*, 461-465.
80   JI Overview, "Mian Tufail Muhammad." March 5, 1998 <http://www.jamaat.org/overview/mtm.html>.
81   *Zindagi* (Lahore), November 10-16, 1989, 60.
82   *Economist,* March 22, 1969.
83   *New York Times,* July 9, 1974.
84   *Dawn* (Karachi), January 25, 1977.
85   As quoted in William Richter, "The Political Dynamics of Islamic Resurgence in Pakistan," *Asian Survey,* Vol. 19, no. 6, 1979, 27.
86   The parties comprising the PNA had diverse ideological backgrounds. Mian Tufail Muhammad's Jamāʿat-e-Islāmī, Maulana Mufti Mahmud's Jamīʿatul ʿUlamā-e-Islām and, Maulana Shah Ahmed Noorani's Jamīʿatul ʿUlamā-e-Pakistan were Islam-based parties. Rtd. Air Marshal Asghar Khan's Teḥrīk-e-istiqlāl, Pir Pagaro's Pakistan Muslim League, Nawabzada Nasrullah Khan's Pakistan Democratic Party, and Azad Kashmir Muslim Conference, headed by Sardar Abdul Qayyum, President of Azad Kashmir (1972-1975), were essentially parties of the "Centre," advocating a return to parliamentary democracy and private enterprise. Sardar Sherbaz Mazari's National Democratic Party and Khan Muhammad Ashraf Khan's Khaksar Tehrik were parties of the left espousing decentralized government and state ownership of the means of production.
87   For details see *Tarjuman-i-Islam* (weekly), Lahore, February 18, 1977, 11-16.
88   Cited in Sarwat Saulat, *Maulana Maududi,* 95. A former Chief Election Commissioner, Mr. Justice Sajjad Ahmad Jan admitted that the March elections were "a complete hoax"; see *Dawn,* November 29, 1977.
89   *Nawā-e-Waqt* (Lahore) March 22, 1977 and *Mashriq*, March 22, 1977.
90   *Mashriq,* March 25, 1977.
91   Niẓām-e-Muṣṭafā refers to the original Islamic social and political order, and the principles of justice, imputed to the rule of the Prophet Muhammad (s.a.w). The term is suggestive of the golden era of social and economic justice. It was a powerful slogan because, it symbolized Islam and the personality of the Prophet (s.a.w). Devotion to Islam was there, but the love that the Prophet's personality inspired for the common man was perhaps even more electrifying. See Khalid Bin Sayeed, *Politics in Pakistan: The Nature and Direction of Change* (New York: Praeger, 1980), 159.

92 Official figures indicated that "the nation wide agitations led to 22 persons being killed, and 369 injured up to March 7, and 242 killed and 1,227 injured thereafter. In addition, 9 persons of the security forces were killed and another 536 injured. No less than 16,863 persons were arrested, 4,290 processions were taken out by members of the public, 262 by women, 95 by lawyers, 19 by ʿulamāʾ, 283 by students and 68 by children. 1,623 vehicles were destroyed and the same was the case with 18 installations, 42 stores, 31 wine shops, 7 hotels, 58 bank branches, 11 cinemas, 7 factories, 23 railway carriages, 57 offices, and 38 shops. In addition, the national economy ground to a halt during the summer month while the flame of violence spread all over the land," See "Brohi's Statement in Begum Bhutto's Petition," *Pakistan Times,* October 13, 1977.

93 See William Border, "Bhutto in Crackdown on Critics Orders Martial Law for Three Cities," *New York Times,* April 22, 1977, Surrendra Nath Kaushik, "Aftermath of the March 1977 General Elections in Pakistan," *South Asian Studies,* Vol. 13, No. 1, 1978, 75.

94 *Dawn,* July 10, 1977.

95 *Far Eastern Economic Review,* July 22, 1977, p. 10. According to Christian Lamb, even Zia's "greatest detractors called him a pious man, and his humility has been described as such that he could convey two handshakes and an embrace in a single glance." *Financial Times,* August 19, 1988.

96 *Nawā-e-waqt,* July 11, 1977.

97 Quoted in Barbara D. Metcalf, "Islamic Argument in Contemporary Pakistan" in William R. Roff ed., *Islam and the Political Economy of Meaning: Contemporary Studies of Muslim Discourse* (Berkeley: University of California Press, 1987), 136.

98 *Pakistan Times,* December 3, 1977.

99 "Brohi's Statement in Begum Bhutto's Petition," *Pakistan Times,* October 13, 1977.

100 Ghafur Ahmad held the portfolio of production and industry; Chaudhri Rahmat Ilahi held the ministry of petroleum, minerals, water, and power; Mahmud A'zam Faruqi was given information and broadcasting; and Professor Khurshid Ahmad was appointed as the minister of planning.

101 Mumtaz Ahmad, "Islamic Fundamentalism in South Asia: The Jamaat-I-Islami and the Tablighi Jamaat of South Asia" in Martin E. Marty and R. Scott Appleby eds., *Fundamentalisms Observed* (Chicago: University of Chicago Press, 1991), 483.

102 *Muslim,* December 2, 1984.

103 See *Dawn*, December 2, 1984; *Pakistan Times*, December 20, 1984; Shahid
     Javed Burki and Craig Baxter, *Pakistan Under the Military: Eleven Years
     of Zia ul-Haq* (Boulder, CO: Westview Press, 1991), 172.
104 *Pakistan Times*, August 13, 1983.
105 *The Muslim*, January 7, 1986. According to the *Pakistan Times*, February
     23, 1986. 157 candidates belonged to the PPP.
106 *The Muslim* February 27, 1985.
107 *Pakistan Times*, February 25, 1985.
108 *The Muslim*, February 27, 1985.
109 Ibid., March 3, 1985.
110 Mumtaz Ahmad, "Islamic Fundamentalism in South Asia...," 483-84.

4   Qazi Hussain and the Jamāᶜat as a Mass Party

1   *Jasarat* (Karachi), March 10, 1990.
2   See Khurram Badr, *Qazi Husain Ahmad* (Karachi: Saba Publications, 1988),
    10-12.
3   JI Pakistan: The Leadership You Can Trust, http://:://www.Jamaat.org/
    leadership/qha.html., May 25, 2000.
4   Mumtaz Ahmad, "Islamic Fundamentalism in South Asia: The Jamaat-I-
    Islami and the Tablighi Jamaat of South Asia" in Martin E. Marty and R.
    Scott Appleby eds., *Fundamentalisms Observed* (Chicago: University of
    Chicago Press, 1991), 494.
5   Ibid.
6   "JI Pakistan:The Basic Facts," http://www.Jamaat.org/overview/
    facts5.html., 3, January 25, 1998.
7   Sayyid Abul Aᶜla Mawdudi, *The Islamic Movement: Dynamics of Values,
    Power and Change* ed., Khurram Murad (Leicester: The Islamic
    Foundation, 1984), 43.
8   Khurram Murad, *Lamḥāt* (Moments) (Mansurah, Lahore: Manshurat,
    2000), 124-25.
9   "Views of Mian Tufail Muhammad on the Policies of the Jamāᶜat-e-Islāmī,"
    Jasarat (Karachi) December 12, 1993.
10 *Jasarat*, June 19, 1988 cited in Mumtaz Ahmad, "Islamic Fundamentalism
    in South Asia...," 484-85.
11 *Nation*, August 18, 1988.
12 *Far Eastern Economic Review*, November 10, 1988.
13 Seyyed Vali Reza Nasr, "Democracy and the Crisis of Governability in
    Pakistan," *Asian Survey*, Vol. 32, No. 6, 1992, 523; also Mohammed
    Waseem, "Pakistan's Lingering Crisis of Dyarchy," *Asian Survey*, Vol. 32,
    No. 7, 1992, 618.

[14] Salamat Ali, "Tarnished Brass: Scandal over Soldiers Playing Politics," *Far Eastern Economic Review,* October 15, 1992.

[15] Seyyed Vali Reza Nasr, *The Vanguard of the Islamic Revolution: Jama'at-i-Islami of Pakistan* (London: I.B. Tauris Publishers, 1994), 209.

[16] *Far Eastern Economic Review,* December 8, 1988.

[17] *The Nation,* August 7, 1990.

[18] Qazi Hussain's interview in *Takbīr,* January 31, 1991, 26 cited in Nasr, *The Vanguard of the Islamic Revolution,* 214.

[19] Khurram Murad, "Defeat in the 1993 Elections: Reasons and Aspects," *Jasarat,* Friday Special, November 5-11, 1993, 24.

[20] Ibid., 25.

[21] Ibid., 24.

[22] Mumtaz Ahmad, "The Politics of War: Islamic Fundamentalisms in Pakistan" in James Piscatori ed., *Islamic Fundamentalisms and the Gulf Crisis* (Chicago: American Academy of Arts and Sciences, 1991), 165.

[23] Ibid., 167.

[24] *Jasarat,* November 2, 1993.

[25] Ibid.

[26] Edward A. Gargan, "President of Pakistan Dismisses Premier and Dissolves Parliament," *The New York Times,* April 19, 1993.

[27] Qazi Hussain Ahmad, "Islamic Front and Our Invitation," *Jasarat,* November 2, 1993.

[28] Ibid.

[29] Interview with Party Vice President, Khurram Murad, "Good government means good people in government," *Impact International,* 10 September – 7 October, 1993, 7.

[30] "Views of Mian Tufail Muhammad on the Policies of the Jamā°at-e-Islāmī."

[31] Ibid.

[32] Qazi Hussain Ahmad, "Islamic Front and Our Invitation."

[33] Ibid.

[34] Interview with Khurram Murad, "Good government means good people in government," 7.

[35] Ibid.

[36] Pakistan Islami Front, *Manifesto* (Mansoorah, Lahore: n.p., 1993), Introduction.

[37] Ibid., 11.

[38] Ibid., 2.

[39] Ibid., 5.

[40] See *Rudād Jamā°at-e-Islāmī* (Lahore: Shu°bah Nashr-o-Isha°at-e-Islāmī, 1996), Vol. I, 50-51.

[41] "Views of Mian Tufail Muhammad on the Policies of the Jamāᶜat-e-Islāmī."

[42] Tahir Amin, "Pakistan in 1993: Some dramatic Changes," *Asian Survey,* Vol. 34, No. 2, 1994, 195.

[43] See Lawrence Ziring, "The Second Stage in Pakistani Politics: The 1993 Elections," *Asian Survey,* Vol. 33, No. 12, 1993, 1175-85.

[44] Khurram Murad, "PIF: Reasons for the defeat in the 1993 Elections," *Jasarat,* Friday Special, 5-11, 1993, 25.

[45] Khurram Murad, "Good government means good people in government," 8.

[46] Mawlana Muhammad Musahib Ali, "Islāmī front kī nākāmī ke asbāb: kārname aur mustaqbal ka la'iḥah ᶜamal" (The reasons for the failure of Islami Front: Activities and future course of action), *Jasarat,* October 18, 1993.

[47] Gallup Pakistan, *Pakistan at the Polls 1997* (Islamabad: Gallup Pakistan, 1997), 23.

[48] Gallup Pakistan, *Pakistan Public Opinion on Important Social Issues* (Islamabad: Pakistan Institute of Public Opinion, 1996), 14.

[49] Riaz Hassan, "Social Structure and Religiousity in Muslim Societies: A Case Study of Indonesia and Pakistan" (A paper presented at the International Conference on Islamization of Sociology & Anthropology: Implications for Social Development of Muslim Countries, Kuala Lumpur, 31 October-2 November 1997),12. The randomly selected 1162 respondents came from Lahore, Faisalabad, Multan, Rawalpindi, Karachi and Peshawar. Of these, 41 percent were classified as religious elite, 26 percent as the elite from other spheres of civil society, and 32 percent as general public. The survey interviews were carried out by the staff of the Social Science Research Center of the University of the Punjab in Lahore from January to May 1997.

[50] Khurram Murad, "Ishārāt" (indications), *Tarjumānul Qur'ān,* Vol. 120, No. 4, April 1994, 10.

[51] Qazi Hussain Ahmad, "Ek hī rāstah: jad-o-jahad" (The Only Way: Struggle), *Tarjumānul Qur'ān,* Vol. 122, No. 12, December 1996, 9.

[52] *Herald,* April 1995, 52-53.

[53] "To contest the election one had to be rich.... So while the official limit on spending was 500,000 rupees (about $25,000), many candidates were spending more than that each day.... Chaudry Shujaat's house in Gujrat, the headquarters for the family's election campaign of four seats, resembled the feeding of the five thousand throughout the thirty-eight-day campaign, with huge marquees erected in the garden to serve up unimaginable quantities of lentil curry and rice." Christina Lamb, *Waiting*

for Allah: Pakistan's Struggle for Democracy (London: Macmillan, 1991), 63-64.

54 Qazi Hussain Ahmad, "Ek hī Rāstah: jad-o-jahad," 9.

55 Ibid., 6. The feudal lord "maintains a legion of servants, owns fine horses, cows and buffaloes... Extravagance in food and dress, gross and vulgar sexual excesses, garish ostentations are the things on which he chooses to devote his income. He has feudal rivalries with the neighbouring landlords and has therefore to maintain a show of power. This he does by commanding a gang of thieves and robbers ... [and by having] in his confidence the police officials. However, "Fear reigns supreme in the life of the hari [tenant] – fear of imprisonment, fear of losing his land, wife or life. The Zamindar [landlord] might, at any time, get annoyed with him and oust him – he might have to leave his crops half ripe, his cattle might also be snatched and he might be beaten out of the village," see M. Masud, *Hari Report: Note of Dissent* (Karachi: Hari Publications, 1948), 2-4.

56 Qazi Hussain Ahmad, "Ek hī Rāstah: jad-o-jahad," 8.

57 According to Duncan, "There are probably only 5000 or so Pakistani landed families that matter, but their political influence is disproportionate to their numbers or even their wealth. Any slice of Pakistani history has the big names playing their part: the Qureshis, Gardezis, Noons, Tiwanas, Soomros, Khuros, Bhuttos, Jatois are a social and political Who's Who of families. The landowners have dominated any sort of parliament in the area, even before Pakistan was created: they have held on to a fat slice of every cabinet and have provided the last two prime ministers of Pakistan, Zulfikar Ali Bhutto and Mohammed Khan Junejo." Emma Duncan, *Breaking the Curfew: A Political Journey Through Pakistan* (London: Macmillan, 1989), 100.

58 For the text of the resolution see "Siyāsī Ṣūrat-e-Ḥāl: Qarārdād Markazī Majlis Shura Munaqidah 6-7, November 1996." (Political Conditions: Resolution of Central Majlis-e-Shura held on 6-7 November 1996), *Tarjumānul Qur'ān,* Vol. 122, No. 12, December 1996, 11-15.

59 Qazi Hussain Ahmad, "Ek hi Rāstah: Jad-o-jahad," 8.

60 Ibid.

61 Similarly in mid 1993, the caretaker prime minister Moeen Qureshi was praised for exposing the names of loan defaulters, drug barons, and tax evaders and the outstanding loans, running into billions. Every newspaper and magazine in Pakistan published the lists and widely commented on these defaulters, who, in many cases, were able to maneuver their way back into the assemblies following the elections of 1993. See *The Guardian,* September 30, 1993.

[62] JI Pakistan, "Abstaining [from] the February 1997 Elections" http://www.Jamaat.org/issues/elections97.html, 4, January 25, 1998.

[63] Election Commission of Pakistan, *1997 General Elections Report*, Volume I (Islamabad: Printing Corporation of Pakistan Press, 1997), 189, 196.

[64] JI Pakistan, "Abstaining [from] the February 1997 Elections," 5.

[65] Personal communication with Qazi Hussain Ahmad, on 6. 15, 1999.

[66] Martin Marty, *The Modern Schism* (New York: Harper and Row, 1969), 101.

[67] Ibid., 5.

[68] Ibid.

[69] JI Pakistan, "Election 1997 and Jamāᶜat-e-Islāmī," http://w.w.w.jamaat.org/crisis/revolution.html, 4, June 15, 1999.

[70] Khurram Murad, "Ishārāt", *Tarjumānul Qur'ān*, Vol. 121, No. 12, December 1995, 7. See also Khurram Murad, "Ishārāt," *Tarjumānul Qur'ān*, Vol. 120, no. 10, October 1994, 3.

[71] JI Pakistan, "Strategy for Change," http://w.w.w.jamaat.org/overview/strategy.html, 2, June 22, 1999.

[72] JI Pakistan, "Resolution on Education," http://w.w.w.jamaat.org/crisis/education.html, 3, June 23, 1999.

[73] Ibid., 4.

[74] JI Pakistan, "Strategy for Change," 3.

[75] Ibid., 4.

[76] Qazi Hussain Ahmad, Editorial: "Sound of Revolution on Pakistan's Doorstep," *Tarjumānul Qur'ān*, Vol. 123, No. 8, August 1997, 6.

[77] JI Pakistan, "The Membership Drive of Jamāᶜat-e-Islāmī," http://w.w.w.jamaat.org/qa/drive.html, 1, February 25, 1998.

[78] "Islam: How Pakistan's Religious Opposition is Challenging the Secular Ruling Elite," *Asiaweek*, Vol. 25, no. 4, January 29, 1999, 33.

[79] http://w.w.w.jamaat.org, June 30, 1999.

[80] Qazi Hussain Ahmad, "Sound of Revolution on Pakistan's Doorstep," 9.

[81] JI Pakistan, "Bloody Revolution or Islamic Revolution?" http://w.w.w.jamaat.org/crisis/revolution.html#Bloody, June 28, 1999, 3.

[82] Cited in Khurram Murad, "Revolution: Through Bullet or Ballot," *Tarjumānul Qur'ān*, Vol. 122, No. 1, January 1996, 6.

[83] Ibid., 9.

[84] Jamāᶜat-e-Islāmī Pakistan provides for elections at its various tiers for a given period. Elections to the post of the *amīr* are regularly held every five years. No one is allowed to present himself as a candidate nor is any form of campaigning allowed. The central *shūrā*, however suggests three names for guidance of the members (*arakin*) who are also free to vote for

any other party member (*rukn*).

85 Thus he stripped the president of the power to dissolve the National Assembly and dismissed the Prime Minister through the 13ᵗʰ constitutional amendment in April 1997. Through the 14ᵗʰ amendment in July 1997, he acquired power to unseat any member of his party from the Parliament and provincial assemblies for violation of party discipline. In December 1997, he succeeded in ousting President Leghari from the office. In October 1998, he forced the Pakistan Army chief, Jehangir Karamat, to resign from office.

86 See "Pakistan Takes a Beating," *The Economist,* Vol. 348, No. 8082, August 22, 1998, 21-22; "The Crumbling of Pakistan," *The Economist,* Vol. 349, No. 8090, October 17, 1998, 27-28.

87 Ajay singh and Ayaz Gul, "Talk About a Mess: Nawaz Sharif is Under Siege," *Asiaweek,* Vol. 24, No. 40, October 16, 1998, 36-37.

88 Ayesha Jalal, "Pakistan's Tangle: The Politics of Conflicting Security and Economic Interests," *Government and Opposition,* Vol. 34, No. 1, Winter 1999, 92.

89 Kargil is situated inside the Indian occupied state of Jammu and Kashmir. In 1999, Pakistan-backed Kashmiri freedom fighters occupied some strategic positions in the region. The Indian military launched intense ground and air attack to dislodge the freedom fighters and in the process, suffered considerable loss of men and materials. The Kargil crisis brought Pakistan and India to an all-out war. The issue was resolved when at the initiative of US President Bill Clinton, Nawaz Sharif agreed to the withdrawal of Kashmiri freedom fighters as well as the regular Pakistani troops from the Kargil region.

90 *Jasarat,* October 13, 1999.

91 Larry Diamond, "Is Pakistan the [Reverse] Wave of the Future?" *Journal of Democracy,* Vol. 11, No. 32, July 2000, 92.

92 JI Pakistan, "JI Resolution on Deposition of Nawaz Government," http:/ /w.w.w.jamaat.org/news/Pr 041599.html, October 23, 1999.

SELECT BIBLIOGRAPHY

BOOKS

Abbot, Freeland. *Islam and Pakistan*. Ithaca, N.Y.: Cornell University Press, 1968.

'Abd, Chaudri 'Abdul-Rahman. *Mufakkir-i Islam: Sayyid Abul A'la Mawdudi* (Thinker of Islam: Mawlana Sayyid Abu'l-A'la Mawdudi). Lahore: Islamic Publication, 1971.

Abu'l-Afaq. *Sayyid Abul A'la Mawdudi: Sawaniḥ, Afkār, Teḥrīk* (Sayyid Abul A'la Mawdudi: Biography, Thought and Movement). Lahore: Islamic Publication, 1971.

Abu Tariq, ed. *Mawlana Mawdudi ki Taqārīr* (Mawlana Mawdudi's Speeches). Lahore: Islamic Publication, 1976.

Afaqi, Abu Tahir. *Fitnah-i Mawdūdiyat* (Discord of Mawdudism). Jawharabad: Idarah-i Adabistan-i Jawharabad, n.d.

Ahmad, Aziz. *Islamic Modernism in India and Pakistan, 1857-1964*. London: Oxford University Press, 1967.

Ahmad, Israr. *Islam Awr Pakistan: Tarīkhī, Siyāsī Awr Thiqāfatī Pasmanzar* (Islam and Pakistan: Historical, Political and Cultural Background). Lahore: Maktabah-e Markazi Anjuman-e Khuddam a'l-Qur'ān, 1983.

Ahmad, Israr. *Tārīkh-e-Jamā'at-e-Islāmī: Ek Gumshudah Bāb* (History of Jamā'at-e-Islāmī: A Lost Chapter). Lahore: Maktabah-e-Jadid Press, 1990.

Ahmad, Israr. *Tarīkh-e-Jamāᶜat-e-Islāmī:Ek Tahqīqī Muṭalaᶜah* (The Movement of Jamāᶜat-e-Islāmī: A Critical Study). Lahore: Dar al Ishāᶜat-e-Islami, 1966.

Ahmad, Khurshid. *The Movement of Jamāᶜat-e-Islāmī, Pakistan.* Lahore: Jamāᶜat-e-Islāmī, Pakistan, 1989.

Ahmad, Khurshid. *The Crisis of the Political System in Pakistan and the Jamāᶜat-e-Islāmī.* Lahore: Secretary Information, Jamāᶜat-e-Islāmī Pakistan, n.d.

Ahmad, Khurshid and Zafar Ishaq Ansari, ed. *Islamic Perspectives: Studies in Honour of Mawlana Sayyid Abul Aᶜla Mawdudi.* Leicester: The Islamic Foundation, 1979.

Ahmad, Mushtaq. *Government and Politics in Pakistan.* New York: Oxford University Press, 1963.

Ahmed, Ishtiaq. *The Concept of an Islamic State: An Analysis of the Ideological Controversy in Pakistan.* New York: St. Martin's Press, 1987.

Aijaz, S. Zakir, tr. *Selected Speeches and Writings of Mawlana Mawdudi.* Karachi: International Islamic Publishers, 1981.

'Ali, Malik Ghulam. *Khilāfat wa Mulūkiyat Par Iᶜtirāzāt ka Tajziyah* (An Analysis of Criticisms made on *Khilāfat wa Mulūkiyat*). Lahore: Islamic Publication, 1972.

Ali, Tariq. *Can Pakistan Survive?* New York: Penguin, 1983.

Badr, Khurram. *Qazi Husain Ahmad.* Karachi: Saba Publications, 1988.

Bahadur, Kalim. *The Jama'at-e-Islami of Pakistan.* New Delhi: Chetana Publications, 1977.

Baxter, Craig. *Zia's Pakistan: Politics and Stability in a Frontline State.* Boulder, Colorado: Westview Press, 1985.

Baxter, Craig, and Syed Razi Wasti, eds. *Pakistan: Authoritarianism in the 1980s.* Lahore: Vanguard, 1991.

Bhutto, Zulfikar Ali. *The Great Tragedy.* Karachi: Pakistan People's Party, 1971.

Binder, Leonard. *Religion and Politics in Pakistan.* Berkeley: University of California Press, 1961.

Burki, Shahid Javed. *Pakistan: A Nation in the Making.* Boulder, Colorado: Westview Press, 1986.

Burki, Shahid Javed. *Pakistan Under Bhutto 1971-1977.* London: Macmillan, 1980.

Burki, Shahid Javed. *Pakistan: The Continuing Search for Nationhood.* Boulder, Colorado: Westview Press, 1991.

Burki, Shahid Javed, and Craig Baxter. *Pakistan Under the Military: Eleven Years of Zia ul-Haq.* Boulder, Colorado: Westview Press, 1991.

Callard, Keith B. *Pakistan: A Political Study.* London: Allen and Unwin, 1957.

Callard, Keith B. *Political Forces in Pakistan, 1947-1959.* New York: Institute of Pacific Relations, 1959.

Choudhury, G. W. *Constitutional Development in Pakistan.*
     Vancouver: Publications Centre, University of
     British Columbia, 1969.

Choudhury, G. W. *The Last Days of United Pakistan.* Bloomington:
     Indiana University Press, 1975.

*Correspondence Between Maulana Maudoodi and Maryam
     Jameelah.* Lahore: Muhammad Yusuf Khan &
     Sons, 1986.

Dastur-e-Jamāᶜat-e-Islāmī, Pakistan (Constitution of Jamāᶜat-e-
     Islāmī Pakistan). Lahore: Jamāᶜat-e-Islāmī, 1989.

Election Manifesto of Jamāᶜat-e-Islāmī. Karachi: Jamāᶜat-e-Islāmī,
     1958.

Election Manifesto. Lahore: Jamāᶜat-e-Islāmī, Pakistan, 1970.

Esposito, John L. *Islam and Politics.* Syracuse: Syracuse University
     Press, 1987.

Esposito, John L., ed., *Voices of Resurgent Islam.* New York: Oxford
     University Press, 1983.

Feldman, Herbert. *Revolution in Pakistan: A Study of the Martial-
     Law Administration.* Karachi: Oxford University
     Press, 1967.

Feldman, Herbert. *From Crisis to Crisis: Pakistan, 1962-1969.*
     London: Oxford University Press, 1972.

Gilani, Sayyid Asᶜad. *Iqbal, Dār al-Islām Awr Mawdudi* (Iqbal,
     Dār al-Islām and Mawdudi). Lahore: Islami
     Academy, 1978.

Gilani, Sayyid As°ad. "Jamā°at-i-Islāmī, 1941-47," Ph.D. dissertation, Department of Political Science, The University of Punjab, 1989-90.

Gilani, Sayyid As°ad. *Maududi: Thought and Movement.* Lahore: Islamic Publication, 1984.

Government of Pakistan. *Ansari Commission's Report on Form of Government, 4ᵗʰ August 1983.* Islamabad: Manager, Printing Corporation of Pakistan Press, 1984.

Hasan, Masudul. *Sayyid Abul Aᶜla Maududi and His Thought*, 2 vols. Lahore: Islamic Publication, 1984.

Hunter, Shireen T, ed. *Islamic Revivalism: Diversity and Unity.* Bloomington, IN: Indiana University Press, 1988.

Hussain, Asaf. *Elite Politics in an Ideological State.* Folkestone, U.K.: Dawson, 1979.

Ijtima' Se Ijtima' Tak (1963-1974); Rudād-e-Jamāᶜat-e-Islāmī, Pakistan (Convention to Convention (1963-1974); Proceedings of Jamā°at-e-Islāmī of Pakistan). Lahore: Jamā°at-e-Islāmī, 1989.

Ijtima' Se Ijtima' Tak (1974-1983); Rudād-e-Jamāᶜat-e-Islāmī, Pakistan (Convention to Convention (1974-1983); Proceedings of Jamā°at-e-Islāmī of Pakistan). Lahore: Jamā°at-e-Islāmī, 1989.

Jahan, Rounaq. *Pakistan: Failure in National Integration.* New York: Columbia University Press, 1972.

Jalal, Ayesha. *The State of Martial Rule: The Origins of Pakistan's Political Economy of Defence.* Lahore: Vanguard, 1991.

Jameelah, Maryam. *Islam in Theory and Practice*. Lahore: Mohammad Yusuf Khan, 1973.

Kennedy, Charles H., ed. *Pakistan: 1992*. Boulder, Colorado: Westview Press, 1991.

Khan, Muhammad Ayub. *Friends Not Masters: A Political Autobiography*. New York: Oxford University Press, 1967.

Lamb, Christina. *Waiting for Allah: Pakistan's Struggle for Democracy*. New York: Viking, 1991.

Murad, Khurram. *Lamḥāt* (Moments). Mansurah, Lahore: Manshurat, 2000.

Malik, Hafeez. *Moslem Nationalism in India and Pakistan*. Washington: Public Affairs Press, 1963.

Manifesto of Jamāʿat-e-Islāmī of Pakistan. Lahore: Jamāʿat-e-Islāmī, 1970.

Marty, Martin E. and R. Scott Appleby, eds., *Fundamentalisms Observed*. Chicago: University of Chicago Press, 1991.

Marty, Martin E. and R. Scott Appleby eds., *Accounting for Fundamentalisms: The Dynamic Character of Movements*. Chicago: University of Chicago Press, 1994.

Mawdudi, Sayyid Abu'l-Aʿla. *ʿAsr-e-Ḥāḍir Main Ummat-e-Muslimah kī Masa'il Awr Unka Hal* (The Problems Of Muslims in Contemporary Times and Their Solution). Khalil Ahmadu'l-Hamidi, ed. Lahore: Idarah-e-Maʿarif-e-Islami, 1988.

Mawdudi, Sayyid Abul A'la. *A Short History of the Revivalist Movement in Islam*. Al-Ash'ari, trans. Lahore: Islamic Publication, 1963.

Mawdudi, Sayyid Abul A'la *Come Let Us Change the World*. Kaukab Siddiq, ed. and tr., Washington D.C.: The Islamic Party of North America, 1972.

Mawdudi, Sayyid Abul A'la. *Human Rights in Islam*. Khurshid Ahmad and Ahmad Said Khan, trans. Leceister: The Islamic Foundation, 1976.

Mawdudi, Sayyid Abul A'la. *Islamic Law and Constitution*. Khurshid Ahmad, ed. Karachi: Jamā'at-e-Islāmī Publication, 1955.

Mawdudi, Sayyid Abul A'la. *Nationalism in India*. Pathankot: Maktab-e-Jamā'at-e-Islāmī, 1947.

Mawdudi, Sayyid Abul A'la. *The Political Situation in Pakistan*. Karachi: Jamā'at-e-Islāmī, 1965.

Mawdudi, Sayyid Abul A'la. *Islāmī Riyāsat* (Islamic State). Lahore: Islamic Publication, 1969.

Mawdudi, Sayyid Abul A'la. *Jamā'at-e-Islāmī: Tarīkh, Maqṣad, Awr La'iḥah-e-'Amal* (Jamā'at-e-Islāmī: History, Aims and Plan of Action). Lahore: Islamic Publication, 1963.

Mawdudi, Sayyid Abul A'la. *Jamā'at-e-Islāmī ke Untīs Sāl* (Twenty Nine Years of Jamā'at-e-Islāmī). Lahore: Shu'bah-e-Nashr wa Ishā'at-e-Jamā'at-e-Islāmī, Pakistan, 1970.

Mawdudi, Sayyid Abul A'la. *Mas'alah-e-Qaumiyat* (Issue of Nationality). Lahore: Islamic Publication, 1982.

Mawdudi, Sayyid Abul Aᶜla. *Musalmān Awr Mawjūdah Siyāsī Kashmakash* (Muslims and the Current Political Crisis). Lahore: Islami Publication, 1938-40.

Mawdudi, Sayyid Abul Aᶜla. *Teḥrīk-e-Pakistān Awr Jamāᶜat-e-Islāmī* (Pakistan Movement and Jamāᶜat-e-Islāmī). Multan: Ikhwan Publication, n.d.

Mawdudi, Sayyid Abul A'la. *Wathā'iq Mawdūdī* (Mawdudi's Documents). Lahore: Idārah-e-Maᶜārif-e-Islāmī, 1986.

Moten, A. Rashid. *Islam and Revolution: Contributions of Sayyid Mawdudi.* Kano, Nigeria: Bureau for Islamic Propagation, 1988.

Moten, A. Rashid. "Political Elites and Political Instability in Pakistan." Unpublished Ph.D. dissertation, Department of Political Science, The University of Alberta, Canada, 1982.

Munir, Muhammad. *From Jinnah to Zia.* Lahore: Vanguard, 1979.

Myrdal, Gunnar. *Asian Drama: An Inquiry into the Poverty of Nations.* Great Britain: The Penguin Press, 1968.

Nasr, Seyyed Vali Reza. *The Vanguard of the Islamic Revolution: The Jamaᶜat-i Islami of Pakistan.* London: I. B. Tauris Publishers, 1994.

Niyazi, Kawthar, *Awr Line Kat Ga'ī* (And the Line was Cut). Lahore: Jang Publication, 1987.

Papanek, Gustav F., *Pakistan's Development: Social Goals and Private Incentives.* Cambridge, M.A.: Harvard University Press, 1967.

Qureshi, Ishtiaq Husain, *Ulema in Politics; A Study Relating to the Political Activities of the Ulema in South Asian Subcontinent from 1566-1947*. Karachi: Ma'aref, 1972.

Report of the Court of Inquiry Constituted Under Punjab Act 11 of 1954 to Enquire into the Punjab Disturbances of 1953. Lahore: Government of Punjab, 1954.

Report on the General Elections of Pakistan 1970-71, 2 vols. Islamabad: Election Commision of Pakistan, n.d.

Report on the General Elections 1985, 3 vols. Islamabad: Election Commision of Pakistan, nd.

Rudād-i Jamāᶜat-i-Islāmī (Proceedings of Jamāᶜat-i-Islāmī), 6 vols, Lahore: Jamāᶜat-i-Islāmī, 1938-83.

Rudād-i-Jamāᶜat-i-Islāmī Pakistan, 1972 (Proceedings of Jamāᶜat-i-Islāmī of Pakistan, 1972). Lahore: Jamāᶜat-i-Islāmī Pakistan, n.d.

Saulat, Sarwar. *Maulana Maududi*. Karachi: International Islamic Publishers, 1979.

Sayeed, Khalid B. *The Political System of Pakistan*. Boston: Houghton Mifflin, 1967.

Sayeed, Khalid B. *Pakistan: The Formative Phase*. London: Oxford University Press, 1968.

Smith, Donald E. *Religion and Political Development*. Boston: Little, Brown, 1970.

Smith, Wilfred Cantwell. *Islam in Modern History*, 2nd ed. Princeton: Princeton University Press, 1977.

Syed, Anwar H. *Pakistan: Islam, Politics, and National Solidarity.*
        New York: Praeger, 1982.

Weiss, Anita M., ed., *Islamic Reassertion in Pakistan.* Syracuse:
        Syracuse University Press, 1986.

Wheeler, Richard S. *The Politics of Pakistan: A Constitutional
        Quest.* Ithaca, N.Y.:   Cornell University Press,
        1970.

Ziring, Lawrence. *The Ayub Khan Era: Politics in Pakistan 1958-
        68.* Syracuse: Syracuse University Press, 1971.

Ziring, Lawrence. *Pakistan: The Enigma of Political Development.*
        Folkestone, U.K.: Dawson, 1990.

ARTICLES

Abbot, Freeland, "The Jamaᶜat-i-Islami of Pakistan," *The Middle
        East Journal,* 11:1 (Winter 1957): 37-51.

Abot, Freeland, "Pakistan and the Secular State," in Donald E,
        Smith, ed., *South Asian Religion and Politics*
        (Princeton: Princeton University Press, 1966): 352-
        70.

Adams, Charles J., "The Ideology of Mawlana Mawdudi," in
        Donald E. Smith, ed., *South Asian Politics and
        Religion* (Princeton: Princeton University Press,
        1966):   371-97.

Adams, Charles J., "Mawdudi and the Islamic State," in John L.
        Esposito ed., *Voices of Resurgent Islam* (New York:
        Oxford University Press, 1983):   99-133.

Ahmad, Aziz, "Mawdudi and Orthodox Fundamentalism of Pakistan," *The Middle East Journal,* 21:3 (Summer 1967): 369-80.

Ahmad, Khurshid and Zafar Ishaq Ansari, "Mawlana Sayyid Abul Aᶜla Mawdudi: An Introduction to His Vision of Islam and Islamic Revival," in Khurshid Ahmad and Zafar Ishaq Ansari, eds., *Islamic Perspectives: Studies in Honour of Mawlana Sayyid Abul Aᶜla Mawdudi* (Leicester: The Islamic Foundation, 1979): 359-84.

Ahmad, Khurshid. "The Nature of Islamic Resurgence," in John L. Esposito, ed., *Voices of Resurgent Islam* (New York: Oxford University Press, 1983): 218-229.

Ahmad, Mumtaz, "Pakistan," in Shireen T. Hunter, ed., *Islamic Revivalism: Diversity and Unity* (Bloomington, IN: Indiana University Press, 1988): 229-46.

Ahmad, Mumtaz. "Islamic Fundamentalism in South Asia: The Jamaᶜat-e-Islami and the Tablighi Jamaat," in Martin E. Marty and R. Scott Appleby, eds., *Fundamentalisms Observed* (Chicago: University of Chicago Press, 1991): 457-530.

Ahmad, Mumtaz. "The Politics of War: Islamic Fundamentalisms in Pakistan," in James Piscatori, ed. *Islamic Fundamentalisms and the Gulf Crisis* (Chicago: American Academy of Arts and Sciences, 1991): 162-184.

Ahmad, Mumtaz. "Islamization and Sectarian Violence in Pakistan," *Intellectual Discourse,* 6:1(1998): 11-37.

Ahmed, Rafiuddin. "Redefining Muslim Identity in South Asia: The Transformation of the Jamaᶜat-I Islami" in Martin E. Marty and R. Scott Appleby eds., *Accounting for Fundamentalisms: The Dynamic Character of Movements* (Chicago: University of Chicago Press, 1994): 699-705.

Alavi, Hamza, "Ethnicity, Muslim Society and the Pakistan Ideology," in Anita M. Weiss, ed., *Islamic Reassertion in Pakistan* (Syracuse: Syracuse University Press, 1986): 21-48.

Amin, Tahir. "Pakistan in 1993: Some Dramatic Changes," *Asian Survey*, 34:2 (February 1994): 191-99.

Brohi, Allahbukhsh K, "Mawlana Abul A'la Mawdudi: The Man, the Scholar, the Reformer," in Khurshid Ahmad and Zafar Ishaq Ansari, eds., *Islamic Perspectives: Studies in Honour of Sayyid Abul A'la Mawdudi* (Leicester: The Islamic Foundation, 1979): 289-312.

Burki, Shahid Javed, "Pakistan Under Zia, 1977-1988," *Asian Survey*: 28:10 (October 1988): 82-100.

Caroll, Lucy. "Nizam-i-Islam: Processes and Conflicts in Pakistan's Programme of Islamisation with Special Reference to the Position of Women," *Journal of Commonwealth and Comparative Politics*, 20 (1982): 57-95.

Esposito, John L., "Islam: Ideology and Politics in Pakistan," in Ali Banuazizi and Myron Weiner, eds., *The State, Religion, and Ethnic Politics: Afghanistan, Iran and Pakistan* (Syracuse: Syracuse University Press, 1986): 333-70.

Jalal, Ayesha. "Pakistan's Tangle: The Politics of Conflicting Security and Economic Interests," *Government and Opposition,* 34:1 (Winter 1999): 77-93.

Jameelah, Maryam. "An Appraisal of Some Aspects of Maulana Sayyid Abul A'la Maudoodi's Life and Thought," *The Islamic Quarterly,* 31:2 (Second Quarter 1987): 116-30.

Kennedy, Charles H. "Islamization in Pakistan: Implementation of Hudood Ordinances," *Asian Survey,* 28:3 (March 1988): 307-16.

Kennedy, Charles H. "Islamization and Legal Reform in Pakistan, 1979-89," *Pacific Affairs,* 63:1(Spring 1990): 62-77.

Mawdudi, Abu Mahmud. "Hamārā Khandān" (Our Family), in Ahmad Munir, *Mawlana Abul A'la Mawdudi.* Lahore: Atashfishan Publication, 1986: 11-14.

Moten, Abdul R. "Pure and Practical Ideology: The Thought of Mawlana Mawdudi," *Islamic Quarterly,* 28:4 (Fourth Quarter 1984): 217-240.

Mujahid, Sharif al, "Pakistan's First General Elections," *Asian Survey:* 11:2 (February 1971): 159-71.

Mujahid, Sharif al, "The 1977 Pakistani Elections: An Analysis," in Manzooruddin Ahmad, ed., *Contemporary Pakistan: Politics, Economy, and Society* (Karachi: Royal Books Company, 1980): 63-91.

Nasr, Seyyed Vali Reza. "Democracy and the Crisis of Governability in Pakistan," *Asian Survey:* 32:6 (June 1992): 521-37.

Nasr, Seyyed Vali Reza. "Students, Islam, and Politics: Islami Jami'at-e Tulaba in Pakistan," *Middle East Journal*, 46:1 (Winter 1992): 59-76.

Rahman, Fazlur. "The Controversy over the Muslim Family Laws," in Donald E. Smith, ed., *South Asian Religion and Politics* (Princeton: Princeton University Press, 1966): 414-27.

Rahman, Fazlur. "Islam in Pakistan," *South Asian and Middle Eastern Studies*, 8:4 (Summer 1985): 34-61.

Richter, William L. "The Political Meaning of Islamisation in Pakistan," in Anita M. Weiss, ed., *Islamic Reassertion in Pakistan: The Application of Islamic Laws in a Modern State* (Syracuse: Syracuse University Press, 1986): 129-140.

Sayeed, Khalid B. "The *Jama'at-e-Islami* Movement in Pakistan," *Pacific Affairs*, 30:2 (March 1957): 59-69.

Weiss, Anita M. "The Historical Debate on Islam and the States of South Asia," in Anita M. Weiss, ed., *Islamic Reassertion in Pakistan. The Application of Islamic Laws in a Modern State* (Syracuse: Syracuse University Press, 1986): 1-20.

Ziring, Lawrence. "From Islamic Republic to Islamic State in Pakistan," *Asian Survey,* 24:9 (September 1984): 931-46.

Ziring, Lawrence. "Dilemma and Challenge in Nawaz Sharif's Pakistan," in Charles H. Kennedy, ed., *Pakistan: 1992* (Boulder, Colorado: Westview Press, 1993).

Ziring, Lawrence. "The Second Stage in Pakistani Politics: The 1993 Elections," *Asian Survey*, 33:12 (December 1993): 1175-85.

INDEX

Note: Arabic names that begin with the definite article al - are alphabetised under the part of the name following the article.